#1 *NEW YORK TIMES* BESTSELLING AUTHOR

MIKE EVANS

CHRISTOPHER COLUMBUS

Secret Jew

TIMEWORTHY
BOOKS

P.O. BOX 30000, PHOENIX, AZ 85046

This book is dedicated,
with great admiration, to my dear friend,
Reuven Rivlin, President of Israel.

He and his ancestors have been
established in Jerusalem since 1809.
Reuven received a law degree from
Hebrew University in Jerusalem.
He and his wife, Nechama have four children.

Preface

In 1492, Columbus sailed the ocean blue . . .

CHRISTOPHER COLUMBUS. The name alone evokes visions of sailing ships, strange lands, adventure and discovery. His likeness carved in marble or cast in bronze stands in cities such as Barcelona, Madeira, Genoa, Havana, Cartagena, San Juan, Santo Domingo, Havana, and Washington, D.C.

Have you ever pondered the reason why Columbus decided to sail in search of a new land in 1492? As we will discover, it was even more important to the Jewish people than it would become to the people of North and South America and the islands of the Caribbean Sea. Queen Isabella and King Ferdinand had issued an edict of ejection regarding the Jews. It decreed that every person of Jewish descent had to leave Spain or be executed. As a result, several Jewish businessmen went to Christopher Columbus, a Genoese Jew whose family had supposedly converted to Christianity under duress, and pledged to finance his efforts to discover a new land. They purchased two of the three ships that carried Columbus and his sailors across the ocean to find the territory that would later become known as the Americas. Why was this so crucial?

King Ferdinand and Queen Isabella were seeking a means to unite the country and had selected Tomás de Torquemada as the Inquisitor General for most of Spain. The harassment began with attempts to drive out Jews, Protestants, and nonbelievers. Benzion Netanyahu, father of Prime Minister Benjamin Netanyahu, wrote of the *Marranos* and *conversos* (Spanish Jews) and the basic reasons behind the attacks on them. According to history professor Netanyahu, the persecution launched against the Jews was based on "racial hatred and political considerations rather than by religious zeal."[1] He continued his explanation with:

> The minority that still adhered to Judaism in the three decades preceding the Inquisition was . . . constantly diminishing in size and influence; that it would have, in all likelihood, soon faded into nothingness, had not the process of assimilation been violently interfered with by the repellent and bewildering actions of the Inquisition; and that, thus, it was due to the Inquisition itself that the dying Marranism in Spain was given a new lease on life. . . . It was not a powerful Marrano movement that provoked the establishment of the Inquisition, but it was the establishment of the Inquisition that caused the temporary resurgence of the Spanish Marrano movement. . . . The aim of the Inquisition, therefore, as I see it, was not to eradicate a Jewish heresy from the midst of the Marrano group, but to eradicate the Marrano group from the midst of the Spanish people.[2]

Christopher Columbus, Secret Jew does not necessarily follow the path that took him to many of those cities named at the beginning of this chapter; rather, it explores the fascination with Jerusalem that impelled him on his journey. It will answer questions that perhaps you may never have known to ask. For instance, were you aware that

- ✧ Columbus was a converso—one who chose to convert to Christianity through coercion?

- ✧ his initial voyage was funded not by Queen Isabella's jewels but by a group of wealthy Jews?

- ✧ he hoped to find a source of gold—perhaps King Solomon's mines—in Asia in order to recapture the city of Jerusalem from the Muslims and fund the restoration of the Temple?

- ✧ on his journey, he hoped to find a place of refuge for Christians and Jews alike in order for them to escape the horrors of persecution descending upon Spain?

- ✧ he traveled with a Jew who spoke Hebrew in hopes of finding the ten lost tribes during his trip to the New World?

The following pages uncover the secrets of Christopher Columbus, the man who plied the ocean in an attempt to aid both Jews and Christians, a man who was devoutly religious, a man who died long before his ultimate dream was fulfilled.

Introduction

THIS IS THE LOG of Christopher Columbus:

"In the Name of Our Lord Jesus Christ. Whereas, Most Christian, high, Excellent and Powerful Princes, King and Queen of Spain and of the Islands of the Sea, our Sovereigns, this present year 1492, after your Highnesses had terminated the war with the Moors reigning in Europe, the same having been brought to an end in the great city of Granada, where on the second day of January, this present year, I saw the royal banners of your Highnesses planted by force of arms upon the towers of the Alhambra, which is the fortress of that city, and saw the Moorish king come out at the gate of the city and kiss the hands of your Highnesses, and of the Prince my Sovereign; and in the present month, in consequence of the information which I had given your Highnesses respecting the countries of India and of a Prince, called Great Khan, which in our language signifies King of Kings, how at many times he, and his predecessors had sent to Rome soliciting instructors who might teach him our holy faith, and the holy Father had never granted his request, whereby great numbers of people were lost, believing in idolatry and doctrines of perdition.

"Therefore, Your Highnesses, as Catholic Christians, and princes who love and promote the holy Christian faith, and are enemies of the doctrine of Mahomet, and of all idolatry and heresy, determined to send me, Christopher Columbus, to the above-mentioned countries of India, to see the said princes, people, and territories, and to learn their disposition and the proper method of converting them to our holy faith; and furthermore directed that I should not proceed by land to the East, as is customary, but by a Westerly route, in which direction we have hitherto no certain evidence that any one has gone . . .

"Thus after expelling the Jews from your domains in the same month of January, your Highness ordered that I should go with sufficient fleet to the same part of India, and for that purpose most graciously elevated me to the title of Don, High Admiral of the sea and perpetual Viceroy and Governor of all the Islands and continents that I should discover and gain both now and hereafter in the ocean sea, and that my son should succeed me so long from generation to generation forever.

"Whereupon, I left the city of Granada on Saturday, May 12, 1492, and came to the town of Palos, a seaport, where I did arm three vessels for such enterprise; and departed from that port well-supplied with provisions and with many sailors, on the third day of August of the same year, being Friday, half an hour before sunrise. I steered for the Canary Islands of your Highness, which are in the said ocean sea that I might thence set out for the Indies to perform the embassy of your Highnesses to the Princes there, so as to comply with my order.

"As part of my duty, I thought it well to write an account of all the voyages most punctually, noting the happenings from day to day, as will hereafter appear. Moreover, I did resolve to describe each night what had passed during the day and to note each day how I navigated at night. I intend to draw up a nautical chart which shall contain the several parts of the ocean and land in their proper situation; and also to compose a book to represent the whole by pictures with latitude and longitude, on which accounts it behooves me to abstain from my sleep and make many trials and navigations, which will demand much labour."

—The Log of Christopher Columbus 1492[3]

—1—

CHRISTOPHER COLUMBUS
Secret Jew

*"By prevailing over all obstacles and distractions,
one may unfailingly arrive at his chosen goal or destination."*
— CHRISTOPHER COLUMBUS

THREE SHIPS lay at anchor in the calm waters off the port of Palos in southwest Spain. They were outfitted with provisions sufficient for a several-months-long voyage of discovery. Standing on the shore gazing at the lamps that lit the darkened caravels was a Genoese explorer who had planned to set sail on Tuesday, August 2, 1492. The departure date had been postponed until the following day, but the captain, Christopher Columbus, had insisted that his crews be on board by 11:00 p.m. that evening. Why? Monarchs Ferdinand and Isabella had issued an expulsion order that would have made it illegal after midnight for any Jew to remain on Spanish soil. The Jews had already been expelled from the Andalusia region in 1483, a prelude to this later move.

There were Jews (conversos) on the three sailing ships whose lives would have been affected by the decree—who would have faced exile or worse had it not been for their mentor and leader. It is commonly thought by historians that discovering the Americas and adjacent islands and the ejection of the Jews were two measures that had the most sweeping significance for the future of Spain.

In order to understand this, we must go back in time to the morning hours of a fall day in 1451, when the cries of a baby boy could be heard reverberating through a neighborhood in the Republic of Genoa. Christopher was Genoese in every respect—his birth and ethnicity—a true child of the Italian Renaissance.

The exact date of his birth was governed by the feast day of the child's patron saint, not by the date the baby emerged from the womb. The lusty wails of the newborn heralded the birth of Cristoforo Colombo, or in Spanish, Cristóbal Colón. Of course, in the Western Hemisphere, he is known as Christopher Columbus, discoverer of the New World. Although perhaps one of the best known in history, it is not his name that is important in the telling of this story; rather, it is his life, his ancestry, his achievements, and his legacy that echo through the chronicle of days.

According to author Mosco Galimir:

> In Tortosa, Salonica and Amsterdam, the name of Colón is found; all bearers of this name are Sephardic Jews." Galimar continues: "Colombo is a Spanish name. The change of name was a custom amongst Jews. Palumbus, Palombo, Columbus, Colombo. Thus the evolution to Colombo, Colón. The Colombos were Jews from Catalonia. Colón is a common Jewish name found on the Mayorcas.[4]

The name *Christopher* means "Christ-bearer." He bears the same name as St. Christopher, who according to legend carried the baby Jesus across a treacherous river. In his book, *Life of the Admiral Christopher Columbus,* his son Ferdinand posited that the surname meant "dove" and was fitting because his father had carried the Gospel of Christ across the Atlantic Ocean to heathens in the New World.[5]

Little is known of Christopher's childhood, which creates questions with few answers: Was he a dedicated religionist, one sent forth at the bidding of Queen Isabella and King Ferdinand to circumnavigate the globe and bring back to Spain untold treasures? Was he a secret Jew who had sailed under the guise of discovery but whose real purpose was to find a safe haven for persecuted Christians and Jews alike? Was his main purpose greed; or was it a deep desire to reclaim the city of Jerusalem from its Muslim captors?

Born to Susanna Fontanarossa and Domenico Colombo, and the eldest of their five children, Christopher would ultimately choose not to follow in his father's footsteps as a wool weaver and owner of a cheese stand. It is likely that his father was a well-known businessman and artisan among the middle class of his day. He held the position of keeper of the Olivella Gate in Genoa—an appointment which paid 85 Genoese pounds per year, or the equivalent of about $160 in gold. It is highly likely that their eldest son would have been born in a house near the gate.

According to author and chronicler Samuel Eliot Morison's description of Domenico Colombohe was

> . . . always making promises he was unable to fulfill,
> buying goods for which he was unable to pay, starting

sidelines like cheese and wine instead of sticking to his loom . . . He was the kind of father who would shut up shop when trade was poor and take the boys fishing; and the sort of wine-seller who was his own best customer.[6]

Two facets of Columbus' youth were meaningful in guiding his career: schooling and family life. Domenico's aspiration to provide schooling for his children transported him from the highland village of Moconesi to Genoa. The instruction accessible to Christopher would take him even farther—from the streets of Genoa to the far vistas of the Atlantic Ocean and beyond.

As a child, Columbus attended the school established by the local wool guild on Pavia Street. There he was taught to read, write and do the most basic arithmetic. His son, Ferdinand, mistakenly thought his father had achieved a higher education at the University of Pavia. Christopher would have learned Latin by memorizing passages from the Bible to assure that he would be able to conduct business in the language. He then moved to more advanced mathematics in order to allow him to master the art of international commerce—which included navigation. It would prove to be invaluable to Columbus the sailor and discoverer.[7] From an early age Christopher chose to follow the outgoing tide as a sailor. One of his brothers, Giovanni, died as a young man, but his brothers Bartholomew and Giacomo (known as Diego) worked alongside Christopher during the first and second quests to the New World.

By the time Christopher settled in Spain, he could speak and correspond fluently in Spanish although his letters were sprinkled with Portuguese, a nod to the years he spent sailing with Portuguese navigators. He also read a smattering of Latin due to his early training; while he spoke Ligurian, a dialect, he never wrote in his native Genoese language.

Following years of research, Estelle Irizarry, a professor of linguistics at Georgetown University, has a different theory regarding the secrecy surrounding the birthplace of Columbus:

> Irizarry says her research clears up the big mystery surrounding Columbus' place of birth, which he never revealed but which different historians have claimed was Genoa, Italy; the French Mediterranean island of Corsica; Portugal; and Greece, as well as Spain. "The people who hid (their origins) more and had reason to do so were the Jews," Irizarry said, referring to the forced conversions and mass expulsions of Jews in late medieval Spain. A scientific project launched three years ago to discover his true origins using DNA comparisons between his family and possible descendants has so far failed to provide conclusive results.[8]

From various accounts, he was "tall, had a long face, a long nose, with clear eyes, and with either blond, red, or white hair."[9] In later years, his hair turned totally white as was befitting a man of his rank and reputation.

Angelo Trivigiano, who was acquainted with the famous seaman, wrote of "Christopher Columbus, a Genoese, a man of tall and lofty stature, of ruddy complexion, of great intelligence and with a long face."[10]

Morison quoted Spanish historian Bartolomé de Las Casas:

> He [Columbus] was more than middling tall; face

long and giving an air of authority; aquiline nose, blue eyes, complexion light and tending to bright red; beard and hair red when young but very soon turned gray from his labors.[11]

Yet another writer labeled the discoverer "irascible when annoyed." Christopher's son Ferdinand said his father's contempt for profanity was so strong that he "never heard him utter any other oath than 'by St. Ferdinand!'"[12] This proclivity can help one to understand Christopher's outlook toward religion. Morison again wrote:

> In matters of the Christian religion, without doubt he was a Catholic and of great devotion.... He observed the fasts of the Church most faithfully, confessed and made communion often, read the canonical offices like a churchman or member of a religious order, hated blasphemy and profane swearing.[13]

Bartolomé de Las Casas, a priest who was known as "the Apostle of the Indies" was personally acquainted with Columbus; his father and an uncle sailed with the discoverer. Las Casas offers this further descriptive information:

> He [Columbus] was extraordinarily zealous for the divine service; he desired and was eager for the conversion of these people [Native Americans], and that in every region the faith of Jesus Christ be planted and enhanced. And he was especially affected and devoted to the idea that God should deem him worthy of aiding somewhat in recovering the Holy Sepulchre... He was

a gentleman of great force of spirit, of lofty thoughts, naturally inclined to undertake worthy deeds and signal enterprises; patient and long-suffering, and a forgiver of injuries, and wished nothing more than that those who offended against him should recognize their errors, and that the delinquents be reconciled with him; most constant and endowed with forbearance in the hardships and adversities which were always occurring and which were incredible and infinite; ever holding great confidence in divine Providence.[14]

Although little is actually known about the early naval career of Columbus it is widely accepted that he was drawn to the sea because of the location of Genoa's busy harbor. Given that his father was a tradesman and importer of fine wool, it is likely that he spent a great deal of time watching for the arrival and departure of ships from other lands. The busy seaport was on the trade route that led from Italy and France, and it was probably in the midst of just such hustle and bustle that the young sailor developed a love for the seafarer's life. Antonio Gallo, a historian from Genoa, intimated that the Columbus brothers set sail as teenagers.[15]

To further substantiate his early sailing experience, Columbus wrote in a missive to Ferdinand and Isabella:

> I have passed more than forty years in this business and have traveled to every place where there is navigation up to the present time.[16]

Calculations would actually place this initiation to sea life at about the age of ten years. There are other writers who concur and place his introduction to sailing at around 1461. (This was the same year King Enrique IV petitioned Pope Pius II to approve the creation of an Inquisition in Castile to punish suspected heretics in the kingdom. The request was approved on March 15, 1462, with his papal bull *Dum Fidei Catholicae* (or *While the Catholic Faith*).

Christopher penned in his private journal in 1492: "I have been at sea 23 years without leaving it for any time worth telling." That would place the launch of his career at about the age of eighteen years.[17] Regardless of when he first set sail, it is apparent that it was a vocation he loved as he followed the tides for the remainder of his life.

The future self-proclaimed Admiral's trips took him to ports in the Mediterranean and Aegean seas before he set sail on his momentous voyage of discovery. It was excellent experience for the fruitful journeys that would follow.

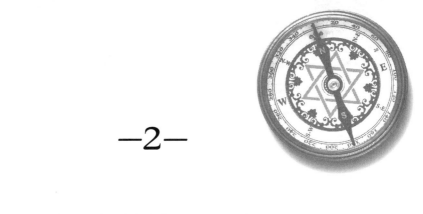

—2—

CHRISTOPHER
COLUMBUS
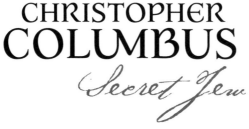
Secret Jew

*"And the sea will grant each man new hope . . .
his sleep brings dreams of home."*
— CHRISTOPHER COLUMBUS

HIS FIRST TRIP aboard ship took Columbus to the Island of Chios near modern-day Greece, a voyage that would take him as close as he would ever sail to Asia. The log for the trip notes that the ship on which he sailed, the *Roxana*, carried soldiers, seamen and *tessitori* or weavers. The intrepid merchant/sailor would likely have traveled as a representative of his father's business in order to purchase wool.

It would have been on this and other earlier trips before his voyage of discovery that he learned the language of sailing and the sea as well as how to properly raise and lower anchors, estimate distances, and other skills necessary to eventually become a ship's captain.

Soon after his return from Chios, Christopher set sail on board what was probably the *Bechalla*, a vessel of Flemish origin, for a trip to Lisbon, England, and Flanders (today the northern portion of Belgium). Since his name does not appear on the passenger list, he may have served as an ordinary seaman. As it sailed along the northern coast of Portugal in mid-August 1476, the ship was attacked by thirteen or more ships of the Franco-Portuguese war fleet. Although Genoa had an active treaty with France, the *Bechalla* flew a Burgundy flag—a country with which France was at war.

The heated battle between the Genoese fleet and the warships commanded by noted naval captain Guillaume de Casenove raged violently as first one and then another of the ships sank in the roiling waters. As night closed in on the combat, the ship on which Columbus had sailed sank. As it settled into the waters, Columbus, like the prophet Jonah whose most notable sea voyage was in the belly of a whale before being spit out on dry land, was forced to abandon ship. Morison described the young sailor's predicament:

> He leaped into the sea, grasped a sweep [oar] that floated free, and by pushing it ahead of him and resting on it when he was exhausted (for he had been wounded in the battle) he managed to reach the shore, over six miles distant. The people of Lagos treated the survivors kindly, and Columbus eventually made his way to Lisbon where he was taken in by some member of the local Genoese colony, and cured of his wounds.[18]

Through a series of voyages which included ones to Thule [Iceland], Ireland, Tunisia, and points north, Columbus honed his seafaring proficiencies. It was, however, his unceremonious landing on the shores of Portugal that would prove to be the turning point in the life of the budding sailor. Why? He had landed in the center of marine travel and discovery.

> Portuguese sailors were at the vanguard of European overseas exploration, discovering and mapping the coasts of Africa, Asia and Brazil, in what has become known as the Age of Discovery. Methodical expeditions started in 1419 along West Africa's coast under the sponsorship of Prince Henry the Navigator, with [explorer] Bartolomeu Dias reaching the Cape of Good Hope and entering the Indian Ocean in 1488.[19]

Added to that list is the discovery and habitation of the Azores and the Cape Verde Islands, and reaching the Gold and Ivory coasts of West Africa.

Christopher would be able to learn the Portuguese and Castilian languages used by seamen; Latin in greater depth, shipbuilding, and other skills needed to pursue voyages of discovery. In his *Book of Prophecies*, Columbus wrote in his own hand:

> I prayed to the most merciful Lord about my heart's great desire, and He gave me the spirit and the intelligence for the task: seafaring, astronomy, geometry, arithmetic, skill in drafting spherical maps and placing correctly the cities, rivers, mountains and ports. I also studied cosmology, history, chronology and philosophy.[20]

Historians and chroniclers are unsure just how long his sojourn in

Portugal lasted, but it is thought that he was there for eight or nine years.

While in Lisbon, Christopher became a skilled cartographer. This was reinforced by his later detailed sketch of Northern Haiti—the only mapmaking effort to survive from his various journeys. It was also in Lisbon that he met his wife, Dona Felipa Perestrelo e Moniz, the mother of Diego, Columbus' firstborn son. The question has been raised: How could a virtually homeless Genoese native with little to recommend him have been allowed to wed the offspring of nobility? It is thought by some that Felipa was—to use the common vernacular—an old maid at the tender age of twenty-five. Perhaps her father was delighted to have finally found a husband for his daughter. There are several other explanations as to how this castaway, a Genoese sailor, managed to win the heart of one of the Lisbon nobility. Among them is that the two met following Mass at the chapel of the Convento dos Santos in Lisbon, a boarding school for aristocracy. On her mother's side, Felipa's grandfather, Gil Ayres Moniz, was lord over one of the richest domains of the Algarve, a coastal region in South Portugal that stretched for 1,958 square miles. Moniz had captured the lands from the Moors before traveling with Henry the Navigator. He was the perfect in-law for Christopher, as was Felipa's father, Bartolomeu Perestrelo, who in 1446 was recipient of a fiefdom of the island of Porto Santo near Madeira in the North Atlantic. The story is told of Bartolomeu's first attempt at colonizing the island. On his maiden voyage, he supposedly took with him a doe rabbit and her litter of newborns. "Breeding like rabbits" soon became not a joke but a catastrophe for Perestrello and his island. The adorable bunnies bred so rapidly that within a year the island had been stripped of its greenery and was overrun by the furry—and famished—creatures. The founding of a village had to be postponed until the course of nature had been restored. Felipa's mother is said to have loved sharing that story of her husband's initial failure at settling Porto Santo.

Not only did Felipa's mother, Dona Isabella, share stories of her late husband, she gifted her son-in-law with his writings and sea charts. Soon after their marriage, Columbus and Felipa moved to Porto Santo, where their only child, Diego, as born.

In his book *Sails of Hope*, Simon Wiesenthal wrote:

> How could a foreign maker of maps, and what is more one of low birth, have been permitted to marry the daughter of Portuguese nobility? . . . There are also scholars who have looked into the genealogy of the Moniz-Perestrello family, hoping to find a clue there. Marranos usually intermarried. It was customary among them for the bridegroom and bride to produce proofs of their Jewish lineage . . . The investigators have actually found Marrano ancestors for Felipa Moniz. On her mother's side she was of Jewish descent; but her forebears had long ago converted to Christianity.[21]

Another clue as to Columbus' heritage was uncovered by Estelle Irizarry, a linguistics professor at Georgetown University who scrutinized the semantics and sentence structure of hundreds of letters, journals and other papers penned by Columbus. Following many years of methodical analysis she determined that the explorer wrote and spoke the Spanish language known as "Ladino," which was purported to be the common language of Sephardic Jews. Her conclusions effectively and scientifically substantiated the speculation that Columbus was a converso, described as someone who had converted to Christianity 1) as a yearning for a less constricting life; 2) an alteration in religious beliefs; or 3) as a life-saving action while under duress. Another clue may be that Columbus frequently called on a Jew in Lisbon, the same man for whom he provided in his last will and testament.

Investigative journalist Simcha Jacobovici determined that

> Columbus was a converso, surrounded by conversos and financed by *conversos*, making a desperate bid to find a land where they could all be openly Jewish. They never did find the lost tribes of Israel ... They did, however, find a haven for Jews and I'm sure Columbus and the various members of the Torres family that supported him would have found gratification in the fact that the State of Israel has been reborn and its greatest supporter is the country that they founded. After all, Luis de Torres was the first European settler in the New World.[22]

And, although able to open doors to the upper class for her husband, Felipa is never mentioned by name in any of her husband's writings that have survived the ravages of time and tide. Sadly, within a year of the birth of Diego, Felipa died.

Following her death, Christopher wasted little time in moving his family to a more hospitable locale, that of the town of Funchal on the island of Madeira. It would have afforded opportunities to ply his trade and undertake several voyages. It may have been there in the company of seafarers that his appetite was whetted for further exploration. The location of the island would have made its beaches ripe for detritus washed ashore from distant lands.[23]

His sojourn in Madeira and the voyages undertaken from its shores taught Columbus many things that would stand him in good stead by the time he set sail on his journey of discovery in 1492:

> . . . how to handle a caravel in head wind and sea, how to claw off a lee shore, what kind of sea stores to take on a long voyage and how to stow them properly, and what sort of trading truck goes with primitive people. Every voyage he sailed under the flag of Portugal made it more likely that he would succeed in the great enterprise that was already in his brain. Above all, he learned from the Portuguese confidence that with a good ship under him and God's assistance, the boundaries of the known world might be indefinitely enlarged; that the Age of Discovery had just begun.[24]

After years of hard work, at the still comparatively youthful age of thirty, it is obvious that Columbus had become a skilled and knowledgeable sailor. He could boast connections to houses of commerce and banking, and was linked by matrimony to two eminent families in Portugal. By all standards except his, the young man had succeeded; but his heart yearned for adventure; he longed to set sail for the countries of his imagination—the lands that lay beyond the horizon. His desire was to reach the Indies by sailing westward; in actuality he had little interest in possibly discovering another continent. There was nothing in the annals of sailors' logs to indicate that anything as large as the Americas lay in the direct path of Columbus' sailing ships. He hoped only to find an island large enough to support his wish to establish a safe port for Christians and Jews, and from which to launch future voyages to Asia.

For early seamen, detecting ghostly islands and fading coastlines was a routine happening of ocean voyages. A bank of clouds on the horizon might appear to be an island to a land-hungry searcher. In the days in which Columbus sailed, a lookout might spot a phantom island in the setting sun and steer a course for landfall. When dawn broke on the high seas, he might suppose the ship had sailed past it in the night. Columbus actually spotted two such points during his first voyage; both determined to be false. Author Samuel Morison determined that if the apparitions had been real as some supposed, "They would be as close together as the Florida Keys."[25]

After years of honing his wishes to sail westward to Asia, Columbus was finally ready to present his plan. He prepared an assortment of convincing papers to validate his proposal and sought an audience with the Portuguese king, John II (a.k.a João II). Given his residence in the country and his marriage to aristocracy, Christopher felt compelled to go first to the king of his adopted land. He finally received a summons in 1484.

Under King John II, Portugal had become the foremost maritime power on the European continent; Portuguese vessels plied the waters of the known world. The monarch had a scientific council that advised him on nautical matters and voyages of discovery. From time to time he granted allowance for expeditions to pursue the discovery of unknown but likely populated lands. The primary route for such expeditions was southward along the western coastline of Africa. Vendors followed the mariners and the affluence of King John's empire burgeoned. While Columbus felt the Portuguese had the right plan for land development, he was by no means convinced that it was in the direction the ships now sailed. Christopher believed the discovery of a sea route to India that would bypass the Muslims—Arabs and Turks—the marauders would lose their ability to exploit European merchants. Such a discovery would create a monopoly on trade between India and the West.

Columbus' main argument was that a route to the west would open a guaranteed track to India and a veritable cornucopia of goods for import. His argument came just decades after men began to believe that the world was round rather than flat, while death by burning had been pronounced on those heretics who dared argue otherwise. Were Christopher to convince King John II to fund his enterprise, he would have incontrovertible proof of the spherical nature of the world. To put it in perspective, his daring proposal was the modern-day equivalent of stating unequivocally that man could travel to the moon and back.

Upon considering Columbus' petition for monetary support of his plan, John labeled it "incorrect and mathematically improbable."[26] Columbus was disappointed, but his dreams were not crushed. In 1485, Christopher and Diego moved from Portugal—a country in the midst of upheaval—to Spain. It has been speculated that Columbus made his move more for political reasons than monetary ones due to Felipa's family having fallen out of favor with the Crown because of their associations with the powerful Duke of Braganza, a close friend. In 1483, the duke had been put to death for treason. This may be supported by a missive received by Columbus from the king of Portugal on March 20, 1488, which read in part:

> And if you are fearful of our justice in consideration
> of certain of your obligations, so know by the present
> letter that neither during your coming, your stay, and

your departure will you be seized, detained, accused, charged, or prosecuted for any reason whatsoever, neither under the civil nor the criminal law, no matter what the cause.[27]

Nothing is known of what Christopher's infraction might have been, and whatever it was, he took it to his grave.

While little more is known of Columbus' wife, Felipa, the marriage proved to be a great influence in his life. Because of the union, he became a naturalized citizen of Portugal and was afforded open doors that may not otherwise have been available to him. His brother-in-law was the influential Pedro Correa da Cunha, governor of Porto Santo, another association that would have significance.

In 1484, Columbus and Diego set sail for Spain and the port of Palos. After days at sea, the father and son were back on dry land, strolling past merchants hawking their wares in open-air markets—fish, bread, vegetables, and spices. As they traversed a rut-laden road, Columbus spied the monastery of La Rabida. Famished and exhausted, he led Diego toward the gates where they were met by Fray Juan Perez, who provided bread and water to the weary travelers. As the two men talked, Columbus shared his dream of ocean exploration with the friar, who immediately introduced the budding explorer to Fray Antonio de Marchena. The two clerics agreed to provide shelter for little Diego as well as to affording letters introducing Columbus to two very powerful nobles in Spain: Don Enrique de Guzmán, duke of Medina Sidonia and Don Luis de la Cerda, duke of Medinaceli. (Prior to his father's first voyage in 1492 and at the age of twelve years, Diego received an appointment as a page in the royal court, a position he held until 1498.)

While Guzmán had little interest in Columbus' dream of a

westward ocean voyage, Cerda provided patronage for him and eventually was able to gain an audience with royalty in 1486. With his looming interview, the future explorer must have felt great trepidation given his ancestry and the terror of the Inquisition already in full swing. Would he be barred at the gates? Would he be ejected from the gallery? Would he be identified as a converso and jailed?

The seafarer/merchant settled on the city of Cádiz for his base of operations, as it had been a stopover on his travels from Genoa to northern Europe. He was soon employed by an old friend in the shipping business, the duke of Medinaceli. Soon Christopher was sharing an astonishing plan with the duke in an attempt to secure backing for his desire to sail in search of a route to Asia. Perhaps surprisingly, the duke was very much intrigued by the idea and began to calculate just how many caravels (Portuguese sailing ships) would be needed for a one-year voyage. Soon realizing that the endeavor was more suited for the Crown than a lone individual, the duke wrote a letter to his uncle, Cardinal Pedro González de Mendoza, asking for an introduction for Columbus to the court of King Ferdinand and Queen Isabella.

Finally the day of his audience dawned. Columbus donned his best robes, gathered his maps and charts, and set out for the palace. The Genoese sailor could not have helped being impressed by the magnificence of the most noteworthy salon in the Throne Room at the Alcazar Palace in Cordoba. He would have entered the presence of the monarchs through a stunning arch that today still bears its original wooden doors. The cupola overhead is made of cedar and is intricately carved with stars, circles, and other geometric patterns which are gilded with gold and shades of red and blue. He would have made his way down a corridor of marble columns and beneath graceful arches into the presence of the king and queen. There he would have presented his ideas for a westward voyage of discovery. Andres Bernaldez described the scene:

> And so Colon [Columbus] came to the Court of King Don Fernando and of Queen Dona Isabel, and he related to them his imagination, to which they did not give much credit . . . and he talked to them and told them what he said was true and showed them the world map, so that he put them in desire to know about these lands.[28]

Columbus piqued the royals' fancy with his stated desire to return to Spain with sufficient jewels and gold bullion to pay for the recent war in Granada, as well as his hopes to fund a campaign to free the Holy Land. Despite Columbus' impressive discourse, the monarchs neglected to commit to his voyage but allowed him a small stipend while considering his proposal.

By January 1486, Christopher had formally entered the service of the king and queen. Historically, we have no indication as to when he might have honed his plan to launch a voyage of discovery westward, but it is evident that a great deal of time and study had been spent on his plan. Not only was he a pioneer, he was a bit of a psychoanalyst and employed Isabella's religious fervor for his own gain. He rationalized that not only would his westward voyage reveal a new and shorter route to India, it would also give him the opportunity to share the Gospel with any people he met along the way.

But planning a voyage wasn't the only thing that captured Columbus' attention while he waited for Ferdinand and Isabella to approve his travel plans: In 1487, while still biding his time, Columbus visited a local chemist's shop owned by a family that had emigrated from Genoa. It was there that he met Diego de Arana. In Diego's home lived an adopted cousin, Beatriz Enríquez de Arana and her brother Pedro Enríquez de Arana. Beatriz and Pedro had been orphaned at an early age and moved from Santa María de Trasierra to live with their maternal grandmother and aunt in Cordoba. Surprisingly, Beatriz was taught to read and write in an era when neither was of great import for a woman. After the deaths of both their aunt and grandmother, Beatriz became the ward of another close relative, Diego. It was he who presented the thirty-five-year-old Christopher to his cousin, twenty-year-old Beatriz in 1487.

In August 1488, Beatriz bore a son, Ferdinand, also known as Hernando Colon. The couple never married. Ferdinand spent his early years in Cordoba, Spain, where as an adolescent he was appointed as a page to Prince Don Juan, heir apparent to the Spanish Crown. After the prince died at an early age, Ferdinand was reassigned to Queen Isabella's service. He accompanied his father on Columbus' fourth expedition to the New World and later sailed there with his half brother Diego in 1509. Preferring a more sedentary lifestyle, Ferdinand settled in Spain and became known as a scholar and collector of books. Reportedly, his personal library housed as many as 15,000 volumes. Eventually, he penned a biography of his father, *The Life of the Admiral Christopher Columbus by His Son Ferdinand*.

It was during his earlier stay in Portugal that Christopher became a passionate biblical scholar and spent much time studying the works of noted Bible teachers, academics, statisticians, cartographers, and travels of the known world. His books were well marked with notes revealing those writers that most impressed him. It has been said that Columbus pursued the "Judaized" trade of cartographer and calligrapher in Portugal—creating maps and trading in engraved books. Seldom were Muslim or Christian mapmakers employed, which may have been another reason Christopher is thought to have been a secret Jew.

His first love was the Scriptures, followed closely by other favorites: Pierre d'Ailly's *Imago Mundi* (*Image of the World*), Pope Pius II's *Historia Rerum* (*History of the World*), and Marco Polo's *The Description of the World*. Columbus' understanding of geography would be influenced by *Imago Mundi*, which gave the promising explorer a greater knowledge of the ocean. His personal copy of Pierre d'Ailly's book can today be found in the Columbus Library in Seville, Spain. The volume contains almost 900 notes written in the margins by Columbus' own hand.

As he delved more deeply into the writings of those much-admired explorers and sailors, Christopher felt strongly that Marco Polo had been correct in his assumption that China was much closer than had been thought. This belief brought Columbus together with Paolo Toscanelli, a scholar who also concurred with Polo. A respected Florentine medical doctor, Toscanelli played a crucial role in the development of Columbus' grand plan. Eventually he corresponded with the physician who was kind enough to send the budding explorer a copy of a letter and chart that had been sent directly to King Ferdinand. (A copy of that letter was included in Ferdinand Columbus' biography of his famous father.)

The chart mentioned by Toscanelli supposedly described the reach of past explorers as well as descriptions of their travels and destinations. It was this missive and chart that Columbus used as illustrations when trying to convince John II and Ferdinand and Isabella of the viability of his plan. He wrote:

> I have searched out and studied all kinds of texts:
> geographies, histories, chronologies, philosophies and

other subjects. With a hand that could be felt, the Lord opened my mind to the fact that it would be possible to sail from here to the Indies, and He opened my will to desire to accomplish the project. [29]

—3—

CHRISTOPHER COLUMBUS
Secret Jew

No one should fear to undertake any task in the name of our Saviour,
if it is just and if the intention is purely for His holy service.

—CHRISTOPHER COLUMBUS[30]

CHRISTOPHER COLUMBUS was more than a man
eager to explore sea routes to Asia; he was a multifaceted individual—who was by his own pen a devoted religionist with a desire to
be a Christ-bearer to those in foreign lands. He wrote to Amerigo
Vespucci (sometimes spelled Vespucius), an Italian explorer,
financier, navigator, and cartographer with whom he had a deep
friendship:

> I feel persuaded by the many and wonderful mani-
> festations of Divine Providence in my especial favour,
> that I am the chosen instrument of God in bringing
> to pass a great event—no less than the conversion

of millions who are now existing in the darkness of
Paganism.[31]

Unfortunately, in what has become an exceedingly avaricious
society, the motives of Christopher have been labeled primarily
economic—that he was only after gold. In a 1992 article in *Modern
Maturity*, author Dan Carlinsky wrote that Columbus' voyage was
a "business trip . . . his chief motive was one of the oldest and most
powerful of all: money."[32] Perhaps that is true, but not, as we shall
soon see, the altruistic reasons for his desire to gain wealth.

At this point in the narrative, the question must be asked: Was
Columbus determined to search out a route to Asia based on a desire
to convert to Christianity any inhabitants of lands discovered along
the way? Or was his underlying plan to find a place of refuge for
the Marranos and conversos who were about to face either expulsion from Spain or unspeakable horrors in the Inquisition? For it is a
certainty that their only escape from the horrors of the Inquisition
was either extermination or expulsion. One meant certain death, the
other probable demise at the hands of enemies or the elements.

It is therefore impossible to comprehend the intentions and
actions of Columbus without understanding the influence that the
Spanish Inquisition had on secret Jews (Marranos and/or conversos) who had become converts to Christianity—which we believe
Columbus to have been.

The history of the Jewish people contains a thread throughout—
the thread of exile. In 70 BC, the Jews were exiled after the
Babylonians conquered the kingdom of Judah.

After the Romans under Emperor Hadrian marched through
Palestine in 135 BC (the land the Semites called Judea) and enslaved
the Jews, the area remained relatively quiet. With his departure in

132 BC, the Jews rallied to fight for their land under the capable leadership of Shimon Bar Kochba. Jewish fighters overran fifty strongholds and seized almost one thousand towns and villages. They were joined in the battle by more Jews and even some Gentiles from other areas.

Then the Romans began to prevail, pushing their challengers to Bethar, the site of Bar Kochba's command center and home of the Sanhedrin (Jewish High Court).[33] Hadrian's troops surrounded Bethar, and on the Ninth of Av, a date linked down through the ages to a list of catastrophes for the Jewish people and believed cursed by God, the walls of Bethar collapsed under the assault. The Roman army slaughtered every individual in the stronghold and prevented the Jews from burying their dead for six long days.

Although the Romans were successful in ending the last *Bar Kochba* revolt, murdering or enslaving the remaining Jewish population, the land was not totally cleansed of Jews. While many were scattered and exiled, there has been a constant representation of Jews in Palestine through the centuries.

While the Romans conquered Palestine and the Jews were exiled, their connection to the Land was preserved in the *Torah* and in daily prayers that called for returning to and rebuilding Jerusalem. However, no Jew was permitted to live inside the walls of Jerusalem while the Romans were in control. Each time the Jews would regain oversight of their homeland, another expulsion followed—and not only in Palestine. Seemingly, wherever the children of Israel sought refuge, trouble ensued. Jews in England were expelled in AD 1290. In 1396, Jews were banished from France, and thousands were forced to flee Austria in 1421. Homelessness has ever been a close companion of the Jewish people; and nowhere was this as evident as it was to become in Spain.

The upheaval that was to engulf Spain began with the secret marriage of Isabella of Castile and Ferdinand II of Aragon. The two were wed on October 18, 1469, in the city of Valladolid—a move to unite the two regions that would eventually become the kingdom of Spain. Secrecy was necessary as Juan Pacheco (one of the great nobles of Castile), was working feverishly to prevent a union between Isabella and the son of Juan II, but the future queen took matters in her own hands and married Ferdinand, the heir apparent to the throne of Aragon. A special papal dispensation was required for the two to wed, as they were second cousins and forbidden by Roman law to marry.

The union was the beginning of bigger, but not always better, things. The two monarchs would prove to be resourceful, robust, and successful rulers and were able to unite two separate and chaotic states into a cohesive and reformed nation. Isabella was a shy, unyielding, zealously devout woman. An authoritarian advocate of the divine right to govern, she was persuaded that the monarchy was her God-given birthright. Together she and Ferdinand would revolutionize Spain. Even though their goals were sometimes neither ethical nor honorable, theirs became a powerful royal court with great influence and authority.

When the marriage of Ferdinand and his cousin Isabella was suggested, the coffers of King Juan were all but empty. Ferdinand could raise no suitable bridal gift to present to his intended. A number of influential Marranos, led by Pedro de la Caballeria, silenced the opposition, and wealthy Marranos from both kingdoms purchased a necklace worth 40,000 ducats (based on the price of gold in twenty-first-century markets, it translates into millions of today's dollars) as a gift for the future queen.[34] The wedding took place in 1469. (Would the contributors have been so eager had they known the future sovereigns would back the Inquisition?)

Ferdinand, rather than being grateful to the Marranos for their luxurious gift, was jealous of their wealth and imposed higher taxes. Isabella, far from being a compassionate ruler, would ride weekly into a city in Castile to dispense justice to supposed offenders. If a wealthy defendant were convicted, his property would be confiscated and claimed by the Crown. Many of the sentences handed down were comparable to those later imposed during the Inquisition.

By April of 1479, Ferdinand and Isabella had assembled the parliament (Cortes) to vote on tax revenues and establish the *Santa Hermandad*, the Holy Brotherhood. This general police force was given powers to invoke sentence without a trial, even in capital cases. Its brutality was notoriously loathsome. The rough and ready justice of the Santa Hermandades became noted for its brutality.[35] Isabella's troops were ultimately placed at the service of the interrogators during the Inquisition and acquired great influence.

It would replace the Cortes as the chief source of royal funding, thus decreasing the power of the nobility and cementing royal rule. The convocation took the first step toward imposing more stringent restrictions on Jews who were instructed to wear a round badge of identification.[36] Perhaps it was from Spain that Adolf Hitler gleaned the idea of having all Jews wear a yellow ID badge.

In recent years, several European countries including Germany and Sweden have considered banning the practice of circumcision of young children for religious reasons. A measure to ban circumcision found its way onto a San Francisco ballot in 2014.[37] We may readily conclude that anti-Semitism will find a way of expression anywhere and at any time.

When and how did Jews come to be in what is now Spain? Don

Isaac Abravanel, a contemporary of Columbus and a prominent Jewish scholar, philosopher, and brilliant communicator during the fifteenth century revealed in his writings that his ancestors arrived in Spain in vessels under the care of Phiros, a colleague of King Nebuchadnezzar of Babylon. The exiles were descendants of the tribes of Judah, Benjamin, Shimon, and Levi and had been transported from Judea during the siege of Jerusalem (see Jeremiah 39).[38] His father and grandfather had held positions of importance in the courts of kings in Castile and in Portugal. It was from them that the young Abravanel learned the fine art of finances and diplomacy.

Abravanel wrote that the deportees settled in Lucena in Andalusia, and in the area of Toledo (which means "wandering" in Hebrew). The earlier refugees were later joined by approximately 80,000[39] outcasts originally displaced by Titus from in and around Jerusalem circa 70 BC. The apostle Paul wrote of the presence of Jews in Spain in Romans 15:24, 28 (NIV):

> I plan to do so when I go to Spain. I hope to see you while passing through and to have you assist me on my journey there, after I have enjoyed your company for a while . . . . So after I have completed this task and have made sure that they have received this contribution, I will go to Spain and visit you on the way.

By the fifth century, nomadic Germanic tribes of Visigoths had conquered most of the Iberian Peninsula. Fortunately for the Jewish inhabitants, the invaders had little regard for the various religious creeds over which they ruled.[40] That changed when Alaric II came to power and summarily espoused the edicts of the conquered Romans.[41] When Visigoth ruler Recared embraced Catholicism in the late sixth century, an antagonistic plan regarding treatment of the Jews was promptly enacted.

Under Recared's leadership, the Third Council of Toledo adopted a law requiring children of mixed marriages to be baptized, including offspring of unions between Christians and Jews. Christian women were forbidden to have intercourse with Jewish men—even husbands with wives—and circumcision was banned. The action did not meet with overwhelming success, as not all Visigoths had converted to Catholicism and were, therefore, more lenient toward their Jewish neighbors. The reprieve was not to last forever.

In 613 a new ruler, Sisebut, took the reins of power on the peninsula, and resurrected Recared's program with rekindled energy. Not only did he reinforce the earlier edict of mandatory baptism for children of multicultural unions, Sisebut launched the first proclamation of conversion or expulsion against the Jews. It is thought that nearly 100,000 became conversos (New Christians), while some fled the country for the region of Gaul with others going to North Africa. According to author Yom Tov Assis, many of the supposed converts continued to practice Judaism in secret.[42] For many Jews, the "conversions" lasted only until the more lenient reign of Sisebut's successor, Swintila, when many of the conversos reverted to Judaism.

The Fourth Council of Toledo voted to eliminate the practice of compulsory baptism for children of mixed marriages, but added that if a converso was in actuality a practicing Jew, any offspring would be taken from the parents and enrolled in a monastery or entrusted to the household of a confirmed Christian. In this way, all Jews who had reverted to Judaism under the rule of Swintila were to be forced to convert to Christianity.[43]

Each succeeding Council of Toledo seemed to impose even harsher laws governing Jews in the kingdom. The Eighth Council forbade Jews the rites of circumcision and observing Shabbat. Conversos were forced to agree to either burn or stone to death any of their colleagues who reverted to Judaism. According to Katz, anyone regardless of race or religion who enabled the practice of Judaism was penalized one-quarter of their personal property and then excommunicated from the Church.[44] Through the years and Councils the fate of Jews rose and fell with various rulers—some inclined to relax the punishment of the Jews for perceived wrongdoing, others raising the bar and instituting even more stringent laws.

This disturbing trend instituted under the various Catholic Visigoth rulers was one of growing oppression. So grueling were the demands against Jews that they felt compelled to seek assistance from the Moorish tribes to the south. Charges of conspiring with the enemy were leveled against the Jews and the intolerance only intensified; Jews were subjugated and their property seized.[45]

The Seventeenth Council of Toledo in 694 under Egica decreed:

As the Jews have added to their other crimes this that they endeavoured to overthrow the country and the people, they must be severely punished. They have done this after they had (in appearance) received baptism, which, however, by faithlessness they have again stained. They shall be deprived of their property for the benefit of the exchequer, and shall be made slaves forever. Those to whom the King sends them as slaves must watch that they may no longer practise Jewish usages, and their children must be separated from them, when they are seven years of age, and subsequently married with Christians.[46]

Under various edicts issued by the Church and/or rulers in Spain, a Christian woman, married or single, daughter or prostitute, was forbidden to enter the home of a Jew. A woman who broke this law had to forfeit the dress she was wearing; a married woman was required to pay a fine of four hundred *maravedis* (a gold or silver Spanish coin); and a prostitute faced one hundred lashes and expulsion from her place of lodging. A Jew who was intimate with a Christian woman, even if it was his wife, faced being burned at the stake.

The Muslim invasion under Tariq Ibn Ziyad vividly changed the lives of Spanish Jews on the Iberian Peninsula. Historians of the time recount the beneficial aid provided to the Moors by the Jews.[47] Having been totally disillusioned and estranged by the edicts handed down from the Catholic Church, the Jews saw the Moors as an emancipating force and chose to help the invaders.[48] The period of Muslim rule on the Iberian Peninsula came to be known as the Golden Age by the Sephardic Jews who settled in the area.

In *The Origin of the Inquisition*, Benzion Netanyahu wrote:

> The Moorish-Arab conquest of the Iberian Peninsula in 711-714, ended the first cycle of Jewish life in Christian Spain. In the isolated spots of northern Spain that remained under Christian control, no Jews lived after 714; nor did Jews live in any of the territories "reconquered" by the Spaniards in the course of the eighth and the early ninth centuries. Those who did not flee southward to the Muslims were killed by Christian raiders or conquerors.[49]

It was during this so-called "Golden Age" that the Jews built the two surviving synagogues in Toledo from that era: A synagogue which had once been a church—Santa Maria Blanca—boasts grand curved arches and carvings that resemble lace. The second occupies a nondescript building, El Transito, or the Great Synagogue. The interior belies the unadorned outside. Jane Frances Amler described it:

> Though some of the Hebrew letters have crumbled, one can still read the psalms of David in gold letters circling the perimeter of the sanctuary. Brilliant colors of peacock blue, orange, red, and sea green, though softened with age, still grace what had been the mudejar [architectural style] balcony for women. On the left and right of where the Ark was displayed are the fading royal crests of the castle and the lion.[50]

Madriaga wrote of Toledo:

> Jewish tradition goes back as far as the days of Solomon for the first settlement of the Jews in Spain, and even credits them with founding of Toledo, the name of which has been considered by some rabbis as a form of the Hebrew word *Tholedoth*, meaning generations.[51]

—4—

CHRISTOPHER COLUMBUS
Secret Jew

A defence [sic] in the Inquisition is of little use to the prisoner,
for a suspicion only is deemed sufficient cause of condemnation,
and the greater his wealth the greater his danger.

—JOHN FOXE, *FOXE'S BOOK OF MARTYRS*

ΛS ΤΗΕ SUN began to set on the régime of the Moors in the
Iberian Peninsula, Christian forces from the north set their sights
on reclaiming the land lost to the Muslims. Consequently, life for
Jews who had prospered in Moorish Spain was soon to change—for
the worse—as repression and retaliation again waited just around
the corner.

Among the most noted leaders of the recovery of southern Spain
was Ferdinand III of Castile (1199–1252), whose rule also proved to
be a catalyst for change in the lives of the Spanish Jews. On April 15,
1250, Pope Innocent IV issued a papal bull (named for the seal used
to authenticate the missives). In it:

[He denied] Jews in Cordova permission to build a synagogue that they wanted. It also forbids them from proselytizing to Christians, from living in the same house as Christians, from eating or drinking with Christians, or even just generally associating with Christians in any way.

Jews can't employ Christians as servants or prepare medicine for Christians. Finally, every Jew has to wear a distinctive [yellow] badge while out in public—though they aren't allowed to be out in public at all on Good Friday.[52]

Jews caught without the reprehensible identity badge were subjected to a fine of ten gold Iberian coins (maravedis) or being beaten with ten lashes.

Alfonso, called "the Wise," adopted as truth a scurrilous legend in which Jews were accused of crucifying a Christian child each year on Good Friday. So taken was he with the fable that he included it in his *Libro de las Cantigas (Book of Songs)*. Despite its fabrication, Alfonso insisted that any Jew suspected of that crime appear before him and, if found guilty, sentenced to death. Alfonso was the successor of Enrique IV who was said to have been a friend of the Marranos. So reprehensible was that idea to those whose hatred for the converted Jews knew no bounds that a statue of the king was carved. The statue was carried onto a field where it was symbolically stripped of its crown and scepter and demolished with great outrage. Following the demolition, his half brother, Alfonso, then only eleven, was symbolically crowned as his successor. As jubilation spread throughout the cities of Seville, Cordova, Valladolid, Toledo, and other towns and villages of Spain, Enrique's officials were ousted.

Only one individual spoke against the uproar—converso and theologian Don Francisco de Toledo. He recognized the "harmful intentions of the Marquis and the iniquitous ambition of some grandees,"[53] and while the young king was not anti-Marrano, his kingdom was controlled by dignitaries and Old Christians whose sole agenda was to persecute the Jews who had converted to Catholicism. The attitude was one of government by false accusations, intrigue, incitement, and prevarication. Don Alfonso's supporters sought simply to annihilate the Marrano race.

The Marranos tried valiantly to mount an advance against the reprehensible charges against them under a covert rebel force. Armed with what chronicler Alfonso Fernández de Palencia called "arrogant resolution" and the best weapons available, they tried valiantly but to no avail to counter the assault against them. The jealousy of the Marranos' wealth was at the root of the Old Christian complaints against them, and the resulting malice led to new and even fouler accusations.

The fortune of the Jews seemed to change with each new king, noble, mayor, or other head of local government. The fourteenth century saw an increase in anti-Semitism that would eventually lead to the horrors of the Inquisition launched against conversos and Marranos throughout Spain.

In 1366, according to early historians:

> Villadiego (whose Jewish community numbered many scholars), Aguilar, and many other towns were totally destroyed. The inhabitants of Valladolid . . . robbed the Jews, destroyed their houses and synagogues, and tore their Torah scrolls to pieces. Paredes, Palencia, and several other communities met with a

like fate, and 300 Jewish families from Jaen were taken prisoner to Granada . . . in Toledo . . . no less than 8,000 persons died through famine and the hardships of war.[54]

It must be noted that by attacking the Jews, the Spaniards were condemning a group of people whose chief contribution to the region and its rulers was monetary, not military. The Jews who were sent to repopulate areas taken back from the Moors were farmers, tradesmen, craftsmen, and importers of commodities needed to sustain the recaptured villages and towns.

In his book *Structure of Spanish History*, Américo Castro posited that "Diligent Jews occupied the place vacated by the Christians in the life of the nation . . . [they] constituted the economic base of the peninsular medieval society." Castro went on to surmise, "The history of Spain has risen on the basis of a Jewish economy."[55]

Eventually, the influence of the Jewish population reached to "physicians, land surveyors, engineers, mathematicians, salt miners, tax collectors, tax farmers, administrators, translators, diplomatic emissaries, and functionaries in a variety of other professions . . . Most of these professions were of tremendous value to the development of Spain's economy, to its fiscal administration, to its diplomatic efforts and to its military accomplishments."[56]

On the surface all seemed to point to an easy union between Jews and Spanish Christians, but beneath the surface churned the ever-present fuel of anti-Semitism. One spark could ignite a backlash that would result in the slaughter of hundreds, if not thousands, of Jews in the forms of turbulence, pogroms, and massacres. Why? No matter how settled the children of Israel appeared to be in Spain or any other European country during the Middle Ages, they were and would always be "aliens in a strange land" (Exodus 18:3 KJV).

Tolerated only until Christians in the land could perform the same activities as had they, the green-eyed monster of jealousy reared its ugly head and the Jews would then be forced out. Shielded in part by the Spanish monarchy, the Jews managed to survive in the region for approximately four centuries before being expelled from Spain. Even those who had converted to Christianity under duress did not escape the scythe of the Grim Reaper during the Spanish Inquisition. As you will see, Marranos and conversos alike were targeted by the Crown and the Church.

As Jews in the land were elevated to various posts of authority, so anti-Semitism[57] grew. The desire among the Spanish peoples to halt the rise of policies favorable to the Jews was spurred by bald-faced hatred. The Jews were often labeled shameless and wicked people. These so-called wrongdoers were said to achieve numerous lies, temptations, and iniquities. They were charged with destroying the kingdom and driving its inhabitants to hopelessness. Christians were said to be subjugated and their lives controlled through taxes owed to Jewish businessmen who were themselves censured for dressing in finery, riding mules, and given Christian names.

It is easy to see how old roots of Jew-hatred thought to be dormant were given new life and justified because of jealousy. In the Cortes (or Parliament) of Toro, Jewish men and women were labeled "enemies of God and all Christians."[58] By 1412, the Laws of Catalina were enacted; Jews were banned from having any economic interchange with Christians. It effectively denied the Jews a source of income and left them in dire economic straits. It also barred them from social interaction with their neighbors.

The implementation of the Laws was systematic and merciless, and triggered insufferable torments to many. Author Solomon Alami described their conditions in vivid terms:

> People who had been well protected in their homes were ousted from their dwellings to find shelter in caves. Others live in huts in summer and in winter, with hungry infants crying in the bosoms of their mothers, and with boys and girls dying from exposure to the cold and the snow.[59]

Early Church pronouncements barred Jewish doctors, specialists, and pharmacists from caring for Christian patients and making prescriptions for them; but the Laws of Catalina outlawed them altogether in medical pursuits. This move deprived the Jews a chief means of revenue and prohibited the growth of friendly interactions between Christians and Jewish physicians who attempted to cure them. The same objective ordained the laws that barred Jews from visiting "Christians in their illness, or give them medicines, or talk idly to them, or send them presents of dried herbs, or spices, or any article of food."[60]

The period between 1391 and 1417 was called the Age of Conversions and was launched by a reeling attack against Jews. (It is thought that some 600,000 Jews were forced to accept conversion during that span.) It began with Ferran Martinez, a Castilian priest. He was said to be a man of little learning but great charisma. He apparently used his own hatred to move the lower-class masses to a frenzied passion against the Jews. He launched his campaign for expulsion of Jews from Spain in about 1378 but achieved little immediate success. Martinez bided his time, awaiting the right moment to approach the king, Enrique II, and strike a blow against the Jewish people in the region. His plan backfired due in large part to two Jews who were prominent members of the king's court: Joseph Pichon and the aforementioned Samuel Abravanel.

The message from the king to Martinez was not designed to endear him to the priest: "Do not dare to interfere in judging any dispute which involves any Jew in any manner."[61] The edict forced Martinez to abandon his tactics—but only temporarily.

With the death of Enrique II on May 30, 1379, Martinez saw an opportunity to revive and revitalize his campaign against the Jews under the new king, Juan I. His efforts were once again stymied by the monarch, but he soon ferreted out another avenue by which to limit the authority and reach of the Jews: Martinez began a campaign to convert to Christianity slaves owned by Jews in Seville. The law stated that Jews could not own Christian slaves, so with conversion, any slaves that embraced Christianity would have to be freed. It would be a blow to the economic interests of the Jews.

The king was angered by the priest's tactics and ordered Martinez in no uncertain terms to cease and desist: "If you do not abstain from this behavior, we shall punish you so that you will regret what you have done and no other person will dare to do likewise."[62] The order simply forced Martinez underground yet again but failed to halt his crusade against Jews in Spain.

Four years slipped by before the priest overtly launched yet another attack, demanding the partition of Christians and Jews according to the law and orders from the archbishop of Seville. Martinez demanded that all synagogues be closed and leveled, that all Jews be expelled from their midst, and no interaction was to be had with them. Forestalled by the archbishop, the priest was again forced to retreat, a position which lasted until July 1390 when Archbishop

Barrose died. Three months later, Juan I also succumbed, leaving the door open for the priest and his followers to attack the Jews in the region with unabashed ferocity.

Martinez issued orders to various clergy in the region to immediately seize and destroy the synagogues in their area. Priests in Ecija, Alcala de Guadaira, Coria, and Cantillana carried out the order.

On June 4, 1391, a pogrom against Jews in Seville erupted as riots broke out in the city—something that had not occurred in nearly three hundred years, not since 1109. The Jews, within the *Juderia* (Jewish Quarter) had apparently felt the stirrings of an uprising, for the gates had been closed and closely guarded. A plot to burn the wooden gates to gain entrance to the area succeeded. Two days later, a horde descended on the Juderia, murdering 4,000 Jews. Those not slaughtered had chosen baptism as the only possible means of evading a death sentence.

In Cordova, the entire Jewish Quarter was burned to the ground with the men, women, and children brutally butchered. When some semblance of calm returned, homes and synagogues had been destroyed and the bodies of 2,000 Jews were callously piled in the streets. The list of towns and villages where Jewish inhabitants were persecuted, massacred, or forced into Christian baptism grew as the spirit of murder spread across Spain. Toledo, Castilian, Aragon, Marjorca, Valencia, and Barcelona, just to name a few cities, were caught in the frenzy of rioting—and the Jews were the ones to suffer at the hands of hysterical mobs.

Thousands of Jews were wiped from the land, communities obliterated, the perpetrators generally unpunished, and the country suffered from the loss of great minds, gifted artisans, prolific farmers, and productive citizens.

Rabbi Joseph Albo described the scene in Seville during the mob-inspired riots:

> A blood-thirsty mob fell on the Jewish quarter of Seville . . . and mercilessly killed every Jew who fell into their hands and refused to be baptized; many women and children were sold into slavery. A number of Jews, however, managed to escape . . . Within three months most of the flourishing Jewish communities in all the Christian States of Spain—Castille, Aragon, Valencia, Catalonia, as well as the Balearic Islands—were destroyed. One of the eye-witnesses to these massacres and atrocities was the famed Rabbi and scholar Hasdai Crescas . . . The pattern was invariably the same: A wild mob, roused by fanatical priests and monks, stormed into the Jewish quarter. They set fire to Jewish homes, shops and synagogues, giving the Jews one choice: conversion to Christianity or death. They killed mercilessly those who refused to be baptized. Many Jews chose to die as martyrs, at *kiddush hashem*[63]; some saved themselves by outward conversion.[64]

Even though conversion seemed to be the solution to those faced with slaughter, the marauding mobs still plundered and burned homes and lands as the Jews awaited baptism. The area was said to resemble a torched wasteland in the wake of the riots. Many Jews were not given the opportunity to convert but were slaughtered with the broadsword, drowned in rivers, burned alive, or sold into slavery. Entire communities disappeared as Jew-haters swept through towns and villages. It was said that leaders were so frightened by the mob mentality sweeping Spain that they failed to offer any protection against the horror. Sensing the change in attitude, Martinez launched a new attack, describing his adversaries as "incorrigible criminals who attempted to cheat even God himself, and nobody should therefore be surprised that they were cheating the kings and the princes." He reminded them that "Had not Jesus said to his disciples when he sent them to preach the Gospel that anyone who would refuse Jesus' reign should be viewed as His enemy and as son of the devil? Whom does this definition fit more than the Jews, who have consistently rejected His reign . . . ?"[65] Martinez demanded that Jews and Christians be separated and that synagogues be dismantled as the law demanded. And while ecclesiastical law prohibited the murder of Jews simply because of their ancestry, he advocated that the multitudes do exactly that, assuring them immunity from retribution by the powers that be.

Martinez was duly famous for his obstinacy and the tenacity to attain his goals. Discipline, joined with his cruelty and ingenuity, as well as his corruptness and determination made him essentially uncontainable. Due to this amalgamation of abilities he triumphed over the forcefulness of kings, the archbishop of Seville, and the nobility. His celebrity and reputation were enhanced by his rhetoric, which must have been rousing and particularly befitting to move the multitudes. (We have to think no further back in history than Adolf Hitler.)

It was principally by this eloquence that Martinez captured the fancy of the lower class that saw him as defender of their Christian cause. The only reason they had held back from inflicting terror on their Jewish neighbors was fear of what the monarchs might do in retaliation. Martinez schooled them in overcoming that fear. He taught them that in terrorizing and even murdering Jews, they were performing a service to the Crown, not disobeying the laws of the land. His cunning and shrewd activities lasted more than fourteen years as he instigated conflict between the Jews and their countrymen. Had he been given the blessing of the Church and the Crown, it is highly likely that his reign of terror would have eventually encompassed the whole of Spain and all the Jews therein. Those in charge of the towns and cities failed to suppress the riots, fearing the mob more than the monarch. For example, in Valencia, some Jews fled but the majority took up crosses, rushed to the cathedrals, and voiced their wish to be baptized. Their conversion led to the total annihilation of the Jewish society in that city. As likely as not, when they returned from awaiting baptism at the local church, they found their homes ransacked and personal effects either looted or destroyed. Many of the converts lost their business partners, either to death or dispersion. Conversos were forced to find and inveigle a Christian to employ them at a vastly lower rate of pay and work longer hours in order to provide for their families.

Thus Martinez was responsible for inflaming the masses and launching the devastating riots of 1391 that resulted in the butcher of thousands of Jewish men and the conversion of some 20,000 Jews. Such success only intensified the determination of Martinez and his gang of henchmen to further expand their activities across Spain. It was only the arrest and incarceration of Martinez's nephew, also a priest, that signaled the halt of the pogrom launched by his anti-Semitic uncle.

The attributes of the pogrom of 1391 perhaps describes the vast swarm of conversions in each of the neighborhoods attacked even before the assaults began. Royal edicts proposing conversion as an option to death engendered an almost total conversion in many Jewish communities. The riots of 1391 merged the methods followed by intimidating governments and those of other pogroms inflamed by the masses whose purpose was primarily hatred and greed. The result was a sizeable number of converts and a comparably lesser sum of martyrs for the faith.

The Jews had been forced to make one of only three choices: Expulsion from Spain, conversion to Christianity, or death. Given the reach of the Spanish Inquisition, conversion would eventually mean death for many of the conversos.

—5—

CHRISTOPHER
COLUMBUS
Secret Jew

A prisoner in the Inquisition is never allowed to see the face of
his accuser, or of the witnesses against him, but every method is
taken by threats and tortures, to oblige him to accuse himself,
and by that means corroborate their evidence.

—JOHN FOXE, AUTHOR

THE FORCED conversions in Spain during the 1391 riots and pogroms were the precursor to the Inquisition launched under the direction of King Ferdinand and Queen Isabella. The number of Jews who submitted to the coercion of forcible conversion was quite large and included the wealthy who ultimately became bitter enemies and oppressors of their Jewish brethren. Thus the conversos and Marranos became the targets of the inquisitors who would invent and/or endorse the most heinous of acts against the supposed betrayers of the Faith and the Church.

No widespread epidemic hostile to Jews in the Middle Ages produced such staggering loss as did the riots and pogroms of 1391.

Jewish fatalities in the Rhineland[66] all through the first Crusade in 1096 or in Germany during the Black Death of 1348[67] were no harsher than those of the Jews in Spain in 1391. If we consider those Jews who abandoned their faith because of intimidation during the riots, the demise of Spain's Jews far outstripped those encountered elsewhere. Within two or three years, Spain's Jewish society, the biggest in the known world, was diminished by almost thirty-three percent—the utmost calamity that had yet transpired among Jews in Europe.

Neither the Marranos nor the conversos were held in especially high esteem by their fellow countrymen. The word *Marrano* comes from an Arabic word that means "forbidden, anathematized." In fifteenth-century Spain it came to mean "pig" and "dirty." It was a racist epithet used in a prejudicial way. There have been various explanations as to the etymology of the word, including the Aramaic-Hebrew *Mar Anus* or "forced convert"; and the second word of the religious oath *anathema maranatha* or "cursed at the final judgment." No matter the origin, it was meant to be derisive. *Converso* simply meant to have converted from Judaism to Christianity. In reality, Spain was boiling with frustration, and the pressure resulting from the addition of all the new converts was taxing the tolerance of the Church and its people.

Being forced to convert under duress presented an entirely new set of problems for the conversos. Under constant scrutiny, Jews were forced to forego any semblance of their former lives or rituals, were required to work on religious holidays, and were banned from working on the Christian Sabbath and festivals. Eventually, Judaic traditions among the conversos declined, while Christian practices blossomed.

Late in the fifteenth century the position of the aristocracy as well as that of the lower classes changed regarding the conversos.

It is believed that they hid their Jewishness beneath a façade of Christianity. By 1449 conversos were banned from holding public office in Toledo no matter how long since their families had converted to Catholicism.[68] This same law presented another concept, that of the *limpieza de sangre*, the "purity of the blood," reminiscent of Nuremberg Laws established by the Nazis in the twentieth century.[69] A division between Old Christians and conversos was created in which conversos were deemed to be subordinate. The newly instituted rule was censured by theologians who determined that all persons who had been baptized into the Church were Christians and should not fall into condemnation. Suddenly, the Old Christians saw themselves, not the Jewish converts, as the oppressed. Actually, they were no worse off but perceived that they had become socially and economically debased because of their converso neighbors. They felt there was no way to change the government's favorable policies toward the New Christians, thus the anti-Marrano/converso faction would be forced to take the law into their own hands. A steady tide of social, economic, and political advancement among conversos would prove to be the catalyst for the Toledan laws enacted in 1449.

Soon, the first flash of hatred as a result of the newly enacted laws against the Marranos arced and would rapidly consume the entire group. It quickly advanced from spark to inferno, and launched a new period of struggle between Old Christians and New in Spain.

The laws signaled the start of an anti-converso movement among the inhabitants of both Castile and Aragon. Hatred of Marranos and conversos flared, as did the violence leveled against them. It was comprised of two parts: 1) a Preamble setting forth a judgment of the social and religious conduct of the conversos; and 2) legal limitations that were to be imposed on them. The law was given a name which reflected the two segments: *Sentencia-Estatuto* (Judgment and

Statute). Benzion Netanyahu wrote, "Each of these documents bears witness to the motives, attitudes, doctrines, and convictions that shaped the views of the anti-Marrano party."[70] The Jewish people were regarded as a problem that could not be resolved by baptism and conversion to Christianity. The statute deprived conversos of the ability to hold any public office, to effectively defend themselves in the courts, and instituted a ban against making a living as clergy in the Church. The laws extended to their descendants in perpetuity. The tenets were designed to strip conversos of all Christian fellowship.

The *Sentencia* (judgment) portion of the document embraced the ideology that conversos filled most public offices in Toledo that dealt with fiscal issues. This, the anti-Marranos exposed, was what allowed them to dominate Old Christians in the entire region. Conspiracy theories against the Jews—both practicing and converts—abounded in Spain in the Middle Ages. The charge required no substantiation; it was enough that those accused had Jewish blood flowing through their veins. Fingers pointed to the converso management of the king's fiscal administration; they were accused of "having stolen large and innumerable quantities of maravedis and silver from the King our Lord and from his revenues, taxes, and tributes . . . [and] have brought devastation upon the estates of many noble ladies, caballeros and hijos dalgo [little children] . . . [and] have oppressed, destroyed, robbed and deprived most of the old houses and estates of Old Christians of this city, its territory and jurisdiction."[71]

The Toledan Petition, as it came to be known, was the initial manifestation of the anti-Marrano attitude that was prevalent in the country but previously had been officially inhibited. It was the prescribed position adopted by a sector of the people of Spain toward the Marranos and what many considered the Marrano problem. Additionally, it was the initial manifestation of a viewpoint that was to permeate every aspect of Spanish existence. It was a giant step toward the horror that would engulf Spain at the hands of the inquisitors, and a perfect parallel to Psalm 83:3 (ESV): "They lay crafty plans against your people; they consult together against your treasured ones." The conversos were too easy a target for the frequent charges of conspiracy. They were charged with seeking jurisdiction over key court positions by attempting to control and oppress the Old Christians of Spain.

The forces which brought about the launch of the Inquisition were based on religious, socio-economic, and racial factors. In his book on the life of Jewish statesman and philosopher Don Isaac Abravanel, Benzion Netanyahu wrote:

> It was in the year of 1480—the year in which the Cortes of Toledo helped the kings break the powers of the feudal aristocracy—that the Spanish monarchy embarked upon a determined and unrelenting anti-Jewish course. In that year steps were initiated for the segregation of the Jews and their elimination from Spanish life, and it was in that year that the Inquisition was established. The Inquisition, although directed not against Jews but against Jewish converts and their descendants, was nevertheless the most radical anti-Jewish measure taken at any time in the Middle Ages . . . Spain was the only country in the Middle Ages where Jews were converted to Christianity on a mass scale . . . . The moment a Jew embraced Christianity, all discrimination against him was to end. But this was not the attitude of the burgher. The

latter sought, not the Jews conversion, but rather his annihilation or expulsion.[72]

Even with the institution of the Inquisition and the war against Marranos who had long been converts to Catholicism, Abravanel rebelled against the idea that those tortured and burned at the stake were secret Jews who still practiced the tenets of the faith. Abravanel felt that Marranos, by and large, were traitors to Judaism and had deserted their race to "intermingle" with the gentiles. He turned to the prophet Hosea 7:8 (KJV) to support his belief of what had happened to the Marranos: "Ephraim has mixed himself among the peoples; Ephraim is a cake unturned."

Abravanel would probably have liked the *New Living Translation*'s succinct statement:

> "The people of Israel mingle with godless foreigners, making themselves as worthless as a half-baked cake!"

The Marranos had been exposed to the fire; a just punishment for their apostasy. Abravanel's unrelenting disdain for the Marranos seems a clear indication that many had embraced Catholicism and were true converts, and thus there was no reason for them to be subjected to the terrors of the Inquisition. The charges that they were secret Jews, still practicing the rites of their religion, were unfounded and sprang basically from covetousness. So little credence has been given to the idea that this charge was at the root of the Inquisition that it has been largely unexplored by historians. As Netanyahu indicated:

The Old Christians thus came to realize the fateful mistake they had made when they forced the Jews to embrace Christianity, thereby by their own hands opening for them the way to all the advantages and positions which they had so vehemently fought to deny them.[73]

The general consensus is that the Marranos were, indeed, Christians, and not Jews covertly clinging to Judaism. It is inordinately sad that the Old Christians resented the Marranos for having embraced the very religion they were forced to accept upon threat of death. Can we then assume that the Marranos might very well have been singled out for the same reason so many of Israel's children are so unpopular today? They are Jews; the offspring of Abraham, Isaac, and Jacob. They are the children of the covenant between God and His people.

Centuries before the term "Nazism" was introduced into the language, there were racists. Long before Hitler's troops goose-stepped through the capitals of Europe, anti-Semitism reigned supreme. Years before the Jews were charged with creating the chaos that was Germany's economic upheaval, Jew-hatred permeated that society. Holocaust historian Raul Hilberg wrote, "The Nazis did not discard the past, they built on it. They did not begin a development. They completed it."[74]

It did not even begin in Spain in the Middle Ages. It began when the children of Israel resolved to be a distinctive group of people, set apart by their faith in one God (Jehovah) and by the denunciation of the predominant religion of the day. They then, all too often, were charged with being the culprits, real or imagined, for whatever adversities were visited upon the world. The anti-Semites down through the ages might well have quoted author Andrew Bernaldez:

> Once the fire has been ignited, it will be necessary for it to go on burning until all the Judaizers are consumed and dead, and none of them remains.[75]

According to the Southern Institute for Education and Research at Tulane University in New Orleans, Louisiana:

> In the late 19th century, the debate on the Jewish question entered a new chapter. Hitherto, the Jews had been viewed as different and unacceptable because of their religion. In 1873, with the publication of the book *The Victory of Judaism over Germanism* by Wilhelm Marr, the Jewish question became one of race. The Jews, it was argued, were different because of who they were, not what they thought. They were different because of birth. They were different because of blood. An "alien" people, the Jews could never be Germans. It was in this book that the term anti-Semitism first appeared. This so-called scientific basis of anti-Semitism excluded any possibility of Jews being assimilated into German culture. Once defined as such in the popular mind, a major obstacle to Jewish destruction, the common bond in humanity, was overcome.
>
> Social Darwinism took root. This was the belief that people of different races were in competition with one another, and only the strongest of the races

would ultimately survive. [Heinrich Gotthard von] Treitschke, the German philosopher, noted, "The Jews are our misfortune." The expression captured the spirit of the age.[76]

✦   ✦   ✦

It was in the shadow of the coming Inquisition that in 1484 Abravanel was summoned to the court of Ferdinand and Isabella. He was there to advise them on financial matters, and especially on the way to alleviate their vast debts associated with the ongoing war in Granada. His plan—although undefined—won the respect of the monarchs and a place for Abravanel in service to the royals. Only eight years later, the courtier would be faced with expulsion.

When a Jew was baptized and supposedly embraced Christianity, all bigotry was to stop. Unfortunately, that was not the case at all. This was especially true among the burghers (inhabitants of a bor-ough in medieval European cities).[77] Many burghers were appalled that Jews chose baptism when the real intent had been expulsion from Spain or annihilation. They came to realize much too late that the plan had backfired; the Jews now were candidates for any and all the benefits and status available to other citizens of Spain. With that knowledge came the plots and schemes to subject the conversos and Marranos to the same pressures and intimidation heaped upon the non-converted Jews.

Enough years had passed following the riots of 1391 that the conversos had become strongly entrenched in Spanish culture and had achieved positions of power within the government hierarchy. According to the law, no restrictions could be placed on the new

Christians. All the offices of the Church and state were open to them. They became advisers to the king, teachers in the universities, administrative officials, and married into noble families.

The basic so-called "criminal nature" of the converts from Judaism was reason enough for harassment, and the burghers relied on the clergy to find sentient ways based on religious motives to arouse suspicion and create a climate favorable to renewed persecution. The people, unaware that they were being spoon-fed a steady diet of hatred for the converted Jews, yielded to the bureaucratic hype and began to view the conversos and Marranos as religious criminals.

Among these were what came to be known as crypto-Jews—men and women who "publicly professed Roman Catholicism" but privately adhered to Judaism during the Spanish Inquisition, and particularly after the Alhambra Decree of 1492. Officially they were known as "New Christians," and there was considerable legislation directed against them in both Spain and Portugal and in their colonies, the chief activity of the Inquisition being directed against them.

The pernicious plot to destroy the Marranos was seemingly ignored by the Jewish population, who really had no love for the traitors who embraced Catholicism. This was further fueled by the fact that among the Marrano leaders were those who had become staunch enemies of the Jews still residing in Spain. Benzion Netanyahu explained the reaction of the Jews in this way:

> Their medieval religious outlook and reasoning, coupled with their negative attitude toward the Marranos, gave birth to a theory of the Inquisition which was as convenient as it was false. Furthermore, the Marranos, caught in the storm-center of persecution,

seemed to have diverted toward themselves most of the enmity for the Jews . . . . Just as the Jews of Germany failed to foresee Hitler's rise to power at any time during the period preceding that rise, so the Jews of Spain failed to notice, even a few years before the expulsion, the mountainous wave which was approaching to overwhelm them.[78]

The truth is that by the time the edict was handed down, the Marranos had been assimilated into the Catholic culture and had reached the point of no return. It is likely that there were small groups within the larger designation "Marranos" who were secret Jews, but not the majority. Sadly, not only did much of the Church consider the Marranos and conversos as heretics, so did the Jews consider them to be enemies of Judaism. Thus, those caught in the grip of the Inquisition had no champion on either side of the conflict, and no one to stand in their defense. Many historians agree that the majority of the converso community were devoutly Christian and happy with the decision to convert, and that only a small minority were actually crypto-Jews.

—6—

CHRISTOPHER COLUMBUS
Secret Jew

IN 1478, Pope Sixtus IV sanctioned the Inquisition in Castile to halt what was labeled "the Judaic heresy." The Inquisition was meant to totally uproot tentacles of Judaism that might remain. It would, or so the Church thought, signal the end of any and all Judaic anomaly that remained in the camp of the conversos and Marranos. On September 27, 1480, Spanish sovereigns Ferdinand and Isabella issued an order to establish tribunals in their kingdom to judge cases of "heretical depravity" . . . the royal decree explicitly stating that the Inquisition was instituted to search out and punish converts to Judaism who transgressed against Christianity by secretly adhering to Jewish beliefs and Jewish rites. According to Benzion Netanyahu:

> The Spanish Inquisition attacked the Marranos with a savage ferocity that by then was outmoded; it burned them by the thousands, confiscated their possessions, incarcerated them in dungeons, branded them as outcasts, robbed their sons of their rightful inheritance while denying them the right to public office, and subjected them all to a reign of terror which "turned their lives into something worse than death," as Mariana, the Spanish historian put it.[80]

So ambitious was Ferdinand that he entertained thoughts of subjugating Italy and France but could not do so without funds. These, he was informed by the Dominicans, could readily be obtained through the Inquisition and the confiscated wealth of Marranos, Moors, and Jews. It would be, he was advised, a blow struck against conversos who were painted as being the enemy of Spain and the Church. No other faction was cited, no other reason specified. That alone implies an intimate connection between the invention of the Inquisition and the Jews in Spain. To prove the point, Leonardo de Eli, an affluent Jew from Saragossa, was accused and tried, thus exposing Ferdinand's true aims. Sickened by the ploy, Marrano dignitaries introduced petitions to halt the king's plan. The move failed and the Inquisition was strengthened. The desolate Marranos planned and launched a successful scheme to assassinate the Inquisitor in Saragossa. When an outraged Queen Isabella heard of the death, she demanded vengeance on the Marranos. Those seized were hideously persecuted before being slain.

The Church became enmeshed in the racist myth which led its victims inexorably to the dungeon of torture and ultimately the grave. Often the convicted were burned at the stake. As the wood was torched, a choir would sing *Te Deum Laudamus or* "We Praise Thee O Lord." In an atmosphere of greed, fear, and cruelty pursued by Ferdinand and Isabella and sanctioned by the Church, alleged apostates were flushed from their hiding places and dragged through the streets to the place of inquisition. So numerous were the supposed heretics that cellars of monasteries were converted to torture chambers. Frequently the victims were totally unaware of the charges brought against them until they faced the horrors inflicted by the inquisitors.

Once a victim had been charged, tortured, and convicted in a public ceremony, an *auto da fe* (act of faith) was held during which the "heretic" was sentenced and then executed. It was an agonizingly excruciating charade during which the doomed victim was stripped of all humanity before a leering and jeering crowd. Death was doubtless a welcome release from the torture dispensed by the inquisitors.

There was one huge problem that Ferdinand and Isabella failed to consider: As Marranos, conversos, and practicing Jews were arrested and made to suffer torture unto death, the source of funds was dying with them. It was at that point the Church decided to extend mercy to the beleaguered Marranos. During the questionable grace period, all who desired to be reunited with the Church could do so—for a fee. A number of very naïve, or gullible, Marranos accepted the offer only to be forced to reveal the names of other family members who were observant Jews. Again, it was the choice given all too many times to the Jewish people: acquiesce or die.

Pope Sixtus IV, upon hearing reports of the Inquisition, released a papal bull insisting that modifications be made in the procedures.

Ferdinand bristled at the Pope's recommendations; the pontiff's interference was a violation of his rights as king and he spurned the order. The pope issued no further writs on the subject.

It is not remarkable that many wealthy Marranos chose to leave Spain for Portugal and Granada. Ferdinand and Isabella were not especially concerned about outflow as any treasures abandoned by those fleeing were divvied up by the monarchs and the Church. Disappointed that the gold of the Marranos was insufficient to cover the costs of the Inquisition, church leaders ordered collection boxes placed in the churches and funds solicited. It had quickly become transparent that a great deal of gold would be needed to arrest, try, and convict innocent men, women, and children.

As the Inquisition gained momentum, one Spaniard managed to carve his name in the annals of history in the blood of Marranos, conversos, and Jews. His name: Tomás de Torquemada, of the Spanish Inquisition, of whom more will be written in later chapters. Just as the name Adolf Hitler caused much of the world to cringe when the horrors of the Holocaust were finally revealed, so did the name Torquemada evoke nightmares of a monster in the service of the Church. Writer Anthony Bruno made a comparison among three of history's most notorious murderers:

"Qualitatively Torquemada stands shoulder-to-shoulder with Hitler and Stalin."[81]

The irony surrounding his selection to the infamous post is that his grandmother was a Jewish convert to Christianity. Born in Valladolid, Spain, in 1420, Tomás was the nephew of a highly respected theologian, Cardinal Juan de Torquemada, a distinction that would advance his career. A celibate Dominican priest in his early years, Tomás was later appointed Prior at the Monastery Santa Cruz, a station he held until chosen in 1483 as Inquisitor General by

Pope Innocent VIII. When Isabella was a child, Tomas developed a close relationship with the future queen as her personal confessor. After she married Ferdinand, Tomás was appointed as a counselor to the royal court.

The Inquisition initially targeted Jews and Moors who claimed to have converted to Catholicism, a group whose allegiance to the state was questionable. The quest was to ferret out those conversos and Marranos who might possibly be traitors. This distrust ultimately produced the Alhambra Decree underwritten by Torquemada and leading to the Jews being banished from Spain in 1492. During the early years of the Inquisition, Tomás had been limited to targeting only conversos and aggressively urged Ferdinand and Isabella to issue the edict which would force the remaining Spanish Jews to either leave the country or convert.

The deeds of evil men are all too often undergirded by scriptures chosen to substantiate their wicked desires. This was certainly true of the masterminds of the Inquisition who, while searching to authenticate the torture of preference, chose the words of our Lord from John 15:6 (Latin Vulgate and KJV):

> *Si quis in me non manserit mittetur foras sicut palmes et aruit et colligent eos et in ignem mittunt et ardent.*
>
> Translation: If a man abide not in me, he is cast forth as a branch, and is withered; and men gather them, and cast *them* into the fire, and they are burned.

The horrors were sanctioned by none other than Thomas Aquinas, who declared:

> Heresy is the sin, the guilty of which must be not

only excommunicated, but also taken out of the world by death.[82]

Torquemada, in an attempt to clarify the position of Christians toward Jews, cited Psalm 94:14: "For the Lord will not cast off His people, neither will he forsake His inheritance" (KJV).

He declared that the phrases "His people" and "His inheritance" referred solely to Christians, not Jews. Augustine, trying to aid in clarification, determined:

> I do not see how that people [the Jews] could be called the inheritance of God—a people that did not believe in Christ, whom having rejected and slain, they became reprobate; who refused to believe in Him even after His resurrection, and who, in addition, killed His martyrs.[83]

Thomas Aquinas, a noted medieval philosopher and theologian, believed those who failed to support the Inquisition were breaking God's laws. His "Treatment of Heretics" laid out very stringent measures that were to be taken against anyone accused of heresy (see Appendix I).[84]

The Spanish Inquisition thrived with three main ingredients: bureaucracy, a police force, and a network of informers. The triumvirate from which the participants were drawn each kept a close eye on the other to prevent bribery. The police were held in check by the informers who believed they would secure their own salvation by exposing heretics. It did not hurt that the informers were rewarded with no taxation and leniency in the courts. And the informer was also given a portion of the property confiscated from the victim. The informers were presented with a special medal—a cross flanked by a dagger and olive branch—as a sign of their service. They were also allowed to display the emblem on their houses.

Academic Dagobert D. Runes wrote of that terrible time:

> The Spanish Inquisition was perhaps the most cynical plot in the dark history of Catholicism, aimed at expropriating the property of well-to-do Jews and converts in Spain, for the benefit of the royal court and the Church. Even "dead" suspects had their bones dug up for "trial" so estates could be confiscated from their heirs.[85]

As the Inquisition gained momentum in fifteenth-century Spain, the informers were particularly interested in the conversos and ultimately the Marranos. The homes of conversos would be visited on Friday nights in search of signs of Jewish religious activity. Were there lighted candles? Were family members dressed in their best? Either of these were cause for arrest. If no smoke emanated from the chimney on the Jewish Shabbat, it was believed that the Marranos were practicing Judaism. Suspicions were accompanied by a list of rules by which a backsliding Marrano or converso might be recognized and thus targeted for persecution:

> If they celebrate the Sabbath, wear a clean shirt or better garments, spread a clean tablecloth, light no fire, eat food which has been cooked overnight in the oven, or perform no work on that day; if they eat meat during Lent; if they take neither meat nor drink on the Day of Atonement, go barefoot, or ask forgiveness of

another on that day; if they celebrate the Passover with unleavened bread, or eat bitter herbs; if on the Feast of Tabernacles they use green branches or send fruit as gifts to friends; if they marry according to Jewish customs or take Jewish names; if they circumcise their boys . . . if they wash their hands before praying, bless a cup of wine before meals and pass it round among the people at table; if they pronounce blessings while slaughtering poultry . . . cover the blood with earth, separate the veins from meat, soak the flesh in water before cooking, and cleanse it from blood; if they eat no pork, hare, rabbits, or eels; if, soon after baptizing a child, they wash with water the spot touched by the oil; give Old Testament names to their children . . . if the women do not attend church within forty days after confinement; if the dying turn toward the wall; if they wash a corpse with warm water; if they recite the Psalms without adding at the end: "Glory be to the Father, the Son, and the Holy Ghost."[86]

The inquisitors seemed to entertain a particular hostility toward those conversos who had been appointed by the Crown to high office. As converts continued to gain importance in all walks of life, constraints and prejudice rose against them. By the time the Inquisition was instituted, the majority of Marranos and conversos had little memory of the religion that had been practiced by their parents or grandparents. But in the eyes of the Church, they were as guilty as if they had celebrated Passover weeks before. One decree, the *limpieza de sangre* (purity of blood) ordinance stated:

> We declare the so-called conversos, offspring of perverse Jewish ancestors, must be held by law to be infamous and ignominious, unfit, and unworthy to hold any public office or any benefice within the city of Toledo, or land within its jurisdiction, or to be commissioners for oaths or notaries, or to have any authority over the true Christians of the Holy Catholic Church.[87]

Torquemada was not above using every means available, even falsifying testimony against the Marranos, conversos, and Jews to achieve his objectives. That could not have been more obvious than with the LaGuardia trial, a melodramatic mythological show. The accused were eight conversos and Jews charged with having victimized a Christian child. It had been reported that the condemned had ripped out the heart of a Jewish child in order to summon demon spirits to halt the Inquisition and inflict madness upon Christians. Blatant falsehoods regarding ritual murders of Christians by Jews have been the source of riots, pograms, and murders for centuries. It is often referred to as "blood libel." Actually, quite the opposite has been true; professing Christians have been guilty of ritual murders against Jews—just consider the Spanish Inquisition where approximately 30,000 Jews were killed. For centuries, the attempts at self-defense by the Marranos went unheard as many of the accused were tried *in absentia* in a charade where only the accusers spoke. Their testimonies languished as the Marranos were summarily convicted and executed. Not until 1873 was the first of those documents published; sadly, it made little difference in public or scholastic opinion.

Not to be confused by facts, Torquemada utilized the LaGuardia trial as a tool to convince Ferdinand and Isabella to implement an order of expulsion against the Jews. Upon receiving word of this plot by the Inquisitor General, two wealthy Jews raised 30,000 ducats and offered the sum to Ferdinand and Isabella to halt the deportation edict. Always in need of cash, the two sovereigns were tempted to accept the offer when challenged by Torquemada, who cried melodramatically, "Judas sold his Master for thirty ducats. You would sell Him for thirty thousand ... Take Him and sell Him, but do not let it be said that I have had any share in this transaction."

All eight of the accused were tortured with hot pincers until they confessed to the crime. Ultimately, no body was found, no victim was discovered, yet the men were burned alive at the stake.[88] Such was the atmosphere in which the Inquisition was launched.

Torquemada firmly believed that conversos and Marranos were progeny of a group of people inclined toward corruption and immorality. They were, therefore, powerless to live a Christian life and should be adjudged to be heretics and were racially inferior.

Marcos Garcia de Mora was the driving force behind the anti-Marrano movement in Toledo, and as such was its chief spokesman. He urged his followers to follow the doctrines of Jesus Christ by robbing the conversos of their possessions and distributing them among the poor—namely the Old Christians. He cavalierly pronounced that some Jewish converts deserved admission into the Christian society, but largely saw a totally different solution to the problem of the Jews in Spain.

Garcia admitted that some of the conversos in Toledo had been victimized because they were traitors and heretics for daring to continue to observe some of the Jewish ceremonies. He felt that the punishment meted out was wholly justified and not at all too harsh.

He preached that the plot formulated by conversos was to murder the Old Christians, rob them of their possessions, and then surrender the city into the hands of Garcia's enemy, Alvaro de Luna.[89] His charges were not meant to be suppositions but rather formal charges by which the conversos could be legally tried and executed—by hanging or burning at the stake. This, he felt, was a just reward for the traitors who plotted to turn the city over to de Luna and the conversos who supported him.

Garcia justified the methods of killing with "For it is known that they were found to be heretical, infidels and blasphemers of Christ and His Mother . . . those of them who were burned as heretics were justly burned, for the punishment of the heretic—according to divine, human and customary law—is death by fire . . . [and] he who exults in cruelty against criminals for the sake of justice deserves a reward [for] he is a minister of God."[90] He then turned to an expert in canon law to support his interpretation. It was ruled that heretics could be turned over to the secular branch of the Church for the sole purpose of being subjected to due punishment—or burning at the stake. Garcia stated unequivocally that had the Toledans *not* murdered the Marranos, they would have been equally guilty of the crime of omission. He believed their only error was in not annihilating all Marranos and subjecting every converso in the city, and preferably in all of Spain, to a heinous death.

Like many before and after him, Garcia exploited the Scriptures to support his proclamations against the people he saw as heretics and traitors. He saw the role of the Marranos as one of trying to seduce the Old Christians into abandoning their faith. He gave two reasons specifically forbidding the converts from gaining office:

1.   Because they [conversos] have always played

false (*prevaricaron*) in the faith, and *under the guise of Christians* have always done evil and much harm to *true* Christians; and

2. Because it is a shady and ugly thing to allow him who yesterday recited prayers in the synagogue to sing today in the church.[91]

The judgments were based on Deuteronomy 24:4–8 and specifically the latter portion of verse 7 (NIV): "You must purge the evil from among you." It gave great latitude to those who were charged with defining "evil."

−7−

CHRISTOPHER
COLUMBUS

Secret Jew

*The crimes of Caligula shrink to insignificance compared to
the havoc wrought by Torquemada. The number of victims
of robbers, highwaymen, rapists, gangsters and other
criminals at any period of history is negligible compared to
the massive numbers of those cheerfully slain in the name
of the true religion, just policy or correct ideology.*[92]

—ARTHUR KOESTLER

THE WORD *inquisition* came to be known and feared throughout medieval Europe, but perhaps it was the Spanish Inquisition
that was synonymous with ruthlessness, fierceness, and depravity.
From the issuance of the papal bull by Pope Sixtus IV, Ferdinand
and Isabella began to wield the scythe of destruction against
Marranos, conversos, and Jews in Spain with the express purpose
of rooting out counterfeit Christians. The two sovereigns sparred
for a time over the tribunals that were to be established to conduct
the Inquisition. The Pope and Isabella ultimately won the day and
Ferdinand acquiesced to the wishes of his wife and the head of the

Church. (It appears that Isabella may have, at times, rivaled Queen Jezebel.[93]) An explicit target was those Jews and Moors who had claimed conversion to Christianity but who were still clandestine practitioners of their faith. Nor were the sovereigns shy about collecting any income generated by the Inquisition—from confiscated lands, jewels, gold, and other sources.

It is often thought—quite erroneously—that the Inquisition lasted only a few years; the truth is that it lasted until 1834, an inconceivable 384 years. At that time, then-Queen Mother Cristina declared, " . . . the Tribunal of the Inquisition is definitely suppressed."[94]

The methods used by the inquisitors during the Spanish Inquisition were understandably horrifying. Citizens were coerced into delivering friends, neighbors, business associates, and even family members into the hands of the torturers because of some real or perceived crime against the Church. Those who faced the inquisitors had little recourse: They could not engage a lawyer to plead their case; the name of their accuser could not be revealed; even the charges against the accused could not be known. Confessions were extracted by the most heinous of tortures.

In *The History of the Christian Church*, author William Jones quoted Voltaire:

> Their form of proceeding is an infallible way to destroy whomsoever the inquisitors wish. The prisoners are not confronted with the accuser or informer; nor is there any informer or witness who is not listened to. A public convict, a notorious malefactor, an infamous person, a common prostitute, a child, are in the holy office, though nowhere else, credible accusers

and witnesses. Even the son may depose against his father, the wife against her husband.[95]

Following the cessation of the Inquisition, no other such brutal and aggressive methods were employed by anyone in Western civilization for scarcely one hundred years until the rise of the Third Reich in Germany and the Communists in Soviet countries.

Those charged with carrying out the Inquisition appeared to hold a singular animosity toward conversos and Marranos who held stations of authority in the courts and financial institutions. Often a Jew was appointed to the position of King's Chief Treasurer, a place of great trust. The man in that chair was often gifted with monetary proficiencies and an extensive knowledge of the numerous challenges that influenced economic situations. These assignments were a basis for acrimonious hostility that some Christian aristocrats felt toward Jews who held positions of power within the court.

Men, women, and even children from every stratum were caught in the inquisitors' trap, having been sent there because of the jealousy or hatred of another. The thoroughness and brutality of the Inquisition seemed to particularly target and entrap the greatest number of Jews.

How the words *inquisition* and *church* could conceivably be used in the same sentence has puzzled historians for centuries. How could a religion that teaches love, tolerance, grace, and mercy be remotely connected to the monstrous torture of having individuals burned alive or tortured in the most foul and horrifying ways? How could fanatical minions of the Church misinterpret Scripture in order to justify their actions? In a questionable attempt to find a biblical basis for its acts, leaders turned to Titus 3:10–11:

A man that is an heretick after the first and second admonition reject; Knowing that he that is such is subverted, and sinneth, being condemned of himself (KJV).

The routine for the Inquisitor General seldom varied. Torquemada, overseer of fifteen district tribunals in Spain, and his train of fifty mounted body guards accompanied by 200 foot soldiers would ride majestically into a town or village. But so paranoid was the cleric that he often kept a charm nearby, a unicorn's horn, said to protect him from poisoning.[96] Torquemada would unleash his silver-tongued rhetoric in the town square or local church. His topic: the evils of heresy. The list of tenets regarding how to spot a sinner would be distributed, including instructions as to what to do should a heretic be discovered. It was, frankly, the perfect opportunity to cause havoc in the lives of any enemies, real or perceived.

A grace period of several weeks would follow the debacle in the square during which involuntary confessions among the populace were urged. During this time, testimony of an individual's heresy was solicited from witnesses that numbered as few as one and as many as thousands. The person who came forward and admitted heretical behavior was given less-severe punishment. Those who chose to rely on the mercy of the court were severely disappointed.

After accusations were received by the inquisitors, the individual was bidden to appear before the Inquisition. It was not a mandatory appearance, but failure to do so was perceived as guilt. According to historians Miroslav Hroch and Ann Skybova, there was ample advice on how to handle the interrogation of an accused:

The Inquisitor should behave in a friendly manner

and act as though he already knows the whole story. He should glance at his papers and say, "it's quite clear you are not telling the truth." Or should pick up a document and look surprised, saying: "How can you lie to me like this when what I've got written down here contradicts everything you've told me?" He should then continue: "Just confess—you can see that I know the whole story already.[97]

Secrecy was the order of the day. No information was released to the suspect, although it was not uncommon for a list of those who might carry grudges against them to be solicited. If the names of the accusers appeared on the list, the accused *might* be released. It behooved the suspect to present lengthy lists to the Inquisitor General. It was not permitted to call witnesses in rebuttal to the charges, and if a lawyer was permitted, he could be charged as an accessory if the person was convicted of the crime.

The accused were placed in solitary confinement with contact limited only to the inquisitors, often for three or four years. All expenses associated with the incarceration had to be paid by the defendant. That, coupled with the fact that those adjudged guilty were stripped of their property, was a prime reason the wealthy were often targeted by the Inquisition. The indicted were harassed to confess to heresy in order to save their souls, and if guilt was admitted, they were pressed to reveal the names of other potential heretics. They were then often released with only penances to be paid. In Spain the penance could include scourging or lashing and being forced to wear a large yellow cross or *sanbenito*.

The severest judgments—burning at the stake or total loss of property—were earmarked for those who refused to renounce their heresy or, as in Spain, conversos who continued to secretly practice their faith. Once convicted, the "relapsed" heretics were handed off to secular authorities for punishment in order to spare the Church from having to administer the death penalty. This was based on an ancient principle of the Church: *ecclesia abhorret a sanguine* ("the Church shrinks from blood").[98] Thus, the preferred method of execution—burning at the stake; no blood was shed. (In Spain, offspring of heretics could not hold public office, join holy orders, become doctors, teachers of the young, or lawyers.)

Torture was used beginning in 1252 after having been authorized by Pope Innocent IV, and approximately one-third of all individuals charged with heresy in Spain were subjected to torture.[99] After an admission of heresy was extracted by the most painful means, the accused would be forced to verify his confession. Refusal meant back to the torture chamber.

The inquisitors invented or customized techniques of torture that were designed to extract confessions—whether valid or not. The methods were designed to inflict the most pain possible just short of death. These horrific torture devices included:

✧ The Strappado: The victim's hands were tied behind his back and a rope attached by which he was suspended and repeatedly raised and dropped.

✧ The Rack: A rectangular frame with rollers at both ends. The victim's hands and feet were secured to the rollers by ropes. A handle attached to the rollers was used to ratchet the ropes/chains tighter and tighter, slowly and excruciatingly dislocating the joints.

✧ The Judas Chair: A pyramid-shaped seat the point of which was inserted into the anus. The defendant was slowly lowered farther and farther onto the seat by overhead ropes.

✧ The Boot: A wooden shoe placed on the victim's foot and tightened incrementally, crushing the bones of the foot and lower leg.

✧ The Thumbscrew: Similar to the boot but used to crush hands and fingers.

✧ The Breast Ripper: A large claw capable of ripping a woman's breast from her body.[100]

✧ Waterboarding: The accused was bound to a board which was placed in a slightly downward angle—the feet higher than the head. The victim's hands and feet were tightly secured so that the bindings cut into the flesh if there was any movement at all. The head was held firmly in place by a band of metal and the mouth forced open with a length of iron. Wood was inserted into the nostrils, and a length of cloth placed over the mouth. Water was slowly poured into the accused's mouth so that each time he was forced to swallow part of the cloth was ingested. Just prior to drowning or suffocation, the inquisitor would yank the cloth from the mouth and begin the process again. After a lengthy torture session, bits of the cloth would adhere to the intestines and the victim would be eviscerated. (This method of torture has a frightening similarity to modern-day methods. Perhaps humanity has not advanced as much as has been thought.)

The writhing, half-dead victims were sarcastically addressed as "Brother in Christ" while every means possible was used—without mercy or any pretense of concern—to extract a confession. These devices of torment were given inoffensive labels to mask the very character of the monstrous actions with which they were associated. The place in which the persecution was inflicted was called *Casa Santa* or "holy house."

In a nearby cathedral, a priest celebrated Mass as the prisoner was dragged from his place of confinement. Bells were rung as the procession slowly marched toward the place of execution, the doomed arrayed in white robes and the anguish endured described as a rite of "purification." In some villages, flames of fire and horrible devil-like creatures were painted on the garments. Each victim was made to parade to the funeral pyre in the town square carrying a tall candle.

The parade-like atmosphere was enhanced by nobles on horseback and members of the Inquisitor General's contingent accompanying the condemned. The judged were forced to bow their knees and place their hands on a prayer book as they repeated their coerced confession. The victim was then excommunicated from the Church before the sentence was carried out.

As Inquisitor General during the reign of Ferdinand and Isabella, Tomás Torquemada was described by Spanish chronicler Sebastián de Olmedo as "the hammer of heretics, the light of Spain, the savior of his country, the honor of his order."[101] Author Jane Gerber wrote:

Ironically, the horror of this first decade of the Inquisition caused a recoil in the *converso* population that sent many of them back to their Jewish roots. The religion and tradition that was painted as a crime by the Christians in Spain became again a source of honor and pride to the Sephardim. In fact, Jews became increasingly willing to risk even the pyre of the *auto-da-fe* [act of faith during which the declared heretic's sins were proclaimed and a public ceremony in which the declared heretic's sins were proclaimed and his sentence was passed] in order to remain faithful to the God of Israel.[102]

The Inquisition was not confined to Spain. Its effects were felt in France, England, the American colonies, Portugal, and Brazil.[103] Nor was the Inquisition the ultimate goal of Ferdinand and Isabella.

—8—

CHRISTOPHER COLUMBUS

Secret Jew

*"You can never cross the ocean unless you have
the courage to lose sight of the shore."*

—ANDRÉ PAUL GUILLAUME GIDE,
French author and winner of Nobel Prize in Literature

CHRISTOPHER COLUMBUS, explorer extraordinaire, arrived in Spain in 1484 in the midst of the horror and infamy of the Inquisition. He had been introduced to the court of Ferdinand and Isabella and had prepared a presentation to the sovereigns in hopes of receiving their blessing to follow the setting sun west in search of a route to Asia.

Not surprisingly, the Inquisition had provoked a fever of exploration; who wouldn't want an opportunity to escape the insanity that had gripped Spain? And Columbus had seen it all! Initially, his consultations to seek support from Ferdinand and Isabella were discouraging. There was little extra in the coffers to support exploration following a lengthy war to retake Granada from the Moors and reunite all of Spain under the banner of the Church. It is also likely that the two rulers thought the demands made by the fledgling explorer were too rich for consideration. Christopher had demanded the title of Admiral as well as an appointment as viceroy over all lands conquered during his adventure. He had also asked for a tenth part of the riches unearthed.

What better time for Columbus to make his bid for a voyage of exploration. It was the golden age of invention for nautical instruments, maps and charts of the then-known waters, and it is not surprising that the Jews of the kingdom were at the forefront of the field. The specialists who dealt with cartography were often referred to as "map Jews" or "compass Jews."[104]

Numerous Jewish scholars were instrumental in developing other nautical instruments:

> . . . the compass, quadrant (predecessor of the sextant), astrolabe, and astronomical tables, from the Arab East to the Christian West. Levi b. Gershom (1288–1344) devised an improved quadrant which continued in use for four centuries and was known as "Jacob's staff"; his invention was itself a refinement of the "Quadrans Judaicus" of Judah b. Machir. The famous "Alfonsine Tables" were translated into Spanish and amended by two Jewish physicians at the court of Aragon in the late 13th century. Majorca was known for its nautical instruments, produced by Jewish craftsmen, and for its Jewish mapmakers, the most renowned of whom were Abraham Cresques (d. 1387) and his son Judah, who completed his father's lifework, a map of the world. Apostatizing after the

massacres of 1391, Judah Cresques entered the service of Prince Henry the Navigator and became director of his nautical academy at Sagres. Abraham Zacuto constructed the first metal astrolabe, compiled astronomical tables, and was consulted by Columbus, Vasco de Gama, and other leading navigators of the Age of Discovery.[105]

The academy boasted numerous Jews who were statisticians and astronomers. The research was designed to help sailors in the midst of the ocean to find and maintain their chosen direction. It would have been suicidal to send ships forth into uncharted waters without proper nautical instruments.

As earlier noted, by the late 1480s most knowledgeable people were aware that the earth was round, yet the practicability of Columbus' plan was disbelieved. He was, in fact, depending on his erroneous assumptions regarding the exact distance from the Azores, the most westward landfall known at the time, to the easternmost part of India. Christopher felt it could be navigated quite readily by the seaworthy ships of his day. However, his opponents in the Portuguese court of King John were more correct than the budding explorer—a reality Columbus would soon discover.

It was the disbelief of those in Portugal which might have supported his scheme that propelled Columbus and his son, Diego, to the shores of Spain where he found more ready acceptance. Once settled there, he found a staunch friend in Diego de Deza, a cleric with a converso background. It was he who gathered a contingent of scientists to hear the plan proffered by Columbus. It was Zacuto, the inventor of the astrolabe, who dismissed any doubts held regarding the proposal by those assembled.

Finance Manager Luis de Santangel and Don Isaac Abravanel were so excited about Columbus' application to the court that they proposed a loan in the princely sum of five million maravedis to the sovereigns so that the explorer could move forward with his plan. This offer circumvented the loan of Isabella's own jewels to finance the trip. Therefore, it was not the queen's "jewels" that financed the undertaking but her court "Jews" who spared the royals the expense of exploration.[106]

Edward E. Hale in his 1891 treatise on the life of Christopher Columbus wrote of his return to the court of Ferdinand and Isabella:

> The king yielded a slow and doubtful assent. Isabella took the enterprise in her own hands. She and Columbus agreed at once, and articles were drawn up which gave him the place of admiral for life on all lands he might discover; gave him one-tenth of all pearls, precious stones, gold, silver, spices and other merchandise to be obtained in his admiralty, and gave him the right to nominate three candidates from whom the governor of each province should be selected by the Crown. He was to be the judge of all disputes arising from such traffic as was proposed; and he was to have one-eighth part of the profit, and bear one-eighth part of the cost of it.
>
> With this glad news he returned at once to Palos . . . . He carried with him a royal order, commanding the people there to fit out two caravels within ten days, and to place them and their crews at the disposal of Columbus. The third vessel proposed was to be fitted out by him and his friends. The crews were to be paid

four months' wages in advance, and Columbus was to have full command, to do what he chose, if he did not interfere with the Portuguese discoveries.[107]

By 1487 Columbus had secured the backing of Abravanel and other conversos. Could that also signal that he was, as some believe, a secret Jew? After all, noted conversos are listed in the annals of Christopher's historic voyage: Alfonso de la Caballeria, Abraham Seneor, and other converted Jews. These relationships could also attest that Columbus was a converso. Research into the topic has produced other questions as well:

- ✧ Why did Columbus date his communications from the time of the demolition of the Second Temple in Jerusalem?

- ✧ What was the odd autograph that seemed to look like the Hebrew ellipsis for "with the help of God" which he pinned to his letters— except those sent to the queen?

- ✧ Why did he have such a sound curiosity about all things Hebrew?

- ✧ Why did he use Old Testament alliteration to describe the dangers of his journey?

- ✧ Why did he first proclaim the outcome of his voyage, not to Ferdinand and Isabella, but to Santangel and Sanchez, two conversos?

Could it also have been that his mother, Susanna (Shoshana in

Hebrew) Fontanarossa, is thought to have been the offspring of a Jewish family, some of the descendants of whom were burned at the stake during the Spanish Inquisition? This lends credence to the supposition that Columbus was a Marrano, a converted Jew.

The world is aware that Ferdinand and Isabella eventually capitulated to the petitions, but few are cognizant that the outcome was ultimately swayed by the intervention of influential Jews and converso nobles who pushed Columbus' objectives and finally reached an agreement for the preponderance of his petitions.

Even as those discussions were taking place, the momentous decree of expulsion evicting all Jews from Spain was being composed for the monarchs. When confronted with the cruel truth of ejection, two of the foremost statesmen and civic leaders, Abraham Seneor and Don Isaac Abravanel, fought to have the writ overturned. Seneor, the court rabbi and chief tax collector of Spain, had functioned as significant go-between during the engagement of the two sovereigns and provided funds for the gift that sealed the matrimonial match between the two. Abravanel, his associate and beneficiary, had also earned the respect of the highest politicos due to his financial advice. He was also thought to have been one of the leading Jewish scholars of his day. The king, willing to attend to the two, accepted a significant bribe from Abravanel—which had no effect on the outcome. Abravanel wrote of his plea to the monarchs to halt the expulsion order:

> I pleaded with the king many times. I supplicated him thus: "Save O king, Why do this to thy servants? Lay on us every tribute and ransom gold and silver and everything that the children of Israel possess they shall willingly give to their fatherland." I sought out

my friends, those who stood near the king and enjoy his confidence, and begged them to beseech and petition him to revoke the evil decree concerning our destruction and annihilation, but all in vain. Like an adder which stoppeth its ears, he remained deaf to our appeals. The queen, also, was standing by his side, but she would not listen to our plea. On the contrary, she argued in favor of carrying out the plan. I neither rested nor speared [sic] myself, yet the calamity was not averted.[108]

Thinking only of his rapidly declining coffers and ways to refill them, Ferdinand obviously gave little consideration to the future of his kingdom. He cared little for the fact that Spain was being stripped of one of its most precious natural resources—the Sephardic Jews. In his bid to appease the Church and empower the state, Ferdinand relinquished the treasure of scientists, craftsmen, physicians, solicitors, educators, poets, and inventors.

While the king was surrendering to the idol of greed, Christopher rapidly validated himself among the most conspicuous converso figures in the court of the Spanish rulers. As with Abravanel, Seneor, Santangel, and Gabriel Sanchez, other Jewish converts to Christianity who served the empire included Alfonso de la Caballeria, vice chancellor and political associate of Aragon, and Juan Cabrero, royal administrator. Apparently, these noblemen were still thought to be trustworthy and were engaged as loyal retainers of Ferdinand and Isabella, even though the Inquisition was an ever-present and threatening demon lurking in the background waiting to rear its ugly head in condemnation of the conversos.

Attempts to execute conversos and Marranos during the

Inquisition were, it seemed, not enough to satisfy the royals. Following the fall of Granada, reports began to spread in court factions that an expulsion decree to banish all unconverted Jews would soon be enacted. Precise dates for the endeavor have been debated, but it was likely signed near the end of January 1492. It was following the definite proclamation of the order that Santangel and Abravanel tried unsuccessfully to compel Ferdinand to withdraw the decree. The king refused to alter his decision and Isabella prodded him to maintain his determination to deport all Jews from Spain.

As the fiery Jewish leader stood before the court in defense of his people, Abravanel was described by Capsali and other historians:

> There he stood like a lion in wisdom and strength, and in the most eloquent language he addressed the king and queen . . . . [He] decided to write [his] words down and to send them to Queen Isabella . . . Thus Don Abravanel sent a letter to Queen Isabella, in which he chastised her mercilessly and showed no respect for her rank. He then arranged to have the letter delivered to the queen while he fled for his life.[109]

In an attempt to stay the departure of Don Isaac Abravanel and Seneor, Ferdinand and Isabella devised a plan to have Abravanel's grandson kidnapped, hoping that the family would convert to Catholicism and remain in Spain. Don Isaac was told of the conspiracy and had the child sent to a relative in Portugal. Abravanel refused to be blackmailed. Seneor was not as strong-willed as his friend; he converted, adopted the name Coronel and was baptized, an event gladly attended by the monarchs.[110]

Author Yitzhak Baer, however, provides more insight into what many saw as Seneor's capitulation to pressure from the Crown:

> The queen had sworn if Don Abraham Seneor were not baptized, she would destroy all the Jewish communities; he did what he did to save the lives of many people, not of his own desire. His son-in-law also followed his example, for both of them fell victim to the queen's design, they having reared her and made her great."[111]

Some scholars believe the expulsion decree was an effort to rid Spain of those thought to be infidels as defined by the Catholic Church. Others point out that the decree appears to be a wholesale invitation to conversion, allowing those who chose to convert to keep their status and riches. There are those who believe Ferdinand was indeed a cunning and greedy monarch who was quite shrewd at hiding his brutality behind a mask of religious sanctimoniousness. He actually protected his Jewish subjects during the 1470s and 1480s while apparently plotting their expulsion. Ferdinand borrowed large sums from Abravanel and his brethren to pay for the war to retake Granada, then ousted them before the debt came due. It is said that Abravanel enjoyed such wealth that he was able to loan the monarchs a tenth of the 12,000,000 reals offered them. He apparently felt blessed that his fortune exceeded that of his ancestors, but after the expulsion his enormous assets—land, jewels, gold, and more—were confiscated by Ferdinand.

Of course, other historians believe Ferdinand and Isabella were coerced into making the move to exorcise the Jews by Tomás de

Torquemada, while others believe Isabella was the determining factor and compare her to the wicked and idolatrous biblical Queen Jezebel.

Capsali wrote of her betrayal of the Jewish people:

> Actually, Isabella had always hated the Jews, and had been involved in an ongoing argument with her husband Ferdinand, for ever since her marriage she had been asking him to exile the Jews of Spain. In this the king was spurred on by the priests . . . When, however, she saw that the king was reluctant to take such a step, she told him: "You no doubt love the Jews, and the reason is that you are of their flesh and blood. In fact, the reason the Jews arranged for you to marry me is so that you would act as their protector." When the King heard this terrible thing, he took his shoe off and threw it at the Queen, hitting her. She then fled the room and the hatred between them continued for a long period of time.[112]

Imagine, if you can, how the Jews and conversos must have felt when the decree ordering them out of Spain was published abroad. They were given four months to wrap up their affairs and forbidden to take their gold, silver, and jewels with them as they fled. The Jews were forced to try to rid themselves of property—homes, lands, vineyards, grain fields, and shops. They had built stunning houses of worship, ceremonial bathhouses, and public rooms. It was impossible for them to sell their possessions in a glutted market where a villa sold for the price of a donkey and diamonds for the price of a linen handkerchief. It is said that some buried their possessions hoping they would be able to return at a later date to repossess their property.

Don Isaac Abravanel and his son-in-law were among the few who were actually granted permission to take the sum of two thousand ducats each in gold and jewelry, a paltry amount for their vast holdings but nearly the equivalent of two million dollars in today's market. In so doing, he relinquished the right to collect any outstanding debts owed him upon his departure from Spain.

Abravanel wrote of the despair that gripped the Jewish community:

> The people heard this evil decree and they mourned. Wherever word of the decree reached, there was great mourning among the Jews. There was great trembling and sorrow the likes of which had not been experienced since the days of the exile of the Jews from their land to the land of foreigners. The Jews encouraged each other: Let us strengthen ourselves on behalf of our faith, on behalf of the Torah of our God . . . if [our enemies] let us live, we will live; and if they kill us, we will die. But we will not profane our covenant, and our hearts will not retrogress; we will walk forward in the name of the Lord our God.[113]

The real challenge was in finding another country in Europe or elsewhere that would welcome these Jewish outcasts from Spain. They were rejected by England, France, Germany, and Italy. North Africa was a possibility for asylum, but getting there was a challenge which many failed as they were victimized by treacherous sea captains in ships that were less than seaworthy. Author Simon

Wiesenthal wrote of an anecdote that dated from 1938 and Hitler's invasion of Austria. He told of a Jewish man who enters a travel agency in Vienna seeking a country to which he might emigrate. The agent sets a globe on the counter and draws an imaginary line from country to country as she recounts the reasons the Jew might not be welcome there. As she exhausts the possibilities, the Jewish man asks, "Is that the only globe you have?"[114]

All Jews regardless of age were ordered to depart by July 31—the day before *Tisha B'Av*—a yearly day of fasting for the Jews. It is an observance of the destruction of the First and Second Temples in Jerusalem, and is said to be the saddest day of the Hebrew calendar. Luis De Torres, a Marrano, wrote in his diary:

> Three hundred thousand people, half the amount that were redeemed from Egyptian slavery, descended to the Mediterranean shore, searching for passage to a new land, to a land where they could openly practice Judaism. I was among them.
>
> However, I was not a refugee; I had been commissioned to join Christopher Columbus's voyage of discovery. I agreed to accompany him because I hoped that if we found Jewish brethren, I would be able to live my life in peace and in freedom. Don Rodriguez, his uncle Don Gabriel Sanchez, Alonso de Loquir, Rodrigo de Triana, Chon Kabrera, Doctor Briena and Doctor Marco, all agreed with my reasoning and joined, but except for Rodrigo, they sailed on the other ships. We were a large group of conversos (Marranos), living in perpetual fear of the Inquisition, hoping that

we would find a way out of the precarious situation we were in . . .

Columbus thought that when he would reach China and the Far East, he would locate the exiled Jews from the Ten Lost Tribes, and he wanted me [with a knowledge of Hebrew] to be able to communicate with them.[115] (Brackets mine.)

Prior to the expulsion date, an exchange of letters was said to have taken place between Jewish leaders in Spain and those in Constantinople. The subject: What should the Jews do to protect themselves under such intolerable conditions? The Jewish head in Constantinople allegedly replied that they were to implement various methods including training their sons as financiers in order to strip the Old Christians of their wealth; learning the art of medicine in order to execute their patients; feign conversion until such time as they could continue to practice Judaism. Copies of the supposed documents were presented to the pope as evidence against the Jews to confirm the malevolence of conversos. There is no evidence to support the erroneous conclusion reached by the Church that Jews in Spain followed the council of their brethren in Constantinople.

Officially, Columbus' departure date of August 2 was postponed by one day because of the influx of Jews into port cities trying to find a way of escape. However, Columbus, the secret Jew, would have postponed the sailing date in order to observe Tisha B'Av.

The first week in July was the beginning of the end for so many of the Jewish families in Spain. They were permitted to take their property provided it was not in gold, silver, or money, which left little other than clothing or livestock. Though some were welcomed in Portugal, King John II only allowed them sanctuary for eight months, after which they had to be prepared to move yet again—or face mandatory conversion, as they had in Spain.

The stories accompanying those who were targeted by Ferdinand and Isabella as well as King John II are heartrending. According to author Jane Gerber, some set out on their journey for the coast but turned back to accept conversion in the panic that followed; some were threatened by Isabella with harsh consequences if they refused to convert, among them Abraham Seneor, the leading Jewish courtier; others were forcibly converted in Portugal upon threat of being enslaved. Samuel Usque, a Portuguese Jewish historian, wrote of the horrors that faced Jewish parents as their children were literally wrested from their arms and auctioned to the highest bidders on the island of São Tomé near West Africa:

> [The island] was inhabited by lizards, snakes, and other venomous reptiles and was devoid of rational beings. Here the king exiled condemned criminals, and he decided to include among them the innocent children of these Jews . . . .
>
> When the luckless hour arrived for this barbarity to be inflicted, mothers scratched their faces in grief as their babes, less than three years old, were taken from their arms . . . The fated children raised their piercing cries to heaven as they were mercilessly torn from their beloved parents . . . One mother, distraught by this horrible unexplained cruelty, lifted her baby in her arms, and paying no heed to its cries, threw herself from the ship into the heaving sea, and drowned embracing her only child . . . .

Finally, when those innocent children arrived at the wilderness of São Tomé, which was to be their grave, they were thrown ashore and were mercilessly left there. Almost all were swallowed up by the huge lizards on the island and the remainder, who escaped these reptiles, wasted away from hunger and abandonment.[116]

Centuries before the expulsion in Spain, the prophet Jeremiah too mourned the loss of Israel's children:

"A voice was heard in Ramah, Lamentation *and* bitter weeping, Rachel weeping for her children, Refusing to be comforted for her children, Because they *are* no more" (Jeremiah 31:15 NKJV).

As the Jews prepared for the march to the Mediterranean it was Don Isaac Abravanel joined by rabbis and other counselors who helped arrange conveyances for their dispossessed countrymen. They arranged for the ships that would take them to Africa, Turkey, and Italy. The people marched forward, the conversos believing that their expulsion was the prelude to the coming of the Messiah. It has been said that the roads along the way were lined with priests begging the Jews to convert. That tactic was thwarted by the treatment—the Inquisition, the torture, the suspicion, the distrust—many had received at the hands of the so-called "Old Christians" of the Church. Why should they believe that anything would be different would they submit to a last-minute conversion?

Benzion Netanyahu wrote of the aftermath of the expulsion in his book about Abravanel. He said of King Ferdinand:

> Having come to the conclusion . . . that Spain could not absorb Jews or Marranos, he wanted to be the one to effect their liquidation, and with maximum immediate advantage . . . The immediate profits of the expulsion of the Jews were incomparably greater than any possible increase in the revenues which the Jews might have brought in decades . . . . Some 7,000,000 maravedis were collected after the expulsion by the government from the moneys and sale of houses and valuables left behind by the Jews in Burgos alone! . . . The expulsion of the Jews presented to them [Ferdinand and Isabella] a way of settling their financial difficulties.[117]

Christopher Columbus, secret Jew, was caught in the midst of that battle between Ferdinand, Isabella, and his Jewish friends. He desperately needed the backing of the Crown in order to launch his voyage of discovery as much as he needed the funding of his fellow Marranos and conversos. But his desire to find a country where they might be safe was not the only reason for his voyage: Christopher was equally interested in finding the lost mines of King Solomon so that he might reclaim the city of Jerusalem and the Temple from the infidels who had overrun them. He believed he had found a way to resolve an age-old conundrum. As a student of the Bible, and a scholar of other ancient chroniclers such as Josephus, he had sought to pinpoint the location of Solomon's source of such great wealth.

Solomon, the wisest king over all Judea, was also the most prosperous. Truthfully, little is known about how he amassed his great wealth. The search for the mines from which the preponderance of the king's gold was said to be taken has been the inspiration for books—fiction and nonfiction—for movies, as well as the well-known Indiana Jones series. Writer H. Rider Haggard's book *King Solomon's Mines*, with a later movie by the same name, is a fictionalized account of an attempt to find the mines thought to have been in Africa. The king's wealth seems to have sprung from gold, silver, ivory, and other precious metals and jewels imported from somewhere other than the land of Canaan. The clues are few but seem to be centered in the Old Testament book of Kings, chapters 9 and 10:

> King Solomon also built a fleet of ships at Ezion Geber, which *is* near Elath on the shore of the Red Sea, in the land of Edom. Then Hiram sent his servants with the fleet, seamen who knew the sea, to work with the servants of Solomon. And they went to Ophir, and acquired four hundred and twenty talents of gold from there, and brought *it* to King Solomon (I Kings 9:26–28 NKJV).
>
> For the king had merchant ships at sea with the fleet of Hiram. Once every three years the merchant ships came bringing gold, silver, ivory, apes, and monkeys. So King Solomon surpassed all the kings of the earth in riches and wisdom (I Kings 10:22–23 NKJV).

Although undiscernible on any map or globe, it was believed that if one could determine just where Ophir and Tarshish were located, wealth beyond imagining would be available to the discoverer. Columbus was among those who believed that the wealth of Solomon was to be had if only the correct route could be found to those two ancient cities. Author Steven Weitzman outlined what

Columbus and others thought they knew about the site of Ophir and Tarshish:

1. They were far away from Canaan. The scriptures in I Kings 10 seem to indicate that it took almost three years to make a round-trip to the region. Realistically, the verses say simply that the ships arrived every three years, not that it took that length of time to make sail out and back home.

2. The ships of Solomon had to travel toward the east. Their cargos indicated that the vessels had returned from Africa or Asia, laden as they were with monkeys and ivory.

3. Isaiah 60:9 (Surely the islands look to me; in the lead are the ships of Tarshish, bringing your children from afar, with their silver and gold . . .) seems to indicate that the ships traveled to islands.[118]

This information, whether properly translated or not, signified to the seafaring sailors that they should look for a port in India, Africa, or Asia. Like the great gulf that separated the rich man and Lazarus in the New Testament parable, the impediments seemed to be insurmountable—distance, danger from hostile Muslims, and despair of what might lay at the journey's end.

—9—

CHRISTOPHER
COLUMBUS
Secret Jew

Thus the story of Christopher Columbus reminds us that all fruitful exploration and discovery begins with a willingness to set one's sails higher, to seek new horizons, and to follow wherever one's imagination and experience might lead. It also reminds us that industry and labor are at the foundation of learning and progress.

—PRESIDENT GEORGE H. W. BUSH

ONE PURPOSE and goal of Columbus was outlined in his *Book of Prophecies*; he wrote of the vast land he hoped to discover— a place that would be home to Christianity and a refuge for the Jewish people. But, as we have just read, that was not his only aim: He wanted to deliver the gold of Ophir, the bounty of King Solomon's mines, to the monarchs who had financed his endeavor. His true goal was thought to have been inspired by the desire to rebuild the Temple in Jerusalem after driving the infidels from the gates of the city. He set sail on his voyage of discovery during the same year Ferdinand and Isabella had declared that with the recapture of Granada and the departure of the Jews, Spain was once again a Christian nation. Christopher was certain the monarchs would soon launch an endeavor to recapture Jerusalem and would require vast amounts of gold and other treasures to finance the battles that must ensue. He wanted to provide the gold from the very same sources that Solomon had used to build the first, magnificent Temple.

Based on calculations of that day, Columbus surmised that there was scarcely more than 155 years remaining before the end of the world and the second coming of Christ. History professor Laura Ackerman Smoller wrote that in a letter to Ferdinand and Isabella, Christopher tried to impress upon them the urgency of the voyage:

> Astrology dictated that the world would endure only some 155 years to come. Preceding its destruction, however, Columbus told the monarchs: all of the races would be converted to Christianity. He saw his own voyages as part of the universal missionizing of the last days.[119]

Citing Augustine, the Admiral asserted that the world "would only last for 7000 years; [Columbus] finds that some other genius had calculated that before the birth of Christ it had existed for 5343 years and 318 days; adds 1501 years from the birth of Christ to his own time . . . and finds that the total is 6844 years; subtracts, and discovers that this earthly globe can only last 155 years longer."[120]

Columbus felt a sense of urgency because of a passage in Matthew:

> And this gospel of the kingdom will be preached in

all the world as a witness to all the nations, and then
the end will come (24:14 NKJV).

The explorer was supposedly quite fond of quoting John 10:16 in
the King James Version:

> And other sheep I have, which are not of this fold:
> them also I must bring, and they shall hear my voice;
> and there shall be one fold, *and* one shepherd.[121] (Ital-
> ics mine.)

In the biography of his father, Ferdinand wrote that Columbus
had received two missives from Paolo Toscanelli, both of which
stressed the importance of spreading the Gospel. In the first letter,
the author wrote of the Great Khan of Cathay and his desire "to
have friendship and dealings with the Christians, and about two
hundred years ago they sent ambassadors to the Pope, asking for
many learned men and teachers to instruct them in our faith; but
these ambassadors, encountering obstacles on the way, turned back
without reaching Rome."[122]

In a subsequent letter, Toscanelli penned that the voyage would
be "to kings and princes who are very eager to have friendly dealings and speech with the Christians of our countries . . . They are
also very eager to know and speak with the learned men of our lands
concerning religion."[123]

Columbus had also mentioned to those willing to listen that
he was seeking a route to India. Why would this have piqued the
interest of Jews in Spain and made some of the wealthy willing to
invest in Christopher's voyage? The answer is a bit convoluted but
provides great insight.

Judah was not the only son of Jacob the patriarch; he also fathered the other eleven tribes of Israel: Reuben, Simeon, Levi, Issachar, Zebulon, Dan, Naphtali, Gad, Asher, Joseph, and Benjamin. From the vagaries of Hebrew history two dominions developed, one in the South (Benjamin and Judah) and one in the North (the remaining ten tribes). Some seven hundred years before Christianity emerged Assyrian kings attacked the northern tribes and carried the inhabitants—except for those in Samaria—to Babylon. The number of captives is impossible to calculate. Three years after the initial invasion, Samaria was captured and its peoples taken into captivity. Judah suffered the same fate, and the Jews in that territory fell under the rule of Nebuchadnezzar. The Jews who had traveled to Spain were descendants of the southern tribes of Judah and Benjamin, as are all Jewish progenies today. Nothing is known of the record of the other ten tribes who had become lost in antiquity.

During the Middle Ages stories would occasionally reach Europe of Jewish enclaves in countries such as India and China. Although early records of Jewish life and history are well documented, that custom waned following the Diaspora, as did the stories of the search for the Ten Lost Tribes of Israel. Today, we know little of the quest for the descendants of Reuben, Simeon, Levi, Issachar, Zebulon, Dan, Naphtali, Gad, Asher, and Joseph; but we have been assured that it was a catalyst for the voyage of Christopher Columbus.

Spanish Jews had come to sense that the budding explorer seemed to realize their frustration and support their beliefs. He alleged to know the best way to reach India by water and was searching for financial and moral support for his project. Perhaps the explorer had visions, once on the shores of the vast continent of India, of discovering members of the Ten Lost Tribes which had been reported scattered throughout Asia and China. And it seems that the many threads which zigzag through the life of Columbus appear to be intertwined with the Jewish people and their predicament in Spain at the time of his voyage.

As a suspected descendant of conversos, Christopher would have embraced Christianity and sought to spread its influence to any lands on which he set foot. And he was not the only converso aboard the three caravels that set sail on August 3, 1492; there were at least six other such men present.

One traveler, Luis de Torres, sailed in the company of five other Marranos, two of whom were his physician and navigator. All Jews on board had submitted to baptism into the Catholic Church the day before the ships sailed. Among the men, de Torres spoke Hebrew—a great part of Columbus' belief that he would need someone conversant in Hebrew if or when he encountered members of the Ten Lost Tribes. He, and others of his time, firmly believed the stories of the wandering Hebrew children who had, after their Babylonian captivity, migrated throughout Asia and imprinted numerous civilizations with their cultural mores. Today, there are Asian people, mostly Muslim, who light candles on Friday nights but have never known where this custom originated. There is said to be a group in Japan who once a year drive a goat over a cliff in a ceremony that resembles the Yom Kippur service observed by the Jews.[124]

What other indications are there that Columbus was a secret Jew, a converso? An earlier chapter contains a list of some of the books he relied on in his search for knowledge. In most of them, he added comments in the margins that made it evident he was well informed regarding the Old Testament. His notes held observations of the Prophets with material befitting the academic world of Judaism. In *Historia rerum unique gestarum*, a tome penned by Pope Pius II, one notation indicates Columbus' familiarity with the Jewish calendar as he gives both the Gregorian year—1481—and the equivalent on the Hebrew timeline—5241. One note in particular is lauded as an even more definitive sign that the explorer was a Jew; he referred to the Second Temple as *Casa secunda*—the second House. This is typically a Jewish rendition unused by gentiles. In yet another book, he wrote in the margin, "Gog Magog."[125] It is a reference to the prophet Ezekiel's words in Ezekiel 38:

> "Therefore, son of man, prophesy against Gog. Give him this message from the Sovereign Lord: When my people are living in peace in their land, then you will rouse yourself. You will come from your homeland in the distant north with your vast cavalry and your mighty army, and you will attack my people Israel, covering their land like a cloud. At that time in the distant future, I will bring you against my land as everyone watches, and my holiness will be displayed by what happens to you, Gog. Then all the nations will know that I am the Lord . . . .But this is what the Sovereign Lord says: When Gog invades the land of Israel, my fury will boil over! In my jealousy and blazing anger, I promise a mighty shaking in the land of Israel on that day. All living things—the fish in the sea, the birds of the sky, the animals of the field, the small animals that scurry along the ground, and all the people on earth—will quake in terror at my presence. Mountains will be thrown down; cliffs will crumble; walls will fall to the earth. I will summon the sword against you on all the hills of Israel, says the Sovereign Lord. Your men will turn their swords against each other. I will punish you

and your armies with disease and bloodshed; I will send torrential rain, hailstones, fire, and burning sulfur! (38:14–16; 18–22 NLT)

Did Columbus equate this passage with events in Spain—the Inquisition, the forced conversion of Jews, the expulsion order signed by Ferdinand and Isabella? Did he see the ruler, Gog, launching a demonic attack against Jews in the known world? No matter, Columbus' ruminations on that particular passage lends credence to the theory that he was indeed a secret Jew and of his mission to find a safe haven for his people.

In his research, Columbus studied the works of medieval scholar and philosopher Pierre d'Ailly, and especially his tome, *Tractatus de Concordia astronomie veritas et narrationis hystorice* (*Treaty of Concordia astronomy and narrative and historical truth*). Apparently Christopher was seeking to learn of the signs and events that would usher in the reign of the Antichrist to include in his *Book of Prophecies*, a personal diary of scriptures and quotations that reflected his thoughts on the subject of end-time events. He reasoned that there would be eight events signaling the return of Christ. In a letter to Ferdinand and Isabella, he wrote:

> Holy Scripture attests in the Old Testament, through the mouths of the prophets, and in the New Testament through our redemptor Jesus Christ, that this world will end. The signs of when this must happen are described in Matthew and Mark and Luke, and the prophets frequently predicted this event . . . . Our Redeemer said that before the consummation of

this world all that had been written by the prophets would have to be fulfilled.[126]

Among them were: the recapture of Mount Zion from the infidels who had taken the holy site; the conversion to Christianity of inhabitants of the world; finding the garden of Eden; and the discovery of a new world (which Columbus felt he would be the one to fulfill).[127] Columbus was equally adamant that the Temple in Jerusalem had to be rebuilt and the Antichrist revealed.

In his writings Columbus reiterated that the world would soon end with the second coming of Christ. His manuscript *Libro de las Profecias* (*Book of Prophecies*) includes a letter of theological proportions which reads:

> At this time I both read and studied all kinds of literature: cosmography, histories, chronicles, and philosophy and other arts, to which our Lord opened my mind unmistakably to the fact that it was possible to navigate from here to the Indies, and He evoked in me the will for the execution of it. . . . All those who heard of my plan disregarded it mockingly and with laughter. All the sciences of which I spoke were of no profit to me nor the authorities in them. . . . Who would doubt that this light did not come from the Holy Spirit, anyway as far as I am concerned, which comforted with rays of marvelous clarity and with its Holy and Sacred Scriptures. . . . In this letter Columbus presses the providential guidance of his Western discoveries as a miracle intended to encourage the undertaking of the restoration of Jerusalem. . . . I have already said that

in order to execute the enterprise of the Indies neither reason, nor mathematics, nor maps profited me; what Isaiah said was fully realized, and this is that which I wish to write here in order to bring to the mind of Your Highnesses, and in order that you rejoice of the other, which I shall tell you about Jerusalem through the same authorities, about whose enterprise, if there is any faith, hold victory for more than certain.[128]

Columbus also faithfully kept a log of his first voyage which records the events of two dates approximately six weeks after his departure, the details of which hearken back to the time of Moses:

Saturday, September 22, 1492—Steered about W.N.W., her head turning from one point to another, varying the course and making about thirty leagues [ninety miles]. Saw few weeds. Some sandpipers seen and another bird. The Admiral [as Columbus often referred to himself in his ship's log entries] here says, *this head wind was very necessary to me, for my crew had grown much alarmed at the thought that in these seas no wind ever blew in the direction of Spain.* Part of the day saw no weeds. Later they were very thick.

Sunday, September 23, 1492—Sailed N.W. and N.W. by N. and at times W. nearly twenty two leagues [sixty-six miles]. Saw a turtle dove, a booby, a river bird, and other white fowl. There was a great deal of weed with crabs in it. The sea being smooth and tranquil, the sailors murmured, saying that they had got into smooth water, where the wind would never blow to carry them back to Spain. Afterward the sea rose without wind, which astonished them. The Admiral says on this occasion, *the rising of the sea was very favorable to me, such as had only happened before in the time of the Jews when they went out of Egypt and murmured against Moses, who delivered them out of captivity.*[129]

The Admiral responded to other situations by equating them with biblical episodes causing scholars over the centuries to determine that he might well have been—to the utter horror of some—of Jewish descent. As additional research is done, more scholars are at least willing to contemplate such a heritage rather than toss it on the scrap heap of antiquity.

Scholars who have pored over Columbus' personal letters have noted another conundrum: A number of letters to his son Diego bear a peculiar cipher in the upper-left-hand corner. Author Maurice David writes:

> On all of these thirteen intimate letters but one, the attentive reader can plainly see at the left top corner a little monogram which may seem cryptic to him, but which is, in fact, nothing more nor less than an old Hebrew greeting or benediction, frequently used among religious Jews all over the world even to this day.
>
> This monogram, consisting of two characters, 'beth,' and 'hai,' the second and fifth letter of the Hebrew alphabet—written from right to left, like all Semitic script—is an abbreviation of the Hebrew words, 'Baruch hashem' (Praised be the Lord). . . . [130]

The thirteenth letter written to Diego is devoid of the inscription. One author believes the avoidance is because the letter was to have been delivered to Queen Isabella, who callously ordered "Jews and Moors to be burned."[131] Another genealogist, Salvadore de Madariaga discounted David's findings because each letter also contained a cross in the signature. This might be disregarded, as a cross could be seen on all letters of this time period. It denoted "in the name of God," and to have neglected to include it on his letter would have invited suspicion in Inquisition-gripped Spain. It would have been typical Marrano behavior to remain as inconspicuous as possible.

Author Walter F. McEntire wrote of the climate in Columbus' adopted land:

> . . . it wasn't very safe in those days in Spain to call yourself a Jew, and Columbus knew that, and called himself "a Genoese navigator". . . . [132]

It seems highly likely that Columbus was not a traditional Catholic, but only followed the ceremonies of the Church in order to escape detection. His writings point toward Messianic Jewish beliefs of a New Testament Christian. One of his greatest treasures seems to have been a book written by Marrano and Moroccan convert to Christianity, Samuel Ibn Abbas. The treatise was written exclusively to convince another man, R. Isaac of Sujurmente, that Jesus of Nazareth was the Messiah.

This compels us to ask two important questions regarding Columbus:

✧ Why was the Admiral so captivated by Jesus

from the standpoint of the fulfilling of Old Testament prophecy?

✧ As simply a Marrano or a traditional Catholic, why would he have cared about Jesus as Messiah?

Apparently, his love for the writings of Abbas revealed his deep love for and interest in the Messiah from the viewpoint of a Jewish man—a true Marrano who honestly esteemed the person of Jesus Christ.

Some historians believe that the secrecy surrounding the strange pyramid-shaped signature of Christopher Columbus has never been fully revealed. There are several suppositions, any of which could have readily pointed to his Jewishness. Others, however, believe that Maurice David solved the mystery in his book, *Who Was "Columbus"?* He writes,

> . . . the mystic signature in the shape of a triangle, considered by Colón [Columbus] as his own family emblem, is nothing less than an abbreviation of the "last confession" of the Jews and also a substitute for the Kaddish—in lieu of the real Kaddish, which was interdicted.

The abbreviation in this case should read as follows:

.S.
.S.A.S.
XMY
:X.p.o.ferens./

In Hebrew:
Shadai, Shadai
Adonoy Shadai
Yehova molai chesed
Nauthai ovon, pesha, chatuo[133]

In Latin:
Sanctus. Sanctus, Adonai, Sanctus.
Chesed Moleh Yehovah.

Shadai, Adonai or Adonoy, and Yehovah are Hebrew names of God. The inscription may have been indicative of a blessing the Admiral wished to leave to his sons. While it does not represent the "mourner's" version of the Kaddish, it is certainly possible Columbus was requesting that his sons substitute the prayer signified by his signature in order not to draw attention to their Jewish roots.

Some historians have also suggested that his seal was adapted from tombstones in old Jewish graveyards in both Spain and France. Others see it as purely decorative. Regardless of the implication, in his last will and testament, Columbus demanded that his descendants use the pyramid version of his signature in perpetuity. His instructions were to

> Sign with my signature which I now employ which is an X with an S over it and an M with a Roman A over it, and over that an S and then a Greek Y with an S over it, preserving the relation of the lines and points.[134]

Some of his missives are signed simply "Christopher," while others end with *El Almirante* or the Admiral.

David wrote:

> The very S . . . leads to the solution of the strange and mystic signature, which means nothing else but the last confession of the Jews as read from right to left with Hebrew words for each initial—abbreviated—it is true—but perfectly acceptable, according to the rabbinical laws . . . it is meant simultaneously as a Kaddish for Colón—or better, as a substitute for a Kaddish—the supreme prayer dreamed of continually by all Jews alike . . . Hence the repeated command to his heirs and their heirs to sign exactly like his signature always and perpetually.[135]

David proposes that because the Inquisition probed every facet of an individual's personal existence, Columbus' sons would be restrained from saying the mourner's Kaddish for their father. David suggests that the signature was in fact an alternative for the Hebrew prayer, the substitution for which was a characteristic of the Marranos who feared the inquisitors' intrusion into their daily lives and the reality of torture and death.

—10—

CHRISTOPHER
COLUMBUS

Secret Jew

*Set sail from the bar of Saltes at eight o'clock and
sailed with a strong breeze till sunset towards the
south for fifteen leagues. Afterwards steered S. W. and
S. by W., which is the direction of the Canaries.*

—CHRISTOPHER COLUMBUS[136]

SIX YEARS after Christopher Columbus entered the service
of King Ferdinand and Queen Isabella, Boabdil, a pacifist and the
last king of the Moors, invited the monarchs to the city to effect
a surrender of the last Moorish holdout in the decades-long wars
between the monarchs and the Moors in Andalusia. On January 1,
1492, followed by their armies, the king and queen rode their steeds
into the city and took possession of Granada, the last city to fall.
The ceremony was enacted before the fortified palace of Alhambra.
Boabdil handed Ferdinand the keys to the magnificent edifice and
then paid homage to the Spanish Crown.

Author Jane S. Gerber wrote of the significance of the fall of Granada:

> [It] was greeted with jubilation throughout Europe but especially in Spain, where the monarchs could now thru their energies to the unresolved question of the conversos and the Jews. In fact, as the final campaign against Granada was reaching its climax, anti-Jewish tracts were being circulated in order to gain even more popular support for a national expulsion.[137]

The wars that stretched over a period of eight hundred years had come to an end and finally the Christian flag flew unchallenged over all Spain. Even as the thrill of victory replaced the agony of defeat across Spain, Columbus was not to be denied his share of the spoils. He was joined at the court by his friend Luis de Santangel who in 1491 had scarcely escaped the wrath of the Inquisition when faced with charges of being a secret Jew. Ferdinand had interceded on his behalf, allowing Santangel to go free. Having obtained high office through their knowledge and affluence, Santangel had been a kind of quartermaster in the court and also held the designation of paymaster general in the city of Castile. A favorite of Ferdinand, Santangel also knew the identity of all the skeletons in the king's closet and kept tabs on his most burdensome business dealings.

This friend of both king and common explorer had invested his money and gambled his standing with the court in order to support Columbus' plan to sail westward to India. He was now a participant in negotiations to seal the plan and allow Christopher to set sail. He was joined in his court appearance by royal chamberlain Juan Cabrero, a converso who had also lost kin in the fires of the Inquisition. He too enjoyed the favor of King Ferdinand; so much was his friendship and expertise valued that Cabrero had been selected as executor of the king's last will and testament.

Now the adventurer could almost smell the sea and salt air that would surround him were he allowed to sail. Victory was close; the time for negotiation was at hand. Once Columbus sensed that he was about to achieve his life's dream, he began to set forth the additional demands mentioned in an earlier chapter.

The king must have gasped in disbelief when he heard the requirements and conditions set forth by the lowly former Genoese sailor. How and why should he approve such preposterous demands? Ferdinand and Isabella had graduated from tolerating the foreigner to actually entertaining his scheme only to be faced with the ridiculous! How dare a mere adventurer without pedigree or wealth make such grandiose demands on the Crown while in the company of Spanish royals! Perhaps shocked silence reigned for a moment before titters and giggles began to spread throughout the royal hall. Were they in the company of a madman or a mastermind? Then, just as quickly, the assemblage realized the king was actually pondering the wild demands as Columbus stood his ground. He reiterated that his plan was worthy of the compensation outlined. After all, he had waited patiently for six years to be heard by the court; his requests were results-oriented, and if successful would be wholly worthy of the perks for which he asked.

Christopher Columbus stood on the cusp of realizing his dream at the age of forty-two. He was about to discover what was behind "door number three." His life was about to change; he could either be outfitted as an adventurer, or banished from the shores of Spain. If he was discovered to be a secret Jew, he would likely face the inquisitors' wrath. What else might have flitted in the shadows of his mind as he stood in the presence of royalty? Did he think of the poverty into which he had been born? Did he recall the aspirations that gripped him at an early age—the desire to sail the oceans and discover far-off lands? Was he reminded of the flame of faith that was kindled in his heart, and the desire to spread the Gospel to the unchurched wherever he set foot ashore? Christopher saw himself as appointed by God to fulfill a mission, and he was not to be denied the fulfillment of his calling.

Was he finally to be able to put aside his cloak of subservience and take on the mantle of success as he had dreamed? Did he dare take advantage of the opportunity afforded him to bargain for the absurd and hope for success? Was he foolish or sensible? Only time would tell; and the answer would not be forthcoming until the king and queen had been afforded the opportunity to discuss the audacious proposal and its originator.

Christopher would have to wait another three long months before being summoned to the court to hear the outcome of his outrageous demands. On April 17, 1492, after refusing to capitulate and lessen his requirements, the following articles were presented to Columbus:

1. He and his heirs forever should have the title and office of Admiral in all the islands and continents of the ocean that he or they might discover, with similar honours and prerogatives to those enjoyed by the High Admiral of Castile;

2. He and his heirs should be Viceroys and Governors-General over all the said lands and

continents, with the right of nominating three candidates for the governing of each island or province, one of whom should be appointed by the Crown;

3.   He and his heirs should be entitled to one-tenth of all precious stones, metals, spices, and other merchandises, however acquired, within his Admiralty, the cost of acquisition being first deducted;

4.   He or his lieutenants in their districts, and the High Admiral of Castile in his district, should be the sole judge in all disputes arising out of traffic between Spain and the new countries;

5.   He then, and he and his heirs at all times, should have the right to contribute the eighth part of the expense of fitting out expeditions, and receive the eighth part of the profits.[138]

And finally, on April 30, 1492, another was drawn up conferring upon our hitherto humble Christopher the right to call himself "Don," and finally raised him, in his own estimation at any rate, to a social level with his proud Spanish friends.

He must have felt much as Moses did when Jehovah told him that he could view the Promised Land:

Then Moses went up from the plains of Moab to Mount Nebo, to the top of Pisgah, which is across from Jericho. And the Lord showed him all the land

of Gilead as far as Dan, all Naphtali and the land of
Ephraim and Manasseh, all the land of Judah as far as
the Western Sea, the South, and the plain of the Valley of Jericho, the city of palm trees, as far as Zoar.
Then the Lord said to him, "This *is* the land of which
I swore to give Abraham, Isaac, and Jacob, saying, 'I
will give it to your descendants'" (Deuteronomy 34:1–
4a NKJV).

From this exalted view, he could look both forward and backward.
He could taste the victory while reliving the struggle to reach that
place in life. He could see the promise of the light to come while
seeing the dark clouds of adversity that hovered over his past. He
could face the future with hope, knowing that the God he served
would sail with him. As he prayed for favor, he rehearsed the scripture in Jeremiah 29:11 (NIV):

For I know the plans I have for you," declares the
LORD, "plans to prosper you and not to harm you,
plans to give you hope and a future."

As Moses must have whispered the names of those who had gone
before him—Abraham, Isaac, Jacob, Joseph—so must Columbus
have silently recounted the names of those who paved the way for
him—Abravanel, Cabrero, Mendoza, and others who contributed
encouragement and support.

Santangel invested 17,000 ducats to help equip the caravels on
which Columbus and his crew would set sail. Account books that
have survived through the centuries testify that Christopher repaid
the loan years after his voyage. But why did he rely so heavily on

his Jewish friends for support? Their dreams of the discovery of a safe haven free from Jew-hatred paralleled those of the explorer. The Marranos and conversos desperately needed a way of escape to a faraway land to avoid the threat of the Inquisition. To Santangel and others, it was a risk compelled by the possibility of a favorable outcome, worth any sum of money to achieve. Should the proposed expedition fail, those friends who provided support would have faced the ultimate and final solution—loss of land, affluence, and/or life. Why? Just one month prior to finalizing the documents for the adventure, Ferdinand and Isabella had signed the Order of Expulsion, forcing the Jews from Spain. But the men made a brave gamble—one that paid off.

Simon Wiesenthal wrote:

> During this period, when the inquisition was the most virulent and when victims of the tribunal were being burned in the squares of Spanish cities, one would think that people of Jewish descent had other matters to attend to than to lend aid to a foreigner who had come to Castile with some hare-brained notion of touring the Indies. The experts had pronounced the man's plans to be too risky or even basically unsound. Yet those very Jews and Christianized descendants of Jews, who were reputed to be so astute, put themselves behind a man whom the king's scientific advisory council had rejected . . . . A single slip and they would have forfeited the good opinion of the king. And that good opinion . . . stood between them and their ruin.[139]

After all the documents were signed, Columbus set out for the port of Palos to oversee the building and outfitting of the three caravels that would take him and his crews on their historic voyage. The port where the *Niña, Pinta,* and *Santa Maria* were outfitted for the voyage is no longer in existence. Today, it is little more than a narrow lane crowded on either side by forlorn and crumbling houses—an insult to its former bustling seaport. Fleets of ships no longer lie at anchor outside the sand bar that separated the Palos from the Saltes River. Today, ships bypass the desolate village headed for the bustling ports of Huelva or Cadiz.

Palos was home to the Pinzon family—Martin, Vicente, and Francisco—who would play an important role in the voyages of Columbus. Martin not only invested 500,000 maravedis in the venture, he sailed with the Admiral as captain of the *Pinta.* But he performed a role that was much more important to the success of the enterprise. Due to his expertise as a sailor and his business reputation, he was able to recruit a suitable crew for the voyage. During the interminable wait to set sail, some of his recruits abandoned the venture. It was only due to the harsh recruiting tactics of the Pinzons and the introduction of a letter from Ferdinand and Isabella that a crew was finally assembled.

Martin's first act as partner in the venture was to totally discount the ships that Columbus had confiscated by order of the Crown and to supply two caravels from his own fleet—the *Pinta* and *Niña.* As one writer surmised, no endeavor since the building of the Ark as recounted in the book of Genesis was so closely controlled by one family.[140]

Pinzon outfitted his two vessels with the most qualified sailors to be found on Palos, relegating the miscellany of other ports to the *Santa Maria* with Columbus. While Columbus was assigned the largest of the three ships, she was perhaps not the most seaworthy of the three. According to Jerry Woodfill of NASA:

> All discussion of the characteristics of the *Santa Maria* must begin with the comment: "No one knows exactly what Columbus's mother-ship was like." The best we can determine is to examine similar ships of the era. It is known the ship had a length of 75 feet with a beam (width) of 25 feet. Her draft (depth beneath the surface of the ocean) was 6 feet. There were five sails attached to the vessel's three masts. Most of the driving force of the craft was from the largest mainsail with the remaining sails used for "trimming." Though many mariners viewed the *Santa Maria* as an adequate vessel for her day, Columbus was not so kind with his assessment, "a dull sailer and unfit for discovery." Because of the deep draft (6 feet), the vessel was not suited for sailing near reefs and shallow island waters. In fact, the craft ran aground off Hispaniola and had to be abandoned. The *Santa Maria* was a rented vessel owned by Juan de la Cosa, who sailed with Columbus as the first officer. Formerly known as the *La Gallega* since its owner was from Galicia, Columbus renamed the vessel *Santa Maria*.[141]

The flagship was three-masted and bore a crew of fifty-two individuals. We can only wonder where they stowed not only their gear but themselves, given the confining size of the conveyance. The *Pinta*, the swiftest of the three vessels, was a midsized caravel, and the *Niña*, with Vincenti Pinzon at the helm, was the smallest of the three and carried a crew of eighteen. So fearful were the inhabitants of Spain with regard to the route of the three ships that Columbus was unable to cajole his priest to accompany him. This must have greatly grieved the head of the expedition because of his love for Scripture. Of the crewmen, four were criminals who had been offered amnesty by the Crown as an inducement to join the Admiral on his journey.[142] The Pinzons were also able to enlist the services of two physicians, a goldsmith, and Luis de Torres, a converso and interpreter who spoke Hebrew.[143] So few writers focus on the language in which Torres was fluent.

It is notable that scant consideration has been paid to the fact that there was an interpreter on board. Why had de Torres been recruited to accompany Columbus? Hebrew was not a language formally employed by any country known to the planner of the expedition. His presence was important because Columbus firmly believed that he would encounter displaced Jews along his journey and he wanted to be prepared to communicate with them. It is likely he would have been one of, if not the first, to set foot on any lands discovered in an attempt to communicate with the peoples who inhabited the far-off lands. It could be that the first words spoken by a member of the crew would have been a greeting in Hebrew. Perhaps he stood in the prow of the boat or on the shore and called out, "Shalom aleichem," (peace be unto you).

Just as Columbus followed in the footsteps of Marco Polo with this practice, it is interesting to note that he was not the only explorer to do so. In 1497, Vasco de Gama employed a Jewish interpreter during his voyage to India via Cape Good Hope. When the ship made land in Calicut on the Malabar Coast in 1498, Joao Nunez was the first to go ashore and speak to the natives in Hebrew. De Gama was aware that there were key Jewish centers of commerce in Calicut and on the island of Chennamangalam.

In a 2006 article in the Jewish news service *Haaretz*, Shalva Weil reported:

> At a site adjacent to the old synagogue in the Keralan town of Chennamangalam there is an old tombstone with a clearly visible inscription in Hebrew letters of the words: "Sara bat Israel" (Sara, the daughter of Israel). The Hebrew date corresponds to 1269, making it the oldest Hebrew inscription in India. How did this old Hebrew inscription reach the quiet, verdant village of Chennamangalam, in the southern state of Kerala? The Jews of Cochin have lived on the Malabar Coast for centuries, some say from the time of King Solomon. Others say the Jews arrived in the first century C.E. following the destruction of the Second Temple . . . . Cochin Jews abandoned their property and their synagogue and after facing several obstacles; most of them immigrated to Israel in 1954. The last trustee of the synagogue died [in 2001].[144]

Sadly, while Columbus and his crew awaited the tide in August 1492, the port of Palos was overrun by Jewish families clamoring to escape Spain under threat of death. Following the Expulsion Order signed into law by Ferdinand and Isabella, wealthy Jews had commissioned willing captains to take as many of their countrymen as possible to other lands. As a result, people were huddled together awaiting a means of transport.

Jewish poet Ludwig August Frankl wrote hauntingly of the plight of those Jews and the hope represented by the voyage of Columbus:

> "Look, they move! No comrades near but curses;
> Tears gleam in beards of men sore with reverses;
> Flowers from fields abandoned, loving nurses;
> Fondly deck the woman's raven hair.
> Faded, scentless flowers that shall remind them
> Of their precious homes and graves behind them;
> Old men, clasping Torah-scrolls, unbind them,
> Lift the parchment flags and silent lead.
> Mock not with thy Height, O sun, our morrow.
> Cease not, cease not, O ye songs of sorrow;
> From what kind a refuge can we borrow,
> Weary, thrust-out, God-forsaken we?
> Could ye, suff'ring souls, peer through the Future,
> From despair ye would awake to rapture;
> Lo! The Genoese boldly steers to capture
> Freedom's realm beyond, an unsailed sea!"[145]

Even as Columbus prepared to have his sailors hoist anchor and set sail, a vast number of Jews awaited a place, no matter how cramped, on ships that could be expected to do little more than stay afloat. They were jammed with the bodies of terrified, saddened and hopeless individuals. After days at sea confined in such close quarters, disease became the likely outcome. The threat of an epidemic kept many of the ill-fated refugees stranded on beaches where scores either died from illness or starved. So desperate were some that they opted to return to Spain and accept forced conversion if it meant being able to feed their children. In his volume on the life of Don Isaac Abravanel, Benzion Netanyahu quoted Genoese historian Bartolomeo Senarega on the condition of the émigrés:

> One might have taken them for specters, so emaciated were they, so cadaverous in their aspect, and with eyes so shrunken; they differed in nothing from the dead except in the power of motion, which indeed they scarcely retained.[146]

Surely in looks they resembled those freed from Nazi concentration camps at the end of World War II; and perhaps they felt much as the children of Israel had after leaving Egypt and trekking into the wilderness of Sinai. They lamented to Moses, "Why did you bring us out here to die in the wilderness? Weren't there enough graves for us in [Spain]?" (Exodus 14:11 NLT, brackets mine.)

Italy was one of the few countries that made provision for the exiles. Ferrante, the king of Naples, allowed the weary travelers to land. Hospitals were set up to treat the pestilence that had gripped the Jews as they journeyed and food was provided for the hungry. It was on the Italian shore that Abravanel set foot. It is a testament to his greatness that he did not long languish in obscurity. He was soon offered a place in the king's court, and later referred to the monarch and his son as "princes of mercy and righteousness."[147] He served in the court until near the end of his life when he was driven to Turkey after the deposing of Ferrante's son and heir to the throne, Alfonso.

Too many of the exiles were forced to cross the Mediterranean to the shores of northern Africa where they were relegated to insect-infested straw huts that sat outside the safety of the walls of towns and villages. Again, many died of starvation and their orphaned children were forced into slavery. Other ports of call accepted the Jews on the basis that they convert to Christianity, and their own brethren rejected them for fear of contracting diseases—including the Plague. There were some, however, who sold their possessions in order to feed their colleagues and, in some instances, liberate them from bondage. When the final ship had landed and the last Jew disembarked, they and their ancestors could be found in Europe and in the New World continents of North and South America, in North Africa, and in the Indies.

Back in Palos, it was midnight on August 2, 1492. The crews had boarded the ships and all were ready for the adventure that awaited them. Historian Samuel Eliot Morison wrote of the events that preceded embarkation:

> Of the many difficulties that Columbus and the Pinzons had to surmount in order to get their people aboard and the vessels ready for sea, no details have survived . . . Tradition designates a fountain near the Church of St. George at Palos, connected by a Roman aqueduct with a spring of sweet water in the hills, where the water casks were filled. Last thing of all, every man and boy had to confess his sins, receive absolution, and make his communion. Columbus, after making his confessions (writes the first historian of the Indies), "received the very holy sacrament of the Eucharist on the very day he entered upon the sea; and in the name of Jesus ordered the sails to be set and left the harbor of Palos for the river of Saltes and the Ocean Sea with three equipped caravels, giving

the commencement to the First Voyage and Discovery of the Indies."[148]

What must it have been like for an adventurer to set sail, not knowing when or if he might return to family and friends? He and his crewmen would be surrounded by a dangerous ocean; captives of both the three small ships and the vagaries of the elements. Before him lay the unknown, a dream sustained only by Christopher's inner belief that there existed a land that would provide a safe haven for his people—both Jews and Christians. As recounted earlier, he envisioned the possibility of a route to the Far East and the discovery of the source of the gold-impregnated mines of King Solomon. He aspired to find the Ten Lost Tribes of Israel, thus the presence of a Hebrew interpreter on board one of the ships. And he hoped to return with enough treasure to afford retaking the city of Jerusalem and the Temple Mount from the infidels holding both captive.

His persistence had finally paid off—the years of imploring first King John II of Portugal and then Ferdinand and Isabella of Spain to support his ambitious plan. As the waters swirled beneath the vessels, perhaps it inspired him to pen the words that began his ship's log: "In the Name of Our Lord Jesus Christ." Surely it was not mere happenstance that the two square sails bore the sign of the cross. Columbus was as prepared for the mission as he could possibly be, so as the sun rose on Friday, August 3, 1492, he gave the order to set sail.

It is likely that the crew were not as mesmerized by the vision as was the Admiral. After all, they were headed for uncharted seas patrolled, they feared, by great monsters—perhaps the leviathan[149] mentioned in Isaiah 27:1 (NLT):

In that day the LORD will take his terrible, swift sword and punish Leviathan, the swiftly moving serpent, the coiling, writhing serpent. He will kill the dragon of the sea.

But on that day, fears were put aside, replaced with cries of "Farewell" and shouts of encouragement from the teeming docks.

—11—

CHRISTOPHER COLUMBUS
Secret Jew

With a hand that could be felt, the Lord opened my mind to the fact that it would be possible to sail from here to the Indies. . . . This was a fire that burned within me who can doubt that this fire was not merely mine, but also of the Holy Spirit.

—CHRISTOPHER COLUMBUS

JUST THREE DAYS' journey from the port of Palos, trouble struck Martin Pinzon and the *Pinta*. The ship's rudder was lost, some think due to sabotage by the ship's owners, Gomaz Rascon and Christoval Quintero. The two were thought to have been responsible for delays that caused problems before the ships' departure. And once again, the men were suspected of interference with another attempt to halt the progress of the journey by the time the trio of ships reached the Canary Islands. They did not figure on the skill of Martin Pinzon, who jury-rigged a temporary steering mechanism with ropes. Although the process had to be repeated the following day, it held long enough for the ships to reach the harbor of Lanzarote in the Canaries.

Leaving the *Pinta* and its crew in the harbor, Columbus set sail for Gomera in an attempt to find a replacement for the *Pinta*. His attempts were unsuccessful, leaving him no choice but to have the caravel beached and a new rudder fashioned and installed on the damaged ship. On September 6, 1492, after having lost a month in the islands, Columbus again gave the order to set a course westward. He was eager to leave the islands behind in hopes of quashing the whining of the crews, many of whom saw a divine warning in every minor occurrence. Columbus ordered a pause just off the shore of Gomera long enough to take on food and water.

Soon after their departure, the land slipped away over the horizon, leaving the *Niña, Pinta,* and *Santa Maria* three mere dots lost in the vastness of the Atlantic Ocean. Once again, the sailors began to bemoan their lot in life—crying and begging the Admiral to return them to the shores of Spain. Yet Columbus, with a vision of the future held steady the course he felt God had set for him. I am reminded of President Ronald Reagan's speech following the Challenger tragedy in 1986. He commended the seven who gave their lives and then reminded us that "the future is not free; the story of all human progress is one of a struggle against all odds."[150]

With the ships under way, Columbus issued instructions to the other captains to set a course westward for seven hundred leagues should they become separated, and to remain at that point for twelve hours. In an attempt to placate the crew of the *Santa Maria*, the Admiral penned accurate information in the ship's log, but indicated that the distance to be traveled was less than denoted. Author Filson Young noted in his treatise on Columbus that the sailors faced a daunting sight on Tuesday, September 11:

On this day he notes that the raw and inexperienced

seamen were giving trouble in other ways, and steering very badly, continually letting the ship's head fall off to the north; and many must have been the angry remonstrance from the captain to the man at the wheel. Altogether rather a trying day for Christopher, who surely has about as much on his hands as ever mortal had; but he knows how to handle ships and how to handle sailors, and so long as this ten-knot breeze lasts, he can walk the high poop of the *Santa Maria* with serenity, and snap his fingers at the dirty rabble below. On Monday they made sixty leagues, the Admiral duly announcing forty-eight; on Tuesday twenty leagues, published as sixteen; and on this day they saw a large piece of a mast which had evidently belonged to a ship of at least 120 tons burden. This was not an altogether cheerful sight for the eighteen souls on board the little *Nina*, who wondered ruefully what was going to happen to them of forty tons when ships three times their size had evidently been unable to live in this abominable sea![151]

During the voyage, the Admiral made only two course corrections: the first was on October 7 and the second on the evening of October 11 just hours before landfall. After spotting a flock of birds overhead on October 7, Columbus "decided to alter course and turn the prow to the WSW [west southwest]."[152] Had he not done so, the ships would have had to sail an extra day before catching sight of land. Just two days prior, the Admiral had been threatened with mutiny by his water-weary crew. Only later would he understand that this course correction just may have saved his life.

After sunset on October 11, the Admiral gave the order to resume the original due-westward course, offering no explanation to the navigator and helmsman. It was a move that again likely saved the expedition from certain disaster. Had he continued the course the ship could have ended up on the shoals along an island in the Caribbean. While some attribute this to "dumb luck," Bartolomé de Las Casas suggested, "God gave this man the keys to the awesome seas, he and no other unlocked the darkness."[153]

The Admiral's son Ferdinand wrote that on the evening before land was sighted, his father "Spoke to the men of the favor that [the] Lord had shown them by conducting them so safely and prosperously with fair winds and a clear course, and by comforting them with signs that daily grew more abundant."[154]

The ship's log outlines the various "sightings" of birds, grasses, and other indications that land could be near—all to no avail; until that very Thursday, October 11, 1492. In the words of Columbus:

> The crew of the *Pinta* saw a cane and a log. They also picked up a stick which appeared to have been carved with an iron, a piece of cane, a plant which grows on land, and a board . . . and a stalk loaded with roseberries . . . . As the *Pinta* was the swiftest sailer and kept ahead of the Admiral, she discovered land and made signals ordered by the Admiral. The land was first seen by a sailor called Rodrigo de Triana, although the Admiral at ten o'clock that evening, being on the castle of the poop, saw a light, but so small a body that he could not affirm it to be land. Calling to Pero Gutierrez, gentleman of the King's bedchamber, he told him he saw the light and bid him look that way, which

he did and saw it . . . . Few thought this an indication of land, but the Admiral held it for certain that land was near.[155]

The men aboard the *Niña, Pinta,* and *Santa Maria* had at long last gazed upon land, a sight some of them may never have thought to see again. For weeks they had heard neither the call of shorebirds nor the sound of wind in the trees, but only the splat of canvas whipping in the wind and the sound of the prow of the ship knifing through the ocean. The crew didn't have to be told twice to shorten the sails or take soundings to determine the depth of the water. At last the ships reached the mark of nine fathoms and the sails dropped to the deck amid a joyous cry. The three ships were brought around into the wind and the anchors dropped into the blue sea. Ropes were stowed as the Admiral gazed at the land over which he had been proclaimed Viceroy and Governor-General. He recorded the events in his log:

> Friday, October 12, 1492: When it grew light, they found themselves near a small island, one of the Lucayos, called in the Indian language Guanahani [San Salvador or Holy Savior, as it was christened by Columbus]; or, to give it its modern name, Watling's Island.
>
> . . . the Admiral called to the two captains and to others who leaped on shore, and to Rodrigo de Escovedo, secretary of the whole fleet and to Rodrigo Sanchez, of Segovia, to bear witness that before all others he took possession of that island for the King and Queen . . . [156]

We have Columbus to thank for the massive notes he kept on his life and voyages, all of which reveal his deeply religious nature. He frequently quotes Scripture or references people of the Bible in relation to various events. In his personal log, he writes that he found land with the help of the Lord. When he landed on the shore of San Salvador, he took possession of it for the Spanish Crown with

> O Lord, Eternal and Almighty God, by thy sacred word thou hast created the heavens, the earth and the sea; blessed and glorified be thy name, and praised be thy Majesty, who hath designed to use thy humble servant to make thy sacred name known and proclaimed in this other part of the world.[157]

Coming from the discreet and reserved climes of Europe and having just invoked God's name over the land of discovery, the men of the three ships must have been stunned when they were greeted by a group of naked men, women, and children timidly advancing toward the landing party. The Admiral wrote a description of the natives:

> All of them go around as naked as their mothers bore them; and the women also, although I did not see more than one quite young girl. And all those that I saw were young people, for none did I see of more than 30 years of age. They are very well formed, with handsome bodies and good faces. Their hair [is] coarse—almost like the tail of a horse—and short.[158]

To that, he added one of the true purposes for his trek westward:

> I recognized that they were people who would be better freed [from error] and converted to our Holy Faith by love than by force[159] . . . I believe that they would become Christians very easily, for it seemed to me that they had no religion.[160]

At some point in his journey, Columbus made the decision to select several of the young men to be taught Castilian and then evangelized. His most successful convert among the Awarak—or Taino—natives was a young man who was christened Diego Colon. The young man became the official translator for the Admiral and was able to explain to his fellow islanders that Columbus was searching for gold—a commodity that was of little value to the carefree natives. Diego was ultimately able to ascertain that gold was thought to be readily available on the island of Cuba (a land the Admiral was certain to be Cathay or China, the mainland he so eagerly sought). But it was on Hispaniola that he ultimately found sufficient gold to at least appease Ferdinand and Isabella.

It was on Cuba that the explorers found a plant that would forever change history—tobacco. Samuel Eliot Morison wrote with some humor of the encounter with "My Lady Nicotine":

> The two Christians [Rodrigo Sanchez and Luis de Torres], met on the way many people who were going to their villages, women and men, with a firebrand in the hand, and herbs to drink the smoke thereof as they are accustomed. . . . Inserting one end in a nostril, they lit the other from a firebrand and inhaled the smoke twice or thrice, after which the cigar was handed to a friend or allowed to go out.[161]

Within one hundred years of Morison's writings, tobacco use had encompassed the known Western world. It was smoked by both sexes notwithstanding the disapproval of monarchs and priests. The tobacco leaf would prove to be of immeasurable value in terms of currency in the New World.

The ships and their crews were warmly received in the various ports by the natives who thought the light-skinned Europeans were gods. The villagers welcomed them with great adoration, kissing their hands and feet and begging to sail with them on their return trip to the heavens.[162]

Robert Poole in an article for Smithsonian.com wrote that the origin for several words in much use today came from the Taino people:

> If you have ever paddled a *canoe*, napped in a *hammock*, savored a *barbecue*, smoked *tobacco* or tracked a *hurricane* across *Cuba*, you have paid tribute to the Taíno, the Indians who invented those words long before they welcomed Christopher Columbus to the New World in 1492.[163]

It was on the island of Haiti that Columbus first heard of gold in the land of Cibao. It was a land the Admiral would eventually name Espanola (later Hispaniola) for his adopted homeland. Although he sailed there on the *Santa Maria* on December 5, 1492, thinking his destination to be a separate island, he soon discovered it was on the same island as Haiti. Today the Dominican Republic and Haiti share the large island still known as Hispaniola. It would be the site of Columbus' first tenure as a governor in the New World, and also of his greatest humiliation—but that story is for a later chapter.

The voyage to Hispaniola had been a difficult one, filled with turbulence and lack of rest and relaxation for the taxed crew. The day before Christmas, the weather became calm; the exhausted crew stretched out on the decks warmed by the Caribbean sun and drifted off to sleep. During the night, it is said that the sleepy pilot turned the wheel over to a boy. The inexperienced helmsman allowed the ship to drift on the tide. The *Santa Maria* ran aground on a coral reef. Silently and gently the ship became stuck and began to take on water. Although none of the crew was lost, the Admiral's flagship had to be abandoned and Columbus was forced to forsake his crew on the island. A temporary fort was thrown up to house thirty-nine members of the stranded crew.[164]

Ever the wordsmith, Columbus put his own spin on the shipwreck in a letter to the Spanish monarchs, Ferdinand and Isabella. Still thinking he was blithely sailing around the islands of the sea near China, he wrote:

> In this Espanola, in the situation most convenient and in the best position for the mines of gold and for all communication with the mainland here as well as there, belonging to the Great Khan, where there will be trade and gain, I have taken possession of a large town. To it I have given the name of La Navidad [or the Nativity, for the wreck occurred on Christmas day]. Here I have constructed a fort which by now will be furnished, and I have left sufficient men and arms and provisions for more than a year and a ship's boat together with a master craftsman to build others.[165]

Martin Pinzon, who had sailed away from the original fleet to search on his own, heard of the shipwreck and quickly returned to the Admiral's side. About the time of his arrival, some of the crew of the *Santa Maria* discovered gold along the banks of the Yaque de Norte River. That with additional reports of finding gold in Jamaica gave Columbus all the ammunition required to substantiate his mission.

(In May 2014, Massachusetts marine investigator Barry Clifford announced that he had discovered what was thought to be the wreckage of Columbus' flagship in the waters off the island of Haiti. Clifford said that "geographical, underwater topography and archaeological evidence strongly suggests that this wreck is . . . the *Santa Maria*."[166])

For three months longer, Columbus and his crew of explorers, now aboard the *Niña*, sailed around the islands of the Caribbean in search of gold, precious jewels, and further proof that he had indeed found a westward route to Asia. The Admiral then began preparations to return to Europe. The crews loaded provisions, water, and the gold, flora, and fauna discovered on the tropical islands. Also on board was a small contingent of the Arawak people, including Diego Colon. On January 6, the ships raised anchors and slipped out of the port into the roiling winter ocean waters of the Atlantic, setting a course for the port of Palos in Spain. It is nothing short of miraculous that the two small caravels survived the violent winds and pounding seas. A week later Columbus penned in his diary, "I have faith in our Lord that He who brought me here will lead me back in His pity and mercy . . . no one else was supportive of me except God, because He knew my heart."[167]

His return route did not follow the journey westward but took him instead toward the northeast and then eastward. The *Niña* and her sister ship the *Pinta* became separated during one particularly ferocious storm in mid-February. The waves crashing over the whole of the *Niña* were so violent that none of the crew thought it, or they, would survive the tempest. Columbus wrote in the ship's log:

> The winds increased and the waves were frightful, one contrary to the other, so they crossed and held back the vessel which could neither go forward nor get out from between them, and the waves broke on her.[168]

Yet survive they did. The morning after the ferocious gale the ship reached the Azores. The relief at reaching any port in the storm was short-lived, for it was but a few days later that another storm smashed into the tiny ship. The sails were ripped to shreds, and it is by God's grace that on March 4, 1493, the waves literally drove the *Niña* near the coast of Lisbon, Portugal. When dawn broke, the Admiral found that his caravel was anchored altogether too close for comfort to a heavily armed Portuguese man-of-war. The Niña was a sitting duck and the great ship a peregrine falcon waiting to pounce. Its ship's master was none other than Bartholomeu Dias, the explorer who discovered the Cape of Good Hope. Dias boarded the Niña and demanded that the Admiral give account of his exploits, which Columbus refused to do.

Columbus seemed to be a magnet for misfortune and his landing in Portugal was no exception. He was then ordered to accompany Dias back to the Portuguese ship to face Captain Alvaro Damao. Again the Admiral refused with all the dignity accorded him as Admiral of the Ocean Sea. The first mate of the *Niña*, Vincente Yanez Pinzon, was then deemed to be an acceptable substitute for Columbus, but again the order was refused. It was a practice for Castilian sailors to face death rather than surrender to an enemy force, and Columbus was not tempted to breach tradition. Dias then demanded Columbus' papers, which the Admiral was only too happy to provide. Upon his return to ship, Dias related the details of the encounter to the captain, who then boarded a skiff and was rowed across to the *Niña*. There he paid a courtesy call on the Admiral of the Ocean Sea and placed himself at the beck and call of the captain of the *Niña*. Winner of the skirmish: Christopher Columbus.

While in Lisbon he was summoned to the court of King Joao. Morison wrote convincingly of the spectacle that must have been Columbus and his entourage weaving its way from dockside to the court:

> Mules were provided by D. Martin, a few gold nose-plugs and other souvenirs of the Indies were doubtless packed in the saddlebags, and as undeniable evidence that he had been to an undiscovered country, Columbus selected some of the healthiest specimens of his captive Indians to share the royal week end . . . as it is likely, they were required to trudge barefoot in the mud, and be stroked and pinched by curious crowds in the streets of Lisbon. A "great pestilence" was then raging along the lower Tagus [River], but *Nina's* company, both white and red, fortunately escaped contamination.[169]

Unfortunately, the Admiral's good sense did not prevail once before the king. He bragged of his conquests in the New World and the great wealth he had discovered, all but goading the monarch for not having sponsored the westward voyage of discovery. So incensed were the nobles at court that some among them plotted to kill the boastful explorer.

The triumphant return he must have imagined in his fertile mind did not come to pass, as finally on March 15 the *Niña* limped into the port of Palos, Spain. Columbus' navigational skills have been touted by many as extraordinary, yet according to some, it was the Admiral's faith in God that made the difference—it was at the crux of his accomplishments.

With great pomp and circumstance the Admiral and his contingent made their way from Palos to Seville. The roadside was crammed with people straining to see the caravan laden with gold, pearls, parrots and other birds, tropical fruits, and the legation of Arawak people who had accompanied Columbus back to Spain.

Author Salvador de Madariaga proposes that Columbus may have fashioned this jubilant parade in honor of the Jews who with broken hearts had trudged to the Mediterranean coast just a year prior. He writes:

> His triumphant progress through Castille [sic] and Aragon was a fit commemoration of the dismal progress of the expelled Jews. He can hardly have failed to think of it while he passed through the same roads and was acclaimed by the same people who one year earlier had watched the tragic exodus in sullen, sad or charitable silence.[170]

One month later, he stood before Ferdinand and Isabella to recount his adventures in the New World. His son, Ferdinand, wrote of the hero's welcome accorded Columbus:

All the Court and the city came out to meet him; and the Catholic Sovereigns received him in public, seated with all majesty and grandeur on rich thrones under a canopy of cloth of gold. When he came forward to kiss their hands, they rose from their thrones as if he were a great lord, and would not let him kiss their hands but made him sit down beside them.[171]

Although, as many point out, Columbus failed to set foot on the North American continent, his exploits opened the door for an invasion of voyagers, aggressors, opportunists, and teachers of the Gospel. Some of the men who made their way across the Atlantic to explore the lands discovered by the Admiral and his crew would accomplish great deeds; others would spread sickness and death among the unsuspecting native population. Author Paolo Emilio Taviani wrote of the devastation wrought by the introduction of disease in the New World:

By some estimates about 350,000 Tainos lived on Hispaniola when the Spanish arrived. By 1508, there were 60,000, and in 1548 . . . no more than 500 survived on the whole island.[172]

One thing is certain: The New World would be forever changed by the influx of adventurers.

—12—

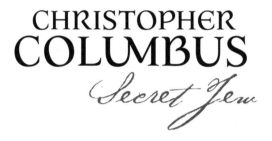

CHRISTOPHER
COLUMBUS
Secret Jew

*By prevailing over all obstacles and distractions,
one may unfailingly arrive at his chosen goal or destination.*

—CHRISTOPHER COLUMBUS

COLUMBUS was the hero of the hour, comparable to a modern movie or rock star. Wherever he went crowds clamored after him. Banners were draped throughout the towns he visited and the streets were lined with the curious and captivated. What an overwhelming welcome for the explorer who was earlier snubbed by the nobility of Spain! Now he was welcomed by masses and monarchs alike.

The Admiral was eager to share his findings and boast of his discoveries in the New World. Accompanied by Arawak natives, he regaled those amassed with their ability to work diligently, their capacity for accepting the Gospel, and his belief that entire islands would eventually convert to Catholicism. He entertained with descriptions of the excellent climate, the trees dripping with flowers or bearing clusters of fruit. He called for the men presenting beautifully colored exotic birds. Next he pulled from his tunic a handful of golden trinkets, and then introduced the natives. Perhaps he likened himself to the dove released from Noah's Ark who flew over the waters and returned with an olive leaf (see Genesis 8:11). Columbus' offerings were simply a tantalizing taste of all that was yet to be discovered and brought back to Ferdinand and Isabella.

The explorer and creative writer used pretentious words and painted glowing pictures of what lay just around the corner and out of sight of the Spanish sovereigns. He took every advantage of the opportunity that had been offered to sail the high seas and return the conquering hero.

After he had exhausted his grandiloquent discourse, so moved were Ferdinand and Isabella that they slipped to their knees in tribute to the One who had brought glory to them and the Church. With that move, the entire assembly followed suit and a choir fervently sang a *Te Deum* (*We Praise Thee, O Lord*). Those in attendance then enjoyed a robust feast in honor of the Admiral.

Suddenly, the son of a Genoese merchant found himself in the exalted circle of nobles and churchmen that surrounded the king and queen. In his early years, he had struggled to find anyone who would even give audience to his plan to sail westward to Asia. Now his every word was repeated; his feats honored; his appetite for pomp and circumstance satiated. With his mane of white hair and his uniform of the admiralty, he must have made quite a stunning and dignified impression. His origins were, at least momentarily, overlooked; the fickleness of human nature temporarily forgotten in the rarefied air of praise and commendations.

During his sabbatical between the first and second voyages to the

New World, Columbus was feted by the man who was deemed to be the third in command after Ferdinand and Isabella, Pedro Gonzales de Mendoza, grand cardinal and primate of Spain. At the sumptuous table set before the conquering explorer, Columbus occupied the seat of honor and indulged in the pageantry normally reserved for nobility. Every dish prepared for the Admiral was sampled by none other than the cardinal himself before being passed to Columbus.[173]

**It was during this interlude of grandeur that the apocryphal story of the egg was first hatched:

> Columbus was dining with many Spanish nobles when one of them said: "Sir Christopher, even if your lordship had not discovered the Indies, there would have been, here in Spain, which is a country abundant with great men knowledgeable in cosmography and literature, one who would have started a similar adventure with the same result." Columbus did not respond to these words but asked for a whole egg to be brought to him. He placed it on the table and said: 'My lords, I will lay a wager with any of you that you are unable to make this egg stand on its end like I will do without any kind of help or aid.' They all tried without success and when the egg was returned to Columbus, he tapped it gently on the table breaking it slightly and, with this, the egg stood on its end. All those present were confounded and understood what he meant: that once the feat has been done, anyone knows how to do it.[174]

The tale is said to be factually inaccurate in view of the other legendary stories told about equally important men in other settings.

Lest the reader think all the Admiral did was attend one fete after another, he was also engaged in other more pressing pursuits: Columbus attended numerous sessions with Ferdinand and Isabella with lengthy discussions regarding the colonization of the New World. They talked of how to convert the islanders and transform them into staunch Christians. The Crown was under obligation to Pope Martin V who had issued a Papal Bull in 1438 requiring them to evangelize the heathen as far west as the Azores, the then-known reaches of the world. With the discovery of a New World, Ferdinand requested from Pope Alexander VI (of the house of Borgia) confirmation that Spain was to have oversight of the new lands located by Columbus (See Appendix F.)

The captive natives that had been taken to Spain aboard the Niña were not much more than a circus attraction—of little more value than the parrots and tobacco leaves gathered from the New World. One of the first acts after landing on the shores of the Old World was to baptize the Awarak Indians into the Catholic faith. Did the natives have any real idea of the meaning of the rite of baptism, or was it as foreign to them as the babble of voices around them? The baptism was surrounded with pomp and circumstance as had been their arrival, with royalty in attendance and the queen, herself, sponsoring the candidates. After Columbus discovered the New World and returned to Spain, Queen Isabella "immediately decreed that the natives (Indians as the Spanish would call them) were her subjects and were morally equal to all her other subjects including the Spaniards themselves. They were to be treated humanely and not to be enslaved, and they were to be Christianized and Europeanized."[175] Isabella fought ardently against the practice of treatment of the natives of the Indies and ultimately ordered some five hundred slaves that had been transported to Spain be freed and returned to their island home.

So pleased were the monarchs with the first journey of discovery launched by Columbus that he was endowed with a coat-of-arms:

> According to the blazon specified in letters patent dated May 20, 1493, Columbus was to bear in the first and the second quarters the royal charges of Castile and Leon—the castle and the lion—but with different tinctures or colors. In the third quarter would be islands in a wavy sea, and in the fourth, the customary arms of his family.

The earliest graphic representation of Columbus's arms is found in his *Book of Privileges* and shows the significant modifications Columbus ordered by his own authority. In addition to the royal charges that were authorized in the top quarters, Columbus adopted the royal colors as well, added a continent among the islands in the third quarter, and for the fourth quarter borrowed five anchors in fess [a broad horizontal band across the center of a coat of arms] from the blazon of the Admiral of Castile. Columbus's bold usurpation of the royal arms, as well as his choice of additional symbols, help to define his personality and his sense of the significance of his service to the Spanish monarchs.[176]

Could it have been the coat-of-arms of the Admiral of which poet Henry David Thoreau wrote:

> Columbus felt the westward tendency more strongly than any before. He obeyed it, and found a New World for Castile and Leon.[177]

Although it took seven long and tedious years for Columbus to gain the favor of Ferdinand and Isabella to sanction his first voyage westward, arrangements for a second voyage were immediately approved and the ships outfitted, in a span of only seven months. Don Juan de Fonseca, Archdeacon of Seville, was directed to procure seventeen vessels and raise an army for the journey. He was joined by Juan de Soria as comptroller and Francisco Pinelo as treasurer. The ships amassed were to transport over a thousand men—crewmen, militia and pioneers—to the New World. The monarchs made it patently clear that the voyage had a dual purpose: 1) to establish colonies; and 2) convert the natives. To that purpose a number of friars were enlisted to sail with the Admiral. Founding colonies of Spaniards to farm the land and raise flocks was to be of primary import, followed then by mining for gold. Approximately one year and two months after his initial voyage westward, Columbus boarded the flagship in the port of Cadiz, Spain, for his second expedition and the massive flotilla set sail.

An indication that converting the natives was uppermost in the Admiral's conviction is found in a letter written to Ferdinand and Isabella just before departure. He proposed "that there be a church [in the new colony] and priests or friars [be sent] for the . . . observance of divine worship and the conversion of the Indians . . . and that one per cent of all the gold obtained be taken for the building of the churches and . . . for the maintenance of the priests or friars."

To avoid the possibility that the settlers might become consumed with the quest for precious metal, Columbus suggested that "the search for gold should be forbidden during some period of the year so that an opportunity be given for the performance of other necessary and profitable labors" . . . and that "no one be allowed the privilege of getting gold except those who settle there and build houses for their dwelling-place in the town."[178]

The expense surrounding the launch of the second of Columbus' four voyages was considerable. The rapid turn-around between the two voyages was terribly costly because of the rush to beat a possible Portuguese race to the New World. In response, the monarchs committed two-thirds of the church tithes and a vast sum amassed by the property confiscated from exiled Jews. This was still insufficient for the need, prompting a loan of five million maravedis from the Duke of Medina Sidonia in order to complete preparations.

Among the myriad of men who assisted with the outfitting of the ships were Juonato Beradi and his assistant Amerigo Vespucci who were charged with securing provisions for the voyage. The men responsible for executing the planned excursion were joined in Seville by the Admiral himself. He soon ran afoul of Fonseca, who was said to have been jealous of Columbus. In a snit over some real or imagined affront, Fonseca wrote to the monarchs to complain. But Ferdinand and Isabella informed the cleric that he was to acquiesce to the wishes of the Admiral. The tables would be turned when Fonseca was named head of the Council for the Indies and then had the power to make things difficult for Columbus.

Among those aboard the armada making its way to the Indies were "the Queen's physician, Dr. Diego Alvarez Chanca, his younger brother Diego, Juan de la Cosa, who would make the first map that showed America, and Juan Ponce de Leon, who would later be the first European to explore Florida."[179] There are no crew logs available with the names of the remainder of the group, as there had been on the first voyage.

The armada set sail on September 25, 1493, and after a brief stop in the Canaries, crossed the ocean in only 21 days—a remarkable feat considering the ships were something less than seaworthy. According to historian Filson Young:

> If his [Columbus'] navigation had been more hap-hazard he might never have found again the islands of his first discovery; and the fact that he made a land-fall exactly where he wished to make it shows a high degree of exactness in his method of ascertaining lati-tude, and is another instance of his skill in estimating his dead-reckoning. If he had been equipped with a modern quadrant and Greenwich chronometers he could not have made a quicker voyage nor a more exact landfall.[180]

When the flotilla arrived in the midst of the islands of the Indies on November 3, 1493, Columbus called all the crew of his flagship the *Mariagalante* to the deck and led them in prayers and psalms, "thanking God for His mercy in letting them reach land."[181] As they lay offshore, the Admiral christened the island near Guadaloupe after his flagship. He then went ashore, took possession of the land in the name of the Spanish Crown, had a cross erected, and cel-ebrated Mass. As they sailed toward their destination, La Navidad, the ships passed islands Columbus named Dominica, Guadeloupe, Nevis, St. Kitts, St. Croix, the Virgin Islands and Puerto Rico, among other lush tropical islands.

The island of Guadaloupe offered a site unseen by the Spanish: Carib Indians. An article on the Caribbean in *St. John's Life* exposes the life and times of the cannibals:

> Columbus first learned about them [the Carib

Indians] from the Lucayos, the Tainos of the Bahamas, whom he encountered on his first voyage. According to the Lucayos, a fierce and warlike people ruled many islands to the east.

Peter Martyr, who interviewed sailors returning from the first transatlantic voyages, documented: "The Caribs emasculated the boys whom they seized and those who were born of the captives, fed them fat and, at their festivals, devoured them."

Entering the Caribs' homes [on the island of Guadaloupe], shore parties found "man's flesh, duck's flesh and goose flesh, all in one pot, and others on the spits ready to be laid to the fire. Entering into their inner lodgings, they found faggots of the bones of men's arms and legs, which they reserve to head arrows, because they lack iron; the other bones they cast away when they have eaten the flesh. They found likewise the head of a young man, fastened to a post, and yet bleeding and drinking vessels made of skulls," wrote Martyr.

On Guadeloupe, Columbus found six women, two children and a young man—Tainos from Boriken (Puerto Rico)—who had been captured by the Caribs. According to Columbus's son Ferdinand, the Tainos begged the Spaniards to help them escape. "They elected to give themselves over to an unknown people so alien to their own, rather than remain amongst those who were so manifestly horrible and cruel and who had eaten their husbands and children."[182]

Unlike the hostile and cannibalistic Caribs, the Tainos were found to be friendly, accommodating, and loyal subjects. To Columbus, subjugating the cannibalistic Caribs seemed politically advantageous to the safety and well-being of the more docile island natives.

Setting sail and following the coastlines of the islands that make up the chain of the Lesser Antilles, Columbus gave Spanish names to the islands between what is today Montserrat and the beautiful Virgin Islands. Sailing past each and foregoing exploration of the island paradises that lay before him, he set his course for La Navidad, only halting for a day and night on the island of Puerto Rico. After taking on provisions—water, fish and game—the Admiral departed at dawn on November 22, and by dusk the ship was anchored off the coast of Haiti. Given the route he had taken to reach his destination and the sheer quantity of islands passed along the way, Columbus still held firmly to the idea that he had reached the outer rim of the mainland of Asia.

Six weeks after their departure from Cadiz, the ships approached La Navidad, the temporary village that had been established by the crew of the sunken *Santa Maria*. Among the thirty-nine men who had remained behind were Diego de Arana, the brother of Columbus' mistress, Beatriz; Pedro Gutierrez, Ferdinand's butler; Rodrigo d'Escobeda, secretary; Luis de Torres, the Hebrew-speaking converso; two surgeons, a carpenter, a cooper and a tailor. The Admiral had expected the men to find a more suitable location for a permanent village and then explore the inlands in search of gold.

Upon arrival, the Admiral and his crew discovered grisly signs of the fate of the men from the *Santa Maria*. The hastily assembled shelters for the crewmen were no longer visible; no survivors were there to joyously greet the returning ships from Spain. A scouting party found only a burned-out hulk where the fort had been. According to Morison's account in *Admiral of the Sea*, the Spaniards had suffered a murderous end due to their treatment of the natives in the nearby villages:

> The Navidad garrison had not long been left to their own devices when the men began to quarrel over women and gold; Rodrigo de Escobedo the secretary and Pedro Gutierrez, the royal butler killed Jacome the Genoese gromet [a boy whose job was to turn the ship's hourglass], and made up a gang that roved the island in search of more gold and women. On their travels they encountered Caonabo . . . said to have been of Carib stock . . . He put the Gutierrez gang to death and promptly descended on Navidad with a strong force to wipe out the source of trouble . . . .In the meantime most of the other Spaniards had split up into predatory gangs, and only ten men were left . . . Caonabo attacked them at night, killed three, and chased the rest into the sea, where they were drowned. The others wandering about the interior were killed off by the Indians whom they had robbed or otherwise wronged.[183]

The Admiral was dismayed over the horrendous events that had taken place at La Navidad, but undeterred in his determination to find a proper place to establish a permanent colony in the Indies. After turning the prow of his ship from Haiti, he set sail eastward. On January 2, 1494, he reached the northern coast of Hispaniola—today the Dominican Republic. Finding a suitable location, he had the 1,500 settlers off-loaded and founded the first Spanish colony in the New World. On January 6, the colonists and ships' crews led by

Benedictine friar, Father Buil celebrated the feast of Epiphany in a makeshift chapel draped with crimson curtains provided by Queen Isabella. Columbus named the spot La Isabela (after the queen.) Six years later, the colony was a mere memory—and a bad one at that.

In their book about Columbus and the settlement of La Isabela, Kathleen Deagan and Jose Maria Cruxent wrote:

> The site of La Isabela provides the only direct phys-ical evidence for the organization of this first, intru-sive European colonial venture in the Americas. Even though the settlement itself was short-lived, the mate-rial world of La Isabela reflects Columbus's and the Spaniards' expectations for America, and how they thought best to master the continent.[184]

One important reason for the demise of La Isabella was its lack of a port. The Admiral, while a gifted mariner, was not the most remarkable administrator. The question has been asked: Why did he fail to choose a locale with no viable port as the first Spanish colony?

Hardly had the Epiphany mass ended when Columbus dis-patched Alonso de Hojeda and Gines de Gorvalan into the interior of the island to search for the ever-elusive gold. In their wanderings, they stumbled upon the Rio Yaque del Norte (renamed the Rio del Oro by Columbus) and according to Peter Martyr:

> In the sands . . . the Indians accompanying the Spaniards gathered gold by scooping out the sand with their hands to a depth of about a foot and a half . . . .From the bottom of the hole they scoop up sand

in their left hand and pick out the gold with their right hand, and just that easily they put nuggets in our hands. . . . I myself later saw a raw nugget like a river rock that weighed nine ounces; Hojeda had found it himself.[185]

Columbus made the decision to trek inland to see the find with his own eyes, a distance of some forty miles from the village of La Isabela. Upon arrival, the Admiral laid out plans for a fort, oversaw the early stages of its assembly, and left fifty cavalrymen under the authority of Mosen Pedro Margarite, a man who along with Friar Buil would later betray him.

In 1495, Columbus instituted a taxing system in the Vega Real (a fertile valley on what is today the Dominican Republic) which required adult Tainos to deliver to the Admiral a hawk's bell (about three ounces) of gold every quarter. Farming in the region was so disrupted by the search for gold that the land was soon gripped by a severe famine. This was worsened by the sheer number of colonists who required food and the debilitating diseases visited upon the unsuspecting Indians.[186] The result was a very strained atmosphere in the region.

Taviani provided clues as to why the Spaniards were so unsuccessful in colonizing the Indies:

> It was quite impossible to provide twelve hundred people with hardtack, oil and wine for eleven months . . . What remained of the hardtack and salt meat brought from Spain or Gomera putrified from the humidity and heat, and the wind turned sour. Those who settled at La Isabela had to get used to cassava bread made from

[root vegetables] yams, sweet potatoes, or yuca. In the sea off La Isabela was an abundance of fish, mollusks and crustaceans, but many of the hidalgos [non-titled nobility] and farmers were not used to seafood . . . .the earth could produce good grain if it was harvested on time. But someone had to cultivate it. The Admiral ordered everyone to work, even the hidalgos, which caused grumbling and resentment . . . .But they did not feel like working; the hidalgos were offended at being forced to do manual labor . . . .and even the farmers felt debilitated by the climate. They not only did not want to work but could not. [187]

After 24 days at anchor off the coast, the Admiral returned to his ship and sailed away, once again searching for the seemingly unattainable gold, leaving his brother, Don Diego, in charge of the newly-established colony. For the next five months, his crew explored the island of Cuba and discovered the beauty of Jamaica before returning to La Isabela.

Before Columbus had reached his destination, Friar Buil and Margarite had conspired to return to Spain aboard the caravel that had brought Columbus' brother, Bartholomew, to the island with new colonists. Rather than follow them in order to refute their charges against him, Columbus chose to stay in the islands.

Columbus' return to the first colony at La Isabela was far from that which he had expected. In just five months' time, the settlers had managed to wreak havoc on the unsuspecting islanders. The crimes that had been perpetrated upon the Haitian natives there had been multiplied. Groups of settlers had taken to roaming the island of

Hispaniola for the sole purposes of raping the women and enslaving the men. The abuses culminated in war between the Spaniards and the Indians in March 1495. The Admiral allowed himself to be drawn into the conflict by virtue of his own ignorance of the politics that constituted government onshore. The trust he had placed in his brother, Don Diego, had been misplaced as the sibling was more fitted to the monastery than to governing the Spanish colony. He had been sorely inept at coping with the vagaries of human nature and the savage character of those under his oversight; thus Columbus found sheer mayhem upon his return to La Isabela. As good as he was at sailing the high seas, the Admiral was hopeless as a governor. Neither he nor his brothers, Bartholomew and Don Diego, were able to control the inward revolt that had sprung up among the Spaniards on Hispaniola, nor could they corral the malicious actions of the Indians in retribution.

In an attempt to satisfy the idealistic aspirations of the monarchs (due largely to the Admiral's braggadocio after his first voyage) Columbus made what was possibly the worst decision of his life: He chose to approve the slave trade. He outlined a plan whereby open season would be declared on the Carib Indians, and would be considered the solution for not having found gold in great quantities in the Indies.

The Admiral's ruling appears to have been a critical point in his career as governor. There is scant confirmation that in the years following, Columbus was blessed with the godly direction he had previously enjoyed. It seemed that he was walking in his own counsel—lurching from one bad decision to the next. From decades of studying the Scriptures, surely Columbus must have known that bad choices would disrupt fellowship with God, and place him at a disadvantage spiritually. Perhaps he considered the words of Job in 16:11 (NKJV), "God has delivered me to the ungodly, And turned me over to the hands of the wicked."

He might have felt as David did when he wrote:

> I pray to you, O LORD, my rock.
> Do not turn a deaf ear to me.
> *For if you are silent,*
> *I might as well give up and die,*
> (Psalms 28:1, NLT, emphasis mine.)

Regardless, the twelve months of 1495 were spent with the Admiral fighting to build an atmosphere of harmony and striving to maintain stability on Hispaniola. He had little success. Salvadore de Madariaga believed Columbus' difficulty in maintaining order on the island was because he and his brothers were conversos:

> As was to be expected, the people in revolt against the Colons [Columbus and his brothers] soon discovered their Jewish origin. We know that anti-Semitism was always a democratic, and pro-Semitism an aristocratic attitude in Spain. It was therefore expected that [in Hispaniola] the "gentlemen and men of quality" would be with Colon and the people against him . . . . Despite his denials, there are signs . . . that the Spanish colony [in Hispaniola] remained convinced, that the Colons were of Jewish extraction.[188]

Could it be that just one of the drawbacks with Columbus as

governor of Hispaniola was that of being a converso who commanded little, if any, respect from the lower-class colonists?

Upon his arrival in Spain, Friar Buil appeared before Ferdinand and Isabella and presented a bleak picture of events on Hispaniola and questioned Columbus' ability to govern. So troubled were the monarchs that they dispatched Juan de Aguado to La Isabela and charged him to report only to them.

Aguado, who had supposedly been commissioned for the voyage to Hispaniola due to his evenhandedness, let his new position of authority go straight to his head. Rather than unobtrusively examining the charges against the Admiral and his family as he had been instructed to do by the Crown, Aguado wrested control from Bartholomew Columbus and immediately usurped Christopher's authority as well. Bartholomew had been a wise and informed leader, but Aguado's actions threw the colony into chaos. With little rhyme or reason, he incarcerated first one and then another while allowing criminals to go free. He instituted change only for the purpose of change. He arrested this person, imprisoned that; ordered that things should be done this way, which had formerly been done that way; and if they had formerly been done that way, then he ordered that they should be done this way—in short he committed every mistake possible for a man in his situation armed with a little brief authority. He did not hesitate to let it be known that he was there to examine the conduct of the Admiral himself; and we may be quite sure that everyone in the colony who had a grievance or an ill tale to relate, carried it to Aguado. His whole attitude was one of enmity and disloyalty to the Admiral who had so handsomely recommended him to the notice of the Sovereigns; and so undisguised was his attitude that even the Indians began to lodge their complaints and to see a chance by which they might escape from the intolerable burden of the gold tribute.

By the spring of 1496, when Aguado set foot on the island, Columbus found it imperative to return to Spain in order to protect his interests and to clear up any accusations leveled against him by some of the other returning sea captains. His choice of a colony had proved to be untenable for a number of reasons; chief among them was that there was no gold to be found in its immediate surrounds. That, coupled with the reality of a less than welcoming port, was enough to begin equipping the ship, *India*, for a return voyage. The Admiral appointed Bartholomew as governor of Hispaniola, and placed his brother Diego second in command. Francisco Roldan was appointed *alcalde* (head of the town) over La Isabela.

In March, the crew weighed anchor and with only a backward glance at La Isabella, the site of such suffering and disappointment, turned their faces toward Spain. The ruins of the first colony in the Indies were thereafter deemed to be haunted by the ghosts of those who had been ill-served at the hands of the colonists.

Before his departure, the Admiral gave the order that a new and more acceptable site be found for a capital. Santo Domingo, as it would become known, filled the bill—a good harbor, a river that could be panned for gold and rich acreage for farming.

All that remains of La Isabella today is a Dominican national park. Within its gates can be found material remnants of the fifteenth-century colony where visitors can learn about the colonists through the relics on display in the museum.

Bartolomé de Las Casas in his last will and testament wrote of the indignities done in the name of Spain. He might well have said the same of both the natives of the Indies and the exiled Jews:

To act here at home on behalf of all those people out in what we call the Indies, the true possessors of those kingdoms, those territories. To act against the unimaginable, unspeakable violence and evil and harm they have suffered from our people, contrary to all reason, all justice, so as to restore them to the original liberty they were lawlessly deprived of, and get them free of death by violence, death they still suffer.[189]

—13—

CHRISTOPHER COLUMBUS

Secret Jew

Hope in the Creator of all men sustains me: His help was always very ready; on another occasion, and not long ago, when I was still more overwhelmed, He raised me with His right arm, saying, 'O man of little faith, arise: it is I; be not afraid.'

—CHRISTOPHER COLUMBUS

ON MARCH 10, 1496, Columbus finally set sail for Spain in order to defend against the accusations brought against him by Friar Buil and Margarite. He sent his friend Antonio de Torres ahead with a cargo of five hundred slaves, an act that angered Queen Isabella; she ordered them released.

The two men had characterized matters in Hispaniola as quite substandard and painted a bleak portrayal of a congested settlement shattered by sickness, its inhabitants ill from a shortage of food. They stressed the debatable value based on the quality of the gold said to be plentiful in the New World. Moreover, they made serious accusations against the Admiral, characterizing him as incompetent to oversee the settlers. He was, they testified, committed to partiality, and guilty of intentionally falsifying his claims of abundance in order to line his own pockets and gain notoriety as an explorer. This was simply false. Columbus spoke of his aspirations for the journey—not for his own purposes, but with a heart filled with faith and longing to find a means to fund an attempt to recapture Jerusalem. His vision was far greater than any Friar Buil and Margarite might have imagined; his intent loftier than those two malicious adversaries could ever have understood.

After a long and tension-fraught journey from Hispaniola to the port at Cadiz, the Admiral reached the shores of Spain and began at once to seek an engagement with Ferdinand and Isabella. He was eager to right the litany of charges that had been made by his enemies. Once on shore, he chose not to don the uniform of a conquering hero. Instead the Admiral dressed in robes befitting a Franciscan monk—brown, homespun, unassuming, and pious apparel. Madariaga wrote of the significance of his chosen attire:

> He knew he would be deeply humiliated; so he deliberately humbled himself. "As he was a very devout worshipper of St. Francis," says Las Casas, "he dressed in brown cloth, and I saw him in Seville, when he came back then, dressed almost like a friar of St. Francis." . . . Colón was by no means a hypocrite or a dissembler in this. He was acting in all sincerity. But there were two deep-lying motives which prompted him to adopt this monastic garb: the first was a "mimetic" instinct, similar to that which makes some insects look like twigs or leaves; he was in outward danger—the displeasure of

the Court; what better garb than that of a Franciscan? The second was an even deeper instinct: he was in inner danger—the fall from the heights of pride to the depths of humiliation; he determined that no one but himself should humble him; he by his own free will, humbled himself down to the bottom of the ladder; henceforth, no man could abase him lower than he himself had done. He was proof against insults.[190]

The response from the monarchs was polite and gracious, but they failed to grant the requested audience. A month later, the Admiral received a letter from the queen asking his advice on the best route for the royal entourage to take from the Bay of Biscay to Flanders for the marriage of her daughter, Juana, to Archduke Philip of Austria. Several months later, the royals had returned to Burgos to celebrate another wedding—that of their son Prince Don Juan to Margaret, the daughter of Maximilian, the Holy Roman emperor. It was there that Columbus was finally granted the much sought-after audience with the Crown.

The Admiral was apprised of the truth: The charges brought to bear by Margarite and Friar Buil had been discounted by the monarchs. They still held nothing but trust and goodwill toward Columbus. It was at that meeting the Admiral made his request for ships and supplies for yet another voyage to the Indies. He wished to further his goal of reaching India via a westward route. It was an arduous undertaking for him as he had lost some public support for his travels. It is interesting to note that preparations for this voyage were helped along by Amerigo Vespucci. It might have been thought that the two would have been rivals rather than friends.

In a letter to his son Diego, Columbus wrote of his fellow voyager:

> He is a very honest man . . . . He goes for my good
> and is very anxious to do everything that may prove
> beneficial to me if it is within his power. I do not know
> of any particular thing in which I might instruct him
> to my benefit, because I do not know exactly what he
> is wanted for there. He goes determined to do for me
> all that he may possibly do . . . [191]

On May 30, 1498, Columbus set forth on his third journey of discovery. It would ultimately prove to be the most humiliating for the explorer. He sailed with a fleet of six ships—three filled with settlers and three with provisions for Hispaniola. Columbus again landed in the Canary Islands where he sent three of the ships to Hispaniola. He, in command of the other three ships set sail for the Cape Verde Islands. Columbus' intention in varying his route was to find a southern course that would eventually take him across the Atlantic Ocean and on to Asia.

After a brief stop at the island of Sao Tiago, a leper colony in the Virgin Islands, Columbus and his crew raised anchor on July 4 and set a southwesterly course for the ships under his command. For several days, the winds were so gentle that the three ships initially made little headway. Finally, the wind increased and Columbus was able to get underway. But, on a fateful Friday the thirteenth, the trade winds that had carried them forward began once again to abate and the Admiral found his ships and crew in the doldrums. It was one of the hottest and most humid of places to be for a Spanish crew. Columbus wrote:

The wind stopped so suddenly and unexpectedly and the supervening heat was so excessive ant immoderate that there was no one who dared go below to look after the casks of wine and water, which burst, snapping the hoops of the pipes; the wheat burned like fire; the bacon and salted meat roasted and putrefied. The heat lasted eight days . . . . or many people must have perished."[192]

Historians have written various opinions as to why the heat was so oppressive to the Spanish sailors. The general consensus seems to be that the woolen clothing worn by the men aboard ship contributed greatly to their discomfort. Early sailors rarely removed their oppressive outer garments that were ill-suited for tropical climates and therefore subjected to tremendous heat, all without benefit of regular baths or deodorant.

On July 31, 1498 Columbus announced a change in course and ordered the three caravels to come about to north by east. Las Casas wrote that by noon on that day, the Admiral had sent a sailor up to the crow's nest to scan the horizon. The spotter, Alonso Perez, shouted that he could see land about fifteen leagues in the distance. Says Las Casas, "He named this land *la ysla de la Trinidad* [Trinity in Spanish] because he had determined that the first land he should discover should be so named."[193] The island bore three mountain peaks that only served to persuade Columbus of the significance of his discovery.

The following day, Columbus had his crew sail in search of a source of fresh water. Along the south coast of Trinidad, he happened upon Punta de la Playa, as he named it, and a bay into which several freshwater streams emptied. The three vessels anchored off-shore and the weary crew hurried ashore to bask in the cool streams and wash off the weeks-long accumulation of sweat and salt spray. Just before reaching the bay, the Admiral had spotted another massive coastline. Soon, Columbus sailed into the Gulf of Paria and for several days followed the coastline of the peninsula. He happened upon the Orinoco River and marveled at its size—it was larger than the Nile River. Always deeply religious, the Admiral thought he might have discovered the outer reaches of the Garden of Eden along the shores of what came to be known as Venezuela.[194]

By August 14, the Admiral had reached the shores of what appeared to be another great continent, but not Africa or Asia. He quickly deduced that neither had he returned to the shores of Europe. He must have been sadly disappointed to have reached such an enormous roadblock in his quest for that desired westward route to India.

Discovering a new continent was a less than stellar moment for the explorer because of painful physical ailments that severely limited his ability to explore the vast land. Columbus, at a mere forty-seven years of age, was suffering from gout, a disease characterized by acute arthritis, and from ophthalmia, a commonplace ocular ailment of sailors, likely related to poor nutrition and eye strain. Taviani recorded:

> He ruined his eyesight by constantly gazing over the prow at the horizon in the morning, with the sun over his shoulder but the light intense and burning; in the afternoon when the westward course made him gaze directly into the sun; and even in the moonless nights, when only starlight brightened the dark waves sheared by the keel. Columbus' eyes were

swollen, weeping, and bloodshot. When he reached land he could not see all he should have. He could not see details that would have helped him better understand the place, could not make the observations that on the other two voyages he had personally verified and investigated. He did not even write in the Journal but probably dictated it, or perhaps it was transcribed from what he said.[195]

The Admiral sent Pedro de Terreros ashore in a skiff to claim the mainland for Ferdinand, Isabella, and the Catholic Church. Soon thereafter a giant wave is said to have persuaded Columbus and his entourage to set sail for Hispaniola in mid-August. He dictated:

> I heard a terrible roaring which came from the southward toward the ship. And I stood by to watch, and I saw the sea lifting from west to east in the shape of a swell as high as the ship, and yet it came toward me little by little, and it was topped by a crest of white water which came roaring along with a very great noise . . . so that even today I feel that fear in my body lest the ship be swamped when she came beneath it.[196]

Due to an uncanny ability to correctly calculate sea routes, Columbus set a northwest course for Hispaniola on August 16. Later that night, the needle on the compass dropped more than a point to the northwest. It was a phenomenon he had noticed while adrift in the doldrums on his way to Trinidad. With this information, he calculated that the earth was not a perfect sphere. It would not be until the twentieth century that scientists confirmed his theory with the use of satellites. How was Columbus able to deduce this with little more than his keen eye and an early version of a sextant? In a letter to Ferdinand and Isabella dated February 6, 1502, the Admiral wrote:

> Whether we admit that the shape of the world is spherical, as many writers affirm it to be, or bow to the decision of science if its conclusion is different, the fact of the diversity of climate within the same zone must remain undisturbed. That diversity will be served on land as well as on the sea.[197]

On August 31, the Admiral and his three ships made harbor at the newly-settled town of Santo Domingo, today the oldest continuously inhabited European city in the Americas. Upon arrival Columbus discovered that Francisco Roldan had usurped power from Bartholomew and ruled the western region of the island; his brother ruled the southern and central portion. The Admiral, much more at home on the sea than on land, could not readily devise a military means to wrest the region from Roldan.

The Admiral elected to have Miguel de Ballester, commander of the fortress at Bonao (Concepcion) negotiate a settlement between the two factions: Columbus wanted to offer the colonists the option of returning to Spain; Roldan wanted much more. After lengthy and sometimes futile discussions, Columbus opted to relinquish control of the situation to Ballester and have him resolve any differences between the two leaders. The land, which had already been divided between the settlers, would no longer be available to the natives on the island. They became little more than serfs in a New World feudal system that mimicked the practices of Europeans.

The move caused great consternation in Hispaniola, requiring Ferdinand and Isabella to dispatch Francisco de Bobadilla to act as an investigative officer of the court. Landing in Hispaniola in August 1500, Bobadilla assumed duties of governor. His appearance and subsequent control of the island fueled gold mining by provisionally stopping the tariff that had been previously been required on the precious metal. He further developed and expanded the mining industry and placed an even heavier burden on the Taino workers and their families.

Author Taviani explained that Diego Columbus' refusal to surrender to Bobadilla's demands by telling him that his brother's authority and merits were "better and more guaranteed,[198]" angered the Crown's envoy, and thus Bobadilla resorted to removing the Admiral and his family from power in Hispaniola. His arrival and subsequent review of the situation would cause great consternation to the Admiral. Columbus, hero, explorer extraordinaire, divinely-inspired discoverer, respected by the royals, and his brothers were soon to be arrested and returned to Spain in chains. The man who presented the Spanish Crown with almost half the world was now a captive! This gripping affair had enormous consequences. One then can feel only anger and censure from Bobadilla, the heavy in this forlorn tragedy.

Arrested in the name of Ferdinand and Isabella, the brothers were taken aboard the *La Gorda*. After the ship was underway, its captain offered to unchain Columbus. He was refused on the basis that having been arrested in the name of the monarchs, only they had the authority to order his chains removed. Despite that decision, he was treated with great deference by the ship's crew.

Once the *La Gorda* reached the port of Cadiz in Spain, the Admiral wrote to Juana de Torres, his long-time friend, nurse to

Prince Don Juan and confidante to Isabella, of his treatment once Bobadilla had landed on Hispaniola. The letter to de Torres was a tangled missive filled with intense dejection, outrage, acquiescence, lacerated self-assurance, self-esteem, and modesty. It was the plaintive whimper of one who is aware of having provided assistance to Spain and the Church for which a satisfactory reward did not occur, the grief of an individual incensed by discrimination, but still able to trust fully in God's provision. In his letter, Columbus outlined Bobadilla's behavior:

> The governor, on his arrival at [Hispaniola], took up his abode in my house, and appropriated to himself all that was therein. Well and good; perhaps he was in want of it; but even a pirate does not behave in this manner toward the merchants that he plunders. That which grieved me most was the seizure of my papers, of which I have never been able to recover one; and those that would have been most useful to me in proving my innocence are precisely those which he has kept most carefully concealed.
>
> Behold the just and honest inquisitor! I am told that he does not at all confine himself to the bounds of justice, but that he acts in all things despotically. God our Saviour retains His power and wisdom as of old; and, above all things, He punishes ingratitude.[199]

Juana used her influence with Isabella, who in turn persuaded Ferdinand to set the Admiral and his brothers free immediately. Furthermore, the queen and king signed and dispatched a missive to Columbus deploring the indignities suffered by him. The three brothers were invited to the Alhambra in Granada for an official and public audience with the monarchs.

Author Martin Dugard wrote of the meeting between the sovereigns and Columbus:

> Columbus was relieved when the sovereigns seemed happy to see him and beckoned to him warmly. Emboldened, he approached Ferdinand and kissed the king's hand. Then, head bowed, he reached for Isabella's. Some great emotion was released as he placed his lips to the back of her small hand—relief, perhaps; maybe affection.
>
> Columbus had knelt before her so many times, petitioning, receiving orders, announcing great triumphs . . . . He began to cry. Tears soon became sobs, and Columbus collapsed to the floor, not caring that his brothers and the king looked on . . . .And then a marvelous thing happened: Isabella cried too. "The Queen in particular consoled him," wrote one observer, "for in truth she more than the king ever favored and defended him, and so the Admiral trusted especially in her." Isabella reassured him that his imprisonment was not at the sovereigns' command and that it had offended them deeply. The guilty parties, Columbus was promised, would be punished.[200]

The Admiral was overjoyed for two reasons: 1) The charges against him were formally obliterated by the monarchs in his presence; and 2) he was informed that Bobadilla's authority had been rescinded and he would be recalled to Spain. It did Columbus' ego little good that he would not be allowed to return to Hispaniola as governor; instead Spanish soldier Nicolas de Ovando was appointed as his replacement on the island.

—14—

CHRISTOPHER
COLUMBUS
Secret Jew

*Columbus did not retire to a castle and
enjoy the wealth he had acquired.
His mind and heart had no room for anyplace
except the world he had discovered.*[201]

—PAOLO EMILIO TAVIANI

UNABLE TO REST on his accolades and past discoveries, the Admiral was determined to persuade Isabella and Ferdinand to allow yet another voyage of discovery to search for the elusive westward passage to Asia. Having discovered a vast landmass to the south of the Equator and having heard from the Taino people of an equally substantial continent to the north, Columbus was eager to pursue a passage between the two that would allow access to the Indian Ocean.

The English, Spaniards and Portuguese had for some time known of a waterway—today the Strait of Malacca—that provided access for ships traversing from the Pacific Ocean to the Bay of Bengal and into the Indian Ocean. The Admiral's sole purpose on his fourth and final voyage would be to find that passage and reach India. He knew he was chasing the Portuguese sailor Vasco de Gama who had already reached Calcutta by sailing eastward. This was a blow to the Spanish Crown as well as their beloved explorer who was intent on finding an even shorter route to Asia by sailing westward. That had not yet happened by the time de Gama and his two ships reached the coast of India.

Columbus would be allowed to sail, and in fact, carried aboard his flagship a letter from the Spanish monarchs to Vasco de Gama to be presented in the event the paths of the two voyagers crossed mid-ocean. The letter explicitly stated that the Admiral was sailing westward, and it was likely the two would meet somewhere along the way.

Within two months of receiving the go-ahead from the Crown, four caravels manned by 150 sailors set sail from the port of Cadiz. Alongside his father stood young Ferdinand, a mere thirteen years of age; and his brother Bartholomew who likewise had chosen to sail with the Admiral yet again. Diego, totally disgusted with the sailor's life, had opted for that of a cleric and remained staunchly ashore. The crossing took the ships to the Lesser Antilles and then to Martinique where they were re-outfitted with food, water and wood and then set sail for Puerto Rico. Hours before June 1502 faded into the history books, the ships reached the coast of Santo Domingo.

Columbus dispatched his trusted mate, Pedro de Terreros, a close friend and crewmember who had accompanied him on all four voyages. It was he who, on the third voyage, had been sent ashore at Paria to claim the South American mainland for the Spanish Crown. De Terreros approached Governor Ovando and explained that one of their ships was no longer totally seaworthy and the Admiral hoped to trade, lease or purchase a replacement. Columbus also sensed that a hurricane was about to make landfall and wanted his representative to secure permission for his ships to seek refuge from the storm.

While waiting for de Terreros to return with a response from Ovando, the Admiral learned of some thirty Spanish galleons laden with gold that were soon to set sail. Although there was no visible evidence of an impending storm, he notified the captains that they should delay their departure. Michele da Cuneo, a close friend of Columbus, wrote of his extraordinary seafaring skills that "Just by seeing a cloud or a star at night he could tell what was coming up and if there would be bad weather. He commanded and stood at the helm, and when the storm was over he raised the sails himself while the others slept."[202]

His ability to read the sky and his sixth sense about the ocean were uncanny. Despite his skill, the warning was soundly ridiculed and the armada sailed regally from the port of Santo Domingo. By the time the fleet had reached the easternmost limits of Hispaniola, the skies darkened ominously, the air smothered with oppressive humidity, and calm seas prevented the ships from turning back to port. Suddenly, the wrath of the hurricane burst upon the galleons tossing them to and fro, smashing keels and shredding sails. When the storm abated, four ships had escaped the fury of the sea but only one, the *Guecha*, reached Spain intact. Taviani tells us that on board the *Guecha* was Columbus' agent, Alonso Sanchez de Carvajal, with a sum of four thousand gold pesos. The monarchs had ordered Bobadilla to surrender the sum specifically to the Admiral. Blind luck or Divine intervention? Columbus would most certainly have opted for the second choice, especially since his four ships had survived the tempest.

On board one of the ships that perished in the howling seas

were Roldan, Bobadilla, the man who had dispatched the Admiral to Spain in chains just months before, and other of Columbus' enemies. Christopher's son Ferdinand wrote of the tragedy:

> I am satisfied it was the hand of God, for had they arrived in Spain they had never been punished as their crimes deserved, but rather been favored and preferred.[203]

Following the ravages of the hurricane, Columbus, his ships and crew found a safe harbor off the coast of Hispaniola where they spent considerable time regaining their strength, repairing any damage to the caravels, and dodging other lesser storms. Finally, during the middle of July, he was able to give the order to hoist the anchors, raise the sails, and turn westward toward the Gulf of Paria. His plan was to follow the coastline until he discovered the mystical passage he was sure existed—the course that would allow him to find the anticipated route to India.

As he proceeded along the coast, the Admiral encountered winds and currents that perplexed even him. He ultimately changed course, and finally determined that he was near the southwestern coast of Cuba—an area he had named the "Gardens." Several days later, he reached the shore of Honduras—Isla de Pinos. Much to the surprise of Columbus and his crew, a massive canoe was spotted, one which bore a covering resembling a small house at its center. It was inhabited by a cacique (a chieftain) and his family. The group bore emblems of a more progressive society than had heretofore been observed during the Admiral's voyages. Author Filson Young wrote:

> They wore clothing; they had copper hatchets, and

bells, and palm-wood swords in the edges of which were set sharp blades of flint. They had a fermented liquor, a kind of maize beer which looked like English ale; they had some kind of money or medium of exchange also, and they told the Admiral that there was land to the west where all these things existed and many more. It is strange and almost inexplicable that he did not follow this trail to the westward; if he had done so he would have discovered Mexico. But one thing at a time always occupied him to the exclusion of everything else; his thoughts were now turned to the eastward, where he supposed the Straits were; and the significance of this canoe full of natives was lost upon him.[204]

The occupants of the large canoe are thought to have been Mayan Indians from around the Bay of Campeche. This industrious group plied the coastline from the Yucatan south to what is now Belize, Guatemala and Honduras. Some of the items in their canoe—specifically those made of copper—were likely from Mexico. But so intent was the Admiral on finding a westward passage he missed what could have been one of his most important discoveries. Not until several years later in 1519 would Spanish conquistadors led by Hernán Cortés reach Mexico and eventually decimate the Aztec empire in central Mexico.

On August 15, Bartholomew Columbus, as his brother's emissary, set foot on the beaches of Honduras and celebrated Mass. The Admiral was much too ill to leave the ship. The natives that met the Spaniards, while friendly, were described as "very black and ugly." Columbus had the ships resupplied with provisions and quickly continued his route along the coastline. His labors were met with squalls, treacherous currents, and a hurricane that left his fleet battered, its tackle demolished and its sails torn. For several weeks the crews faced the fickle seas, their efforts accompanied by flashes of lightning and the noise of thunder. It was a terrifying time for the sailors and their ailing leader whose painful gout made it more and more difficult to even navigate the confines of his ship.

Young wrote of the Admiral and his unfortunate illness:

> But what must it have been thus to have one's sick-bed on the deck of a cockle-shell which was being buffeted and smashed in unknown seas, and to have to think and act not for oneself alone but for the whole of a suffering little fleet! No wonder the Admiral's distress of mind was great; but oddly enough his anxieties . . . were not so much on his own account as on behalf of others . . . . his son Ferdinand, who was only fourteen . . . had to endure the same pain and fatigue as the rest of them, and who was enduring it with such pluck that "it was as if he had been at sea eighty years"; the dangers of Bartholomew, who had not wanted to come on this voyage at all, but was now in the thick of it in the worst ship of the squadron, and fighting for his life amid tempests and treacherous seas; Diego at home, likely to be left an orphan and at the mercy of fickle and doubtful friends—these were the chief causes of the Admiral's anxiety . . . . Dreadful to him, these things, but not dreadful to us; for they show us an Admiral restored to his true temper and vocation, something of the old sea hero breaking out in

him at last through all these misfortunes, like the sun
through the hurrying clouds of a stormy afternoon.[205]

Although Columbus ultimately happened upon a source of the
ever-elusive gold when he reach the shore of Costa Rica in October,
he delayed only long enough to secure several goodly samples of
the natives' ornaments before setting sail yet again in pursuit of
his fantasy—that he was only days away from reaching the Ganges
River in India. After another month of exploration Columbus
reached the cape which Alonso de Hojeda had named Nombre de
Dios. Having plied the waters from Brazil to the Bay of Honduras,
the Admiral was finally forced to admit that there was no ready
passage westward from Spain to India. It was then that he made
the determination to turn back to Veragua in what is now Central
America. Taviani tells us, "From 16 October until 6 January 1503
they spent days, weeks, and months in a wearisome traversing back
and forth along the Atlantic coast of Panama. For by now Columbus
was thinking only of gold; he wanted to found a colony in the richest part of the New Lands, as close as possible to the mines. He had
found the most gold near Vergua . . . There he would return."[206]

By this time, the ships had been riddled with shipworms (*Teredo*
worms sometimes called "termites of the sea") causing them to leak
badly; his crews were ill; provisions were ruined; and the Admiral's
health was worsening. The men were reduced to catching sharks to
supplement their diet. The ships reached a harbor on the coast on
January 9, 1503, and named it Belem, or Bethlehem. It has been called
an ill-fated site. The ships anchored at the mouth of a river that could
be suddenly overrun by rains from the interior flowing torrentially
down the hillsides. One such torrent proved to be catastrophic for
Columbus and his ship. Before the men realized what was happening,

water gushed into the lagoon where the three ships were anchored, tearing one from its moorings and sending it crashing into another of the caravels. The other two were tossed about like matchsticks, sustaining heavy damage. At last, the struggling sailors managed to regain control and anchor the ships once again. As the waters abated, Columbus realized that sand washed down from the mountains and stirred up by the thrashing seas had created new bars, effectively trapping the ships in the lagoon.

As the rains receded and the weather returned to normal, Columbus dispatched Bartholomew on a visit to the area leader, Quibian. The native appeared before the entourage outfitted in gold—a crown, a large ornamental brooch around his neck, and his arms and legs ringed with thick bracelets. After a meeting with the chief that left Quibian leery of the new arrivals, he agreed to show Bartholomew where the gold mines were located. The Admiral's brother discovered later that the wily cacique had simply taken them farther afield and showed them the mines belonging to a neighboring tribal ruler—a cache of gold not nearly as rich as that of Quibian.

Meanwhile back on the boat, Columbus was reminiscing about Bible passages concerning Israelite King David and his son and the gold of Ophir that allowed Solomon to build and decorate the Temple. Columbus concluded that he must indeed have discovered those mines in Veragua rather than on Hispaniola as he had originally thought. The Admiral had the uncanny ability to live totally in the here and now—determining that the lands in which he then resided held the answer to the mystery he so diligently pursued.

Columbus decided the only thing to do was to colonize the area and prepare to confiscate the mines and work them. He laid out an orderly and amenable plan to reach his goal. Quibian, however, also had a strategy very dissimilar in character. He resented the presence of foreigners on his soil and concluded that the interlopers must be massacred. Fortunately for the Admiral and his crew, two of his men, Diego Mendez and Rodrigo de Escobar had seen the preparations for the attack. He ordered Bartholomew to take a contingent and capture Quibian, which he did successfully.

As the chieftain and fifty of his warriors were rowed unceremoniously back to the ship, he complained of his bonds being too constricting. A reckless Spaniard eased the cords and with the slipperiness of an eel, Quibian squirmed over the side of the launch, dove to the floor of the ocean, and somehow managed to reach shore.

Thinking their foe had perished in the salty waters, Columbus prepared the ships to set sail. Several days later, the waters in the lagoon rose enough to propel the ships across the bar and into the sea. Three of the ships escaped the confines of the cove and a fourth with a contingent of eighty men remained. As the three caravels sat offshore, sixty of the men from the small fort that had been erected on Veragua boarded a launch to bid good-bye to their companions. In their absence, Quibian and four hundred natives poured from the jungle and surrounded the small group left behind to defend the stronghold. The twenty Spanish soldiers were no match for the frenzied locals. The Admiral's beloved brother Bartholomew suffered a wound in his chest from a well-aimed spear but continued to fight against the adversary. He would survive his wound and return to the ship with his men, where all night Columbus had wrestled upon his bed in prayer:

> "Wearied and sighing," says he, "I fell into a slumber, when I heard a piteous voice saying to me, 'O fool, and slow to believe and serve thy God, who is the God of all! What did he more for Moses, or for his servant

David, than he has done for thee? From the time of thy birth he has ever had thee under his peculiar care. When he saw thee of a fitting age, he made thy name to resound marvelously throughout the earth, and thou wert obeyed in many lands, and didst acquire honorable fame among Christians. Of the gates of the Ocean Sea, shut up with such mighty chains, he delivered thee the keys; the Indies, those wealthy regions of the world, he gave thee for thine own, and empowered thee to dispose of them to others, according to thy pleasure. Thou hast won noble fame from Christendom. . . . Turn thou to Him and acknowledge thy faults; His mercy is infinite . . . Fear not but have trust."[207]

Aboard ship Columbus was beset with problems presented by the captive family and servants of Quibian. Determined to escape, the natives managed to break through the hatch that kept them confined belowdecks. Many of them managed to dive overboard and reach the shore. Those who were caught and again imprisoned chose death rather than captivity. The morning after the escape attempt, the captors opened the hatch to check on their prisoners. So determined were the natives not to be held captive that during the night all had died, either by hanging or self-strangulation.

When Diego Tristan, who had been sent to refill the freshwater casks, failed to return, the pilot Pedro de Ledesma volunteered to go ashore in search of Tristan and the men who manned his skiff. The Admiral happily acquiesced to the plan. A launch from the ship carried Ledesma as close to the shore as was safely possible. Laying aside his outer garments, the sailor dove into the sea and finally reached the shore, where he cautiously made his way to a village.

Upon reaching the site, Ledesma found chaos:

> They were preparing canoes to take them to the ships, when the weather should moderate, the boat of the caravel being too small; and swore that, if the admiral refused to take them on board, they would embark in the caravel, as soon as it could be extricated from the river, and abandon themselves to the mercy of the seas, rather than remain upon that fatal coast.
>
> [Ledesma] again braved the surf and the breakers, reached the boat which was waiting for him, and was conveyed back to the ships. The disastrous tidings from the land filled the heart of the admiral with grief and alarm . . . . Rather than the settlement should be broken up, he would gladly have joined the Adelantado [governor] with all his people; but in such case how could intelligence be conveyed to the sovereigns of this important discovery, and how could supplies be obtained from Spain? There appeared no alternative, therefore, but to embark all the people, abandon the settlement for the present, and return at some future day, with a force competent to take secure possession of the country.[208]

And so, Columbus and his entourage abandoned Santa Maria de Belen, the first Spanish settlement in Central America.

When Vasco Núñez de Balboa, another Spanish explorer, crossed the Isthmus of Panama in 1513, he was simply following in the wake of the Admiral of the Ocean Sea and his brother Bartholomew.

—15—

CHRISTOPHER COLUMBUS
Secret Jew

No one should fear to undertake any task in the name of our Saviour,
if it is just and if the intention is purely for His holy service.

—CHRISTOPHER COLUMBUS

ON APRIL 16, 1502, Columbus departed Veragua for Hispaniola, where he planned to provision his three remaining ships and set sail for Spain. The crews were kept busy with an exhausting effort to prevent the ships from sinking as a result of the holes bored in the vessels by shipworms. Given the destruction wrought by the tiny creatures, it is doubtful Columbus would have believed this kind of saltwater clam would one day become a delicacy to be eaten with zest. No, at that moment, it is more likely he was cursing the voracious little creature.

In a letter to Ferdinand and Isabella, Columbus apprised them of the near-catastrophic voyage:

> At the end of eight days I resumed my voyage and

at the end of June reached Jamaica, having always contrary winds and the ships in a worse state. With three pumps, pots and kettles, and with all hands working, they could not keep down the water which came into the ship, and there was no other remedy for the havoc which the worm had wrought. I steered a course which should bring me as near as possible to the coast of Española, from which we were twenty-eight leagues distant, and I wished that I had not begun to do so. The other ship, half under water, was obliged to run for port. I struggled to keep the sea against the storm. My ship was sinking under me, when our Lord miraculously brought me to land. Who will believe that which I write here? I declare that in this letter I have not told the hundredth part. Those who were with the admiral can testify to this.[209]

Samuel Eliot Morison said of the *teredo* shipworms and the application of pitch which was supposed to slow their advance through the hull: "If he gets past it, he will go on. And once into a ship's bottom, nothing can stop a *teredo* until he works through, and the planking is completely riddled."[210]

Setting his face toward the east, the Admiral skimmed the coastline until he was able to safely turn the prow toward Cuba. There, he took on provisions from the more friendly natives. Setting a heading for Hispaniola, it was near the island of Jamaica in Don Christopher's Cove on June 25 that Columbus beached the last two remaining ships. It is today known as St. Anne's Bay, although more an indentation in the coastline than an actual bay.

Ferdinand Columbus described the grounding of the two ships:

We ran them ashore as far as we could, grounding them close together board and board, and shoring them up on both sides so they could not budge; and the ships being in the position the tide rose almost to the decks. Upon these and the fore and sterncastles we built cabins where the people could lodge, making our position as strong as possible so the Indians could do us no harm; for at that time the island was not yet inhabited or subdued by Christians.[211]

Not all 140 who had sailed from Cadiz made it back to Jamaica; The Admiral was left with 116 men under his care. Fearing what might have happened if he had given the crew free reign of the island, Columbus forbade the men to leave the beach for the inland area. He appointed Diego Mendez as his emissary to barter with the local caciques for supplies. Daily, canoes would put ashore loaded with foodstuffs to sustain the men.

Not only was Mendez skilled at bartering for food, he presented Ameyro, one of the caciques, with a large brass bowl in exchange for a canoe. It would prove to be priceless when it came time to dispatch a party to Hispaniola. Columbus had given up hope that his adversary, Governor Ovando, would send anyone in search of him and his sailors. He also realized that a lack of precious metals on Jamaica would prevent other explorers from setting foot on its shores.

The Admiral chose the redoubtable Mendez as the man most capable of reaching Hispaniola and putting together a rescue squad. The first attempt almost ended in tragedy as the sailor was captured by natives and barely escaped with his life. After paddling his own canoe back to Santa Gloria, the inlet where Columbus had taken refuge, he began to consider a second attempt.

The plan for another try to reach Hispaniola was to bring Bartolomeo Fieschi, a friend of the Admiral, along in a second canoe and have Bartholomew shadow the canoes as far along the coastline as the topography would permit. Each canoe was manned by a captain, six Spaniards, and ten Indians. So hot was the weather that the water supply for the entire trip was exhausted by the second day. On the third day, the canoes made landfall on an island where they found sufficient water to refill their carriers. A fire was ignited, shellfish gathered, and the men were able to eat. After that refreshment, they again launched the canoes in the evening hours and paddled the remaining thirty miles to Hispaniola.

Mendez finally reached Santo Domingo only to learn that the one man who could approve a rescue operation, Governor Ovando, was in the interior fighting wars against the natives. Mendez set off to find Columbus' nemesis and persuade him to liberate the Admiral. Apparently more than pleased with the plight of his enemy, Ovando delayed making a decision—and delayed Mendez—for an entire year before a caravelon (a smaller version of a caravel) could finally be chartered and dispatched to rescue Columbus and his men.

Meanwhile back on Jamaica, the situation between the Admiral and his disgruntled men had reached the stage of mutiny. There was no viable way for Columbus to keep his men busy, and the inactivity translated to resentment toward the man they felt responsible for their plight. As time passed and neither Mendez nor Fieschi returned with news of rescue, talk of mutiny was whispered through the ranks. When the cauldron bubbles, filth rises to the surface—in this case it took the form of two lazy and thoroughly despicable brothers, Francisco and Diego de Porras. Morison described them perfectly:

Captain Francisco de Porras of *Santiago*, and Diego the crown representative and comptroller, were political appointees, and like many men of that kidney had never done a fair share of the work. Bartholomew Columbus had been the effective though unsalaried captain of *Santiago*, and Diego Porras, except for keeping account of gold coming aboard, had been an idler the entire voyage. Ignorant of seamanship, they were incapable of understanding the good reasons for running the ships ashore; and the men, in their depressed and discontented condition, were only too ready to hear suggestions of foul play. Why, they asked one another, was the Admiral keeping them in Jamaica?[212]

It took only the murmur of mutiny to catapult them into action. Rumors abounded that the two men sent to achieve their liberation had likely perished along the way; or that the Admiral was so disliked in Spain that the Crown had opted to leave him to perish on the Godforsaken Island. The Porras brothers hinted that it would be better for the seditious crewmen to seize canoes from the natives and set out for Hispaniola. Bedridden with gout, the Admiral could easily be left behind. As the days leading to Christmas crept by and the Old Year gave way to a New, Columbus was assailed in his incapacitated state by Francisco, who poured forth a spate of acrimonious criticism and insolence. He heaped accusations upon their leader and charged the Admiral with neglect. Columbus tried vainly to calm Porras, but with little consequence, even after suggesting that he meet with the crew to examine the best avenue to follow.

The enraged mutineer ridiculed the suggestion and instead shouted, "I am for Castile; those who choose may follow me," followed by cries of "I will follow you."[213] The single cry became a chorus heard throughout the two ships. Columbus lurched from his sickbed and stumbled onto the deck while Bartholomew grabbed his armaments and readied for combat. But not all were ready to sacrifice their beloved captain. Among the faithful were enough men to stem the tide of mutiny and with one voice persuaded Bartholomew and Columbus to allow the discontents to leave. The two brothers agreed that the loss of the mutineers would vastly improve morale among the other sailors and allowed them to go ashore.

Forty-eight rebels joined the Porros brothers, seized ten canoes that the Admiral had purchased from the natives, loaded them with stolen provisions, and paddled off into the sunset. Filson Young tells us that the undisciplined crew

> . . . coasted along the shore of Jamaica . . . landing whenever they had a mind to, and robbing and outraging the natives; and they took a particularly mean and dirty revenge on the Admiral by committing all their robbings and outragings as though under his authority, assuring the offended Indians that what they did they did by his command and that what they took he would pay for; so that as they went along they sowed seeds of grievance and hostility against the Admiral. They told the natives, moreover, that Columbus was an enemy of all Indians, and that they would be very well advised to kill him and get him out of the way.[214]

At last the rascals left Jamaica, their canoes making it only as far as approximately fifteen miles offshore before encountering rough waters. Rather than face an angry and turbulent sea, the terrified sailors turned about and headed back to Jamaica. Fearing that the boats would sink in the roiling waters, the Spaniards shoved the intimidated Indians overboard, where they floundered in the waves. As exhaustion overtook them, the Spaniards hacked at them with their broadswords until ultimately each disappeared beneath the waves. Once onshore, the men decided to stay where they had landed until another attempt could be made to reach Hispaniola.

Meanwhile conditions aboard the Admiral's beached ships began to resume a semblance of order. Columbus, though still ill, moved haltingly among his ailing crew members to minister to and encourage them. Just as he began to see the results of his ministrations, he was faced with a native uprising sparked by the vile behavior of the mutineers. The Indians who had previously delivered provisions to the men rebelled and insisted on being paid more for the food they provided. The Admiral's crew, weakened by sickness, was no longer able to forage for supplies.

According to Washington Irving, this led to a dire situation:

> The jealousy of the natives had been universally
> roused by Porras and his followers, and they withheld
> all provisions, in hopes either of starving the admiral
> and his people, or of driving them from the island.
> In this extremity, a fortunate idea presented itself to
> Columbus.[215]

On board his flagship, the Admiral carried two volumes he felt were significant additions to the library of any sailor: One was the "perpetual almanac" compiled by his long-time friend and

Jewish astronomer, Abraham Zacuto. Its more than three hundred pages of astronomical tables had guided numerous sailors to their destinations. The second work was the *Ephemerides*, which offered charts of the stars and other natural bodies in the heavens at specific times. It also allowed sailors to make rather accurate predictions on where certain events will take place, such as a lunar eclipse. As the natives became more and more hostile toward their unwelcome visitors, Columbus resorted to studying the pages of the *Ephemerides*. While perusing its contents, he spotted the mention of a total lunar eclipse that had been predicted on February 29, 1504.

After having calculated the approximate time the event would occur, Columbus sent a member of his party, an Indian from Hispaniola, to invite the caciques to a meeting to be held on the day of the anticipated eclipse. When they had all arrived at the appointed site, the Admiral informed them, through an interpreter, that he worshipped a God who dwelt in the skies; One who honored the men and women who followed His laws and punished evildoers. He continued by saying that this God had protected Diego Mendez when he set forth on his voyage to Hispaniola, but punished the Porras brothers for their revolt.

Columbus added that this great God of the heavens was angry with the natives because they had withheld provisions from his crew. He further informed them that should they not believe him, a sign would appear in the heavens that night—a blood red moon that would rise and then slowly lose its glow. It was, the Admiral opined, symbolic of the awful penalty that awaited the caciques and their followers.

Ferdinand Columbus wrote of his father's trickery and the hysteria among the natives:

The Admiral having spoken, the Indians departed, some frightened and others scoffing at his threats. But at the rising of the moon the eclipse began, and the higher it rose the more complete the eclipse became; at which the Indians became so frightened that with great howling and lamentation they came running from all directions to the ships, laden with provisions, and praying the Admiral to intercede with God that He might not vent His wrath upon them, and promising they would diligently supply all their needs in the future .... From that time forward they were diligent in providing us with all we needed, and were loud in praise of the Christian God.[216]

It seems safe to say that had Columbus miscalculated by one night, had he not had the courage to take such a gamble, the night would have ended tragically. He and his men may have died on the shores of Jamaica.

As he waited for the moon to again be visible on the warm Caribbean evening, perhaps the Admiral thought of years past when the Jews were summarily ousted from Spain with the slash of a pen authenticating the order of expulsion that was signed by King Ferdinand and Queen Isabella. That devastating event was followed soon after by a tetrad of blood moons that were seen approximately six months apart for the following two years. It seemed as though the heavens were mourning the plight of the Jewish people.

The first event of the tetrad took place during the Hebrew observances of Passover on April 2, 1493. That was followed by a second on the Feast of Tabernacles, September 25, 1493. The third occurred on Passover, March 22, 1494, and the fourth on September 15, 1494.

As a converso with Jewish ties, Columbus would have mourned the harsh treatment of the Sephardic Jews: They faced long years of exile during which they were subjected to murder, mayhem, pogroms, and a devastating Holocaust before finally being allowed to return to their God-given homeland in 1948. It is well to note here that after 500 years of waiting, another three tetrads of blood moons would be seen in the heavens around Jewish observances: Passover, April 13, 1949; Sukkoth (Feast of Tabernacles), October 7, 1949; Passover, April 2, 1950; and, Sukkoth (Feast of Tabernacles), September 26, 1950.

In 1947, before the declaration of statehood, continuing conflict at last exploded into the war between the Jews and Arabs as the UN plan to partition the region was revealed. When on May 14, 1948, the State of Israel was acknowledged by both the UN and the United States, the Arab nations surrounding the newly formed country joined forces and launched an all-out attack against the exultant Jews.

The armies of Egypt, Lebanon, Syria, Jordan, and Iraq invaded what had ceased the day before to be the British Mandate. It marked the beginning of the Arab-Israeli War. The newly formed Israel Defense Forces repulsed the Arab League nations from part of the occupied territories, thus extending Israel's borders beyond the original UNSCOP partition.

By December 1948, Israel controlled most of that portion of the Mandate including Palestine west of the Jordan River. The remainder of the Mandate consisted of Jordan, the area that today is called the West Bank (controlled by Jordan), and the Gaza Strip, now controlled by the Palestinian Authority and the terrorist organization Hamas. Prior to and during this conflict, 713,000 Palestinian Arabs fled their original lands to become Palestinian refugees due, in part, to a promise from Arab leaders that they would be able to return when the war had been won. The war came to an end with the signing of the 1949 Armistice Agreements between Israel and each of its Arab neighbors.

The long-ago prophecy of Ezekiel so diligently studied by Columbus was about to be fulfilled:

> For I will take you out of the nations; I will gather you from all the countries and bring you back into your own land. Then you will live in the land I gave your ancestors; you will be my people, and I will be your God (Ezekiel 36:24, 28 NIV).

But that would not be the end of God's intervention; another momentous time in Jewish history would come just twenty years later. In 1967 yet another tetrad of blood moons would begin: Passover, April 24, 1967; Sukkoth (Feast of Tabernacles), October 18, 1967; Passover, April 13, 1968; and Sukkoth (Feast of Tabernacles), October 6, 1968. On June 5, 1967, the Egyptian army amassed troops along the border between Egypt and Israel. Rather than waiting until a devastating attack by its enemies, the Israel Defense Forces launched a surprise attack. The battle that followed was one for the ages—and another of Columbus' dreams would be fulfilled: Jerusalem would be restored to the Jewish people.

The Israelis launched a lightning strike against the Arab states at ten minutes after seven on the morning of June 5. Simultaneously, Israeli ground forces struck the Egyptian army amassed in the Sinai with a fist that virtually demolished Egypt's capacity to respond.

In Tel Aviv, Colonel Mordechai Gur and his 55th Paratroop Brigade had been scheduled for deployment in the Sinai. Things were going so well there, however, that the high command offered their services in Jerusalem. Colonel Gur and his staff arrived in the city a few hours ahead of their paratroopers. The greatest difficulty facing Gur's plan to penetrate the Green line—as the border with Jordan was called—was whether to attack at night or wait for dawn. It seemed to make little sense to wait for daylight; launching a night attack might even give the Israelis an advantage.

The battle for Jerusalem was bloody and costly. The Jordanians had withdrawn to entrenched positions on Ammunition Hill. There, the Israelis encountered massive resistance. In the early morning hours, two prongs of the paratrooper attack crossed just north of the Mandelbaum Gate. One unit headed toward the Old City, the other toward several Arab strongholds. Both groups encountered fierce street-to-street combat. By noon, however, Jordanian resistance had ended.

At the cabinet meeting that night, Prime Minister Levi Eshkol issued orders through Chief of Staff Yitzhak Rabin to take the city. Colonel Mordechai Gur arranged for detachments to enter the Old City through its gates. The main thrust would be through the Lion's Gate opposite the Mount of Olives. Resistance was minimal.

My beloved friend General Mordechai Gur, who was a thirty-seven-year-old colonel at that time, led his 55th Paratroopers Brigade to defend Jerusalem. Years later in his office in Jerusalem he told me, "On Wednesday morning, June 7th, my paratroopers and I stormed into the Old City and advanced on the Temple Mount. I wept as I shouted over my communications system, 'The Temple Mount is in our hands!'"[217]

Chief Rabbi Shlomo Goren related to me:

> I managed to reach the Western Wall even before
> the firing had died down. Like one of Joshua's priests,
> I was running with the ram's horn, the shofar, in my

hand. When I placed it to my lips and blew, I felt like thousands of shofars from the time of King David were blowing all at once.[218]

Jews from every nation were dancing and weeping as they touched the Western Wall. Hardened veterans ran to touch the ancient wall, tears flowing down their faces in gratitude. "Next year, Jerusalem" was no longer a heartrending cry; it was reality. To pray at the Western Wall was no longer a yearning; it was a certainty. The Temple Mount, on which stands the Dome of the Rock, still remained closed to the Jewish people, but they could at least stretch out their fingertips and touch a portion of it. Most importantly, Jerusalem was united in Jewish hands.

While Israel was becoming a force with which to be reckoned with Spain was in decline. The dawn of the 1700s would find the nation inhabited by the Bourbons of France. The 1800s would see essentially all the Spanish empire globally reduced to ashes while the British and French were still dispatching explorers on voyages of discovery. It was, instead, for the Spaniards a time of political and social unrest which saw it effectively bypassed by the Industrial Revolution that had burgeoned in other European countries.

Twentieth-century Spain would be no different. From 1939 until 1975, Spain was ruled by the iron-fisted dictator Francisco Franco Bahamonde—Generalissimo Franco. His repressive governing style was personified by "more than 190 concentration camps, holding 170,000 prisoners in 1938[219] and between 367,000 and half a million prisoners in 1939, were incarcerated during the Spanish Civil War and in the following years."[220] He sanctioned forced labor and is said to have executed between 200,000 and 400,000 thousand of those he considered to be his enemies in the death camps.[221]

There is yet one more tetrad of blood moons in the twenty-first century that is aligned with the Jewish feast days. Will Israel be drawn into another war with her enemies? Only the passage of time will answer that question.

—16—

CHRISTOPHER **COLUMBUS**
Secret Jew

*"And there will be signs in the sun, in the moon,
and in the stars; and on the earth
distress of nations, with perplexity, the sea and
the waves roaring (Luke 21:25 NKJV).*

AS WE HAVE SEEN, every blood moon tetrad has been
tied to events in the history of the Jews. We have yet to see what
this present occurrence will bring—both to Israel and worldwide.
The prophet Joel also had something to say about the heavens:

> And I will show wonders in the heavens . . . . The
> sun shall be turned into darkness, And the moon into
> blood, BEFORE the coming of the great and awesome
> day of the LORD (Joel 2:30, 31 NKJV, emphasis mine).

From the days of Noah, when God set a rainbow in the clouds
through the times of Abraham, Moses, the prophets, the birth and

death of Jesus Christ, and until the end of the age, God has used or will use signs and marvels in the heavens to call man's attention to certain events. He used the myriad of stars in the sky as a measuring stick to show Abraham how great the nation of Israel would become. For Moses and the wandering children of Israel, He provided a pillar of fire by night and a cloud by day.

When the Messiah was born, the heavens resounded with the voices of an angelic choir who sang of His arrival. When He breathed His last sigh, the skies turned black in the middle of the day as heaven mourned the death of God's beloved Son. And throughout the book of Revelation, signs and wonders appear in the heavens as all of creation groans and travails at the terrible destruction sin has brought upon the world.

Looking forward to the return of the Messiah, Columbus began to record his thoughts, Scriptures, and events in a journal he titled, *Libro de las Profecias (Book of Prophecies)*. In the pages of that missive, he frequently appealed to the Bible and the prophets as he gave both credit for his knowledge and direction. He also quoted Jewish and Christian essayists as he strove to establish the timing for the end of the world and the second coming of Christ. The Admiral was determined to give an accounting of the signs and wonders that would precede such a glorious event. The pages of the treatise contain a letter which reads in part:

> At this time I both read and studied all kinds of literature: cosmography, histories, chronicles, and philosophy and other arts, to which our Lord opened my mind unmistakably to the fact that it was possible to navigate from here to the Indies, and He evoked in me the will for the execution of it . . . All those who heard

of my plan disregarded it mockingly and with laughter
... Who would doubt that this light did not come from
the Holy Spirit, anyway as far as I am concerned, which
comforted with rays of marvelous clarity and with its
Holy and Sacred Scriptures?[222]

Based on the belief that he was a Jew whose family had, at some
point, adopted a true belief in Jesus Christ as Messiah, the Admiral
embraced his faith but never forgot his roots. As one writer questioned: "Was not his heart beating for his lost fatherland, Palestine?"[223]

For Columbus, as with most conversos and Marranos, being
circumspect regarding his ancestry was essential. Boasting of one's
Jewishness could quickly result in the loss of a person's possessions as
well as his head. As a result, he simply became Christopher Columbus,
explorer, adventurer, sailor, and visionary. It has been said that within
the pages of his *Libro de las Profecias* were the words of a devout Believer
rather than simply a ritualistic member of the Catholic Church. It is
interesting that Columbus was enchanted with the contents of a book
written by a Marrano of which Dr. Meir Kayserling wrote:

In Spain, he (Columbus) read with religious zeal the
tract on the Messiah, which was written by the proselyte Samuel Ibn Abbas of Morocco, for the purpose of
converting R. Isaac of Sujurmente; it had been translated into Spanish in 1339, and into Latin a hundred
years later. This book interested Columbus so much
that he excerpted three whole chapters.[224]

The Admiral, as we have seen, was sincerely interested in the
prophecies found in the pages of the Scriptures. There are those

who believe that without a strong and abiding faith, he would never have had the fortitude and determination to search for the westward passage. This is especially true in light of the fact that one of his chief motivations was sufficient gold to enable an expedition to Palestine to free the Temple in Jerusalem from the hands of infidels.

In his writings there were constant allusions to the Old Testament—especially from the books of Isaiah and Jeremiah. At the time the Jews were ousted from Spain, the Church and the Inquisition were all-powerful. Columbus mentioned the Jews and their ejection with no word of admiration or praise for the abuse administered in the name of either the Church or the monarchs. It seems that the Admiral may well have sympathized with the plight of the exiles. Words of admiration from someone who had been granted a boon from the Crown would have been anticipated, and yet Columbus boldly stated in a missive to Ferdinand and Isabella of the plight of the Jewish people having been banished from Spain. Did he perhaps feel that by undertaking the voyage in search of a New World he, too, was leaving the country just as other conversos and Marranos had been compelled to do? He took a grim gamble at having mentioned something so heinous as the expulsion. He presented no words of praise of the two royals and offered no censure to those who were being exiled.

Not only his writings but his choice of consolation to his crew has been cited as sure proof that he was of Jewish extract. During the first voyage, he chose a portion of Scripture from Psalm 107 as a prayer:

Those who go down to the sea in ships, Who do business on great waters, They see the works of the

LORD, And His wonders in the deep. For He commands and raises the stormy wind, Which lifts up the waves of the sea. They mount up to the heavens, They go down again to the depths; Their soul melts because of trouble. They reel to and fro, and stagger like a drunken man, And are at their wits' end. Then they cry out to the LORD in their trouble, And He brings them out of their distresses. He calms the storm, So that its waves are still. Then they are glad because they are quiet; So He guides them to their desired haven (Psalm 107:23–30 NKJV).

We touched earlier on the question of an ulterior motive for the Admiral having wanted to discover a new land. It could well have been that he sought a place where Christians of Jewish ancestry as well as Jews themselves could find peace and safety.

In a letter written during his fourth voyage, he cried out in despair and desperation, and was rewarded, he believed, with a message directly from the God of heaven in which he was reminded of His grace, faithfulness, and mercy to Abraham and Sarah, to Moses and David. He wrote:

The privileges and promises which God gives, He breaks them not, nor does He say, after He has received the service that His intention was different and that it must be understood in another way, nor does He give martyrdom to anyone in order to lend some colour to sheer force: He sticks to the letter; all He promises, He fulfills and more: is this customary? I have said what thy Creator has done for thee and does for all. Now

He will show some of the reward for this anxiety and danger which thou has undergone serving others.[225]

The Admiral's faith continued to sustain him as he battled debilitating sickness during the year he and his crew spent on the island of Jamaica while his faithful friend, Diego Mendez, languished on the island of Hispaniola. There Mendez waited for the moment he could secure a vessel and rescue his friend. Finally a group of caravels arrived from Spain. As quickly as he could make arrangements, he purchased one of the smaller vessels, had it laden with bread, fruit, wine, meat, and several sheep and hogs and dispatched it to Jamaica. Mendez then boarded one of the ships returning to Spain in order to deliver a report of the disastrous voyage to Ferdinand and Isabella.

As the caravelon plied the waters on its mission, Mendez sailed eastward toward home. The rescue ship reached Santa Gloria, Jamaica, to the boisterous shouts of the weary castaways. The captain of the vessel threaded his way through the shoals and reefs into an inlet, where he dropped anchor. Author Martin Dugard painted a dismal picture of the sight that Columbus beheld from the deck of the *La Capitana*, his home for the past year:

> It was a terrible ship . . . The sails were in tatters from wind, sun, and neglect. The hull was a sieve. Yet she floated, and to Columbus' crew the caravelon was the finest vessel they had ever seen. The hogs were promptly butchered and the wine casks tapped. A fire was built on shore, and the feasting began.
>
> On Saturday, June 29, after a year and five days trapped at Santa Gloria, Columbus abandoned his

cabin on *La Capitana* and stepped aboard the little caravel for the ride back to Santo Domingo. He was too lame to walk without assistance, so boarding the ship was a most difficult task. The Arawak, watching from the shore, wept. Their visitors from another planet, capable of blocking out the moon, were leaving. During his time in Jamaica, seven more of Columbus's men died, including a ship's boy named Grigorio Sollo, who succumbed between the time the rescue ship arrived and the time it sailed to Hispaniola. The Admiral himself had endured malaria, gout, arthritis, and rheumatism, but much to the chagrin of critics like Porras and Ovando, he was still very much alive.[226]

On Santo Domingo, neither Ovenda nor the Admiral's other critics were overjoyed to hear of his impending rescue. Columbus' nemesis and mutineer, Porros, who had been confined there in chains, was promptly released from prison and returned to Spain to stand trial. He would not be forced to face the Admiral or his accusers on the island of Hispaniola.

The trip to Santo Domingo, a passage that had taken Mendez and Fieschi only four days by canoe, was hampered by storms and contrary winds. The overloaded caravelon carrying the castaways foundered in the wild seas and doubts that she would even make land were rife. Taking on water and settling lower into the sea, she landed temporarily at the port of Jacmel in Haiti. Setting sail once again, the vessel reached Hispaniola after a trying forty-five-day journey. Many of the crewmembers were so distraught they vowed never to board another ship.

Columbus, on the other hand, was eager to reach home. He

remained in Santo Domingo for only four weeks—long enough to charter and refit two ships for the trip to Spain. Ovando invited the Admiral to stay at the governor's palace while the work was being done on the caravels, an offer which he accepted. Ovando's act of hospitality was, in actuality, the result of the reception which had been afforded his rival. Since the people on the island showered Columbus with warmth and devotion, the wily Ovando decided it was incumbent that he be seen as polite and welcoming.

Ferdinand Columbus said of Ovando:

> So the governor's compliments to the Admiral were as false as his smiles and pretense of joy at seeing him. Matters went on this way until our ship had been repaired and another vessel chartered in which sailed the Admiral, his relations, and servants, most of the other choosing to stay in [Hispaniola].[227]

Finally, on September 12, the Admiral and his son Ferdinand climbed aboard one of the ships as paying passengers and watched the shoreline of Santo Domingo recede in the distance as they sailed into the blue waters of the Caribbean. His brother Bartholomew captained the second ship. Would that history could record an eventless journey home for the hapless explorers, but that was not to be. Just five weeks into the voyage, a violent storm descended. The ship was battered by the wind and waves until at last the mast cracked in four places and crashed to the deck below. The caravel was at the mercy of the raging sea.

Rather than see the ship on the bottom of the ocean, Columbus took control from his sickbed. Ferdinand wrote that the Admiral instructed the crew to contrive "a jury mast out of a lateen yard, which we secured firmly about the middle with ropes and planks taken from the stern and forecastles which we tore down . . . "[228] He added that during another storm, "Our mizzen mast was brought down . . . and it was God's will that we should sail in this sorry plight for seven hundred leagues, at the end of which we entered the harbor of Sanlucar de Barrameda."[229]

Christopher Columbus, Admiral of the Ocean Sea, was finally back in Spain. His fourth voyage had ended; his health was broken. The arthritis and gout had stolen his ability to walk. He could barely see and could no longer pursue writing in his journals. On the evening of May 20, 1506, Ferdinand, Diego, Bartholomew, and a host of friends gathered at his bedside when, at the age of fifty-five, he would breathe his last breath. King Ferdinand had forbidden final audience with a very ill Queen Isabella, who was suffering from an unknown cancer.

The Admiral's funeral was held in Valladolid at the church of Santa Maria la Antigua, but it would not be his last resting place. In 1509, his body was exhumed and relocated, but only temporarily, to the Franciscan cemetery in Seville. His son Diego had his father's remains moved once again in 1541, this time to the city cemetery in Santo Domingo. The restless bones of Columbus would be moved two more times—first to Havana, Cuba, and finally to a cathedral in Seville. Still the disputes continued over where the actual bones of the Admiral rested. Even with today's DNA testing, there is still controversy over exactly where he is interred—Seville, Cuba, or the Dominican Republic.

There seems to be further proof in his last will and testament that he was, indeed, a converso. His entire estate was bequeathed to his son Diego. He also entrusted the welfare of his other family members to Diego. These included his brothers Diego and Bartholomew, his son Ferdinand, and his former mistress, Beatriz Enriquez. He wrote:

> I order him [Diego] to be responsible for Beatriz Enriquez, mother of my son Sir Fernando, to provide for her so that she can live decently, because she is a person to whom I owe a great deal. And this must be done to clear my conscience, because this weighs heavily against my soul. It would not be proper to explain here the reason for this.[230]

Upon her death, Beatriz would leave her property to Ferdinand—an estate that included a house, workshop, winepress, two orchards and three plots of land in Santa Maria de Trassierra.[231] The Admiral left a tithe—one tenth of his wealth—to the poor and provided an anonymous legacy to indigent girls; both are Jewish customs. He also asked that an unspecified sum of money be given to a Jew who resided near the gate to the Lisbon Jewish Quarter. Not to be forgotten was his love for Jerusalem and his desire that it be liberated; he left funds in support of freeing the Holy Land. One other request was made of his heirs—that they continue to use the distinctive triangular signature that is said to mimic a Jewish prayer. Is it possible that ultimately he wished the world to know that he was descended from the lineage of Abraham, Isaac, and Jacob, a proud heritage?

For centuries following his death, beneficiaries have waged war against the Spanish crown in an attempt to receive all that had been promised Columbus by King Ferdinand and Queen Isabella. The monarchs were reluctant to define just how much was owed the

Admiral, which led to years of sometimes vitriolic lawsuits as his family fought to secure what had been rightfully his.

And so, the life of Christopher Columbus, secret Jew, came to an end. It was one fraught with adventure, discovery, failure, frustration, trials, and tragedy, but also with great success, opportunity, joy, and reward.

The Admiral's impact upon the lives of the Jewish people must not be underrated. As Rabbi Brad Hirschfield has written:

> Whoever Christopher Columbus was, and however he is remembered, this much we know: he was a boundary crossing explorer who drew on multiple identities and traditions in ways that empowered him to take incredible chances when others would not, see remarkable opportunities where others could not, and accomplish things big enough that their full implications were beyond anyone's understanding. That is the stuff of spiritual greatness.[232]

At a juncture in history when anti-Semitism had reached a fanatical note in Spain, Columbus discovered a New World to which the Jews could escape the oppression of the Church in Europe. With abundant determination and bravery, the Jews eventually won the privilege of observing their religion in that New World.

Appendix A

Edict of the Expulsion of the Jews (1492)

Translated from the Castilian by Edward Peters[233]

(1) King Ferdinand and Queen Isabella, by the grace of God, King and Queen of Castile, Leon, Aragon, Sicily, Granada, Toledo, Valencia, Galicia, the Balearic Islands, Seville, Sardinia, Cordoba, Corsica, Murcia, Jaen, of the Algarve, Algeciras, Gibraltar, and of the Canary Islands, count and countess of Barcelona and lords of Biscay and Molina, dukes of Athens and Neopatria, counts of Rousillon and Cerdana, marquises of Oristan and of Gociano, to the prince Lord Juan, our very dear and muched love son, and to the other royal children, prelates, dukes, marquees, counts, masters of military orders, priors, grandees, knight commanders, governors of castles and fortified places of our kingdoms and lordships, and to councils, magistrates, mayors, constables, district judges, knights, official squires, and all good men of the noble and loyal city of Burgos and other cities, towns, and villages of its bishopric and of other archbishoprics, bishoprics, dioceses of our kingdom and lordships, and to the residential quarters of the Jews of the said city of Burgos and

of all the aforesaid cities, towns, and villages of its bishopric and of the other cities, towns, and villages of our aforementioned kingdoms and lordships, and to all Jews and to all individual Jews of those places, and to barons and women of whatever age they may be, and to all other persons of whatever law, estate, dignity, preeminence, and condition they may be, and to all to whom the matter contained in this charter pertains or may pertain. Salutations and grace.

(2) You know well or ought to know, that whereas we have been informed that in these our kingdoms there were some wicked Christians who Judaized and apostatized from our holy Catholic faith, the great cause of which was interaction between the Jews and these Christians, in the cortes which we held in the city of Toledo in the past year of one thousand, four hundred and eighty, we ordered the separation of the said Jews in all the cities, towns and villages of our kingdoms and lordships and [commanded] that they be given Jewish quarters and separated places where they should live, hoping that by their separation the situation would remedy itself. Furthermore, we procured and gave orders that inquisition should be made in our aforementioned kingships and lordships, which as you know has for twelve years been made and is being made, and by many guilty persons have been discovered, as is very well known, and accordingly we are informed by the inquisitors and by other devout persons, ecclesiastical and secular, that great injury has resulted and still results, since the Christians have engaged in and continue to engage in social interaction and communication they have had means and ways they can to subvert and to steal faithful Christians from our holy Catholic faith and to separate them from it, and to draw them to themselves and subvert them to their own wicked belief and conviction, instructing them in the ceremonies and observances of their law, holding meetings at which they read

and teach that which people must hold and believe according to their law, achieving that the Christians and their children be circumcised, and giving them books from which they may read their prayers and declaring to them the fasts that they must keep, and joining with them to read and teach them the history of their law, indicating to them the festivals before they occur, advising them of what in them they are to hold and observe, carrying to them and giving to them from their houses unleavened bread and meats ritually slaughtered, instructing them about the things from which they must refrain, as much in eating as in other things in order to observe their law, and persuading them as much as they can to hold and observe the law of Moses, convincing them that there is no other law or truth except for that one. This proved by many statements and confessions, both from these same Jews and from those who have been perverted and enticed by them, which has redounded to the great injury, detriment, and opprobrium of our holy Catholic faith.

(3) Notwithstanding that we were informed of the great part of this before now and we knew that the true remedy for all these injuries and inconveniences was to prohibit all interaction between the said Jews and Christians and banish them from all our kingdoms, we desired to content ourselves by commanding them to leave all cities, towns, and villages of Andalusia where it appears that they have done the greatest injury, believing that that would be sufficient so that those of other cities, towns, and villages of our kingdoms and lordships would cease to do and commit the aforesaid acts. And since we are informed that neither that step nor the passing of sentence [of condemnation] against the said Jews who have been most guilty of the said crimes and delicts against our holy Catholic faith have been sufficient as a complete remedy to obviate and correct so great an opprobrium and offense to the faith and the Christian religion,

because every day it is found and appears that the said Jews increase in continuing their evil and wicked purpose wherever they live and congregate, and so that there will not be any place where they further offend our holy faith, and corrupt those whom God has until now most desired to preserve, as well as those who had fallen but amended and returned to Holy Mother Church, the which according to the weakness of our humanity and by diabolical astuteness and suggestion that continually wages war against us may easily occur unless the principal cause of it be removed, which is to banish the said Jews from our kingdoms. Because whenever any grave and detestable crime is committed by members of any organization or corporation, it is reasonable that such an organization or corporation should be dissolved and annihilated and that the lesser members as well as tile greater and everyone for the others be punished, and that those who perturb the good and honest life of cities and towns and by contagion can injure others should be expelled from those places and even if for lighter causes, that may be injurious to the Republic, how Much more for those greater and most dangerous and most contagious crimes such as this.

(4) Therefore, we, with the counsel and advice of prelates, great noblemen of our kingdoms, and other persons of learning and wisdom of our Council, having taken deliberation about this matter, resolve to order the said Jews and Jewesses of our kingdoms to depart and never to return or come back to them or to any of them. And concerning this we command this our charter to be given, by which we order all Jews and Jewesses of whatever age they may be, who live, reside, and exist in our said kingdoms and lordships, as much those who are natives as those who are not, who by whatever manner or whatever cause have come to live and reside therein, that by the end of the month of July next of the present year, they depart from all

of these our said realms and lordships, along with their sons and daughters, menservants and maidservants, Jewish familiars, those who are great as well as the lesser folk, of whatever age they may be, and they shall not dare to return to those places, nor to reside in them, nor to live in any part of them, neither temporarily on the way to somewhere else nor in any other manner, under pain that if they do not perform and comply with this command and should be found in our said kingdom and lordships and should in any manner live in them, they incur the penalty of death and the confiscation of all their possessions by our Chamber of Finance, incurring these penalties by the act itself, without further trial, sentence, or declaration. And we command and forbid that any person or persons of the said kingdoms, of whatever estate, condition, or dignity that they may be, shall dare to receive, protect, defend, nor hold publicly or secretly any Jew or Jewess beyond the date of the end of July and from henceforth forever, in their lands, houses, or in other parts of any of our said kingdoms and lordships, under pain of losing all their possessions, vassals, fortified places, and other inheritances, and beyond this of losing whatever financial grants they hold from us by our Chamber of Finance.

(5) And so that the said Jews and Jewesses during the stated period of time until the end of the said month of July may be better able to dispose of themselves, and their possession, and their estates, for the present we take and receive them under our Security, protection, and royal safeguard, and we secure to them and to their possessions that for the duration of the said time until the said last day of the said month of July they may travel and be safe, they may enter, sell, trade, and alienate all their movable and rooted possessions and dispose of them freely and at their will, and that during the said time, no one shall harm them, nor injure them, no wrong shall be done to

them against justice, in their persons or in their possessions, under the penalty which falls on and is incurred by those who violate the royal safeguard. And we likewise give license and faculty to those said Jews and Jewesses that they be able to export their goods and estates out of these our said kingdoms and lordships by sea or land as long as they do not export gold or silver or coined money or other things prohibited by the laws of our kingdoms, excepting merchandise and things that are not prohibited.

(6) And we command all councils, justices, magistrates, knights, squires, officials, and all good men of the said city of Burgos and of the other cities, towns, and villages of our said kingdoms and lordships and all our new vassals, subjects, and natives that they preserve and comply with and cause to be preserved and complied with this our charter and all that is contained in it, and to give and to cause to be given all assistance and favor in its application under penalty of [being at] our mercy and the confiscation of all their possessions and offices by our Chamber of Finance. And because this must be brought to the notice of all, so that no one may pretend ignorance, we command that this our charter be posted in the customary plazas and places of the said city and of the principal cities, towns, and villages of its bishopric as an announcement and as a public document. And no one shall do any damage to it in any manner under penalty of being at our mercy and the deprivation of their offices and the confiscation of their possessions, which will happen to each one who might do this. Moreover, we command the [man] who shows them this our charter that he summon [those who act against the charter] to appear before us at our court wherever we may be, on the day that they are summoned during the fifteen days following the crime under the said penalty, under which we command whichever

public scribe who would be called for the purpose of reading this our charter that the signed charter with its seal should be shown to you all so that we may know that our command is carried out.

(7) Given in our city of Granada, the XXXI day of the month of March, the year of the birth of our lord Jesus Christ one thousand four hundred and ninety-two years.

I, the King,

I the Queen,

I, Juan de Coloma, secretary of the king and queen our lords, have caused this to be written at their command.

Registered by Cabrera,

(NOTE: On December 16, 1968, four hundred and seventy-six years after the expulsion order by King Ferdinand and Queen Isabella was enforced, the Spanish government declared the order void.)

Appendix B

King Ferdinand & Queen Isabella, Agreements with Columbus of April 17 and April 30, 1492[234]

AGREEMENT OF APRIL 17, 1492

The things supplicated and which your Highnesses give and declare to Christopher Columbus in some satisfaction . . . for the voyage which now, with the aid of God, he is about to make therein, in the service of your Highnesses, are as follows:

Firstly, that your Highnesses as Lords that are of the said oceans, make from this time the said Don Christopher Columbus your Admiral in all those islands and mainlands which by his hand and industry shall be discovered or acquired in the said oceans, during his life, and after his death, his heirs and successors, from one to another perpetually, with all the preeminences and prerogatives belonging to the said office. . . .

Likewise, that your Highnesses make the said Don Christopher your Viceroy and Governor General in all the said islands and mainlands and islands which as has been said, he may discover or acquire in the said seas; and that for the government of each one and of any one of them, he may make selection of three persons for each office, and that your Highnesses may choose and select the one who shall be most serviceable to you, and thus the lands which our Lord shall permit him to discover and acquire will be better governed, in the service of your Highnesses. . . .

Item, that all and whatever merchandise, whether it be pearls, precious stones, gold, silver, spices, and other things whatsoever, and merchandise of whatever kind, name, and manner it may be, which may be bought, bartered, discovered, acquired, or obtained within the limits of the said Admiralty, your Highnesses grant henceforth to the said Don Christopher, and will that he may have and take for himself, the tenth part of all of them, deducting all the expenses which may be incurred therein; so that of what shall remain free and clear, he may have and take the tenth part for himself, and do with it as he wills, the other nine parts remaining for your Highnesses. . . .

Item, that in all the vessels which may be equipped for the said traffic and negotiation each time and whenever and as often as they may be equipped, the said Admiral Don Christopher Columbus may, if be wishes, contribute and pay the eighth part of all that may be expended in the equipment. And also that he may have and take of the profit, the eighth part of all which may result from such equipment. . . .

These are executed and despatched with the responses of your Highnesses at the end of each article in the town of Santa Fe de la Vega de Granada, on the seventeenth day of April in the year of the nativity of our Savior Jesus Christ one thousand four hundred and ninety-two.

AGREEMENT OF APRIL 30, 1492

Forasmuch as you, Christopher Columbus, are going by our command, with some of our ships and with our subjects, to discover and acquire certain islands and mainland in the ocean, and it is hoped that, by the help of God, some of the said islands and mainland in the said ocean will be discovered and acquired by your pains and industry; and therefore it is a just and reasonable thing that since you incur the said danger for our service you should be rewarded for it . . . it is our will and pleasure that you, the said Christopher Columbus, after you have discovered and acquired the said islands and mainland in the said ocean, or any of them whatsoever, shall be our Admiral of the said islands and mainland and Viceroy and Governor therein, and shall be empowered from that time forward to call and entitle yourself Don Christopher Columbus, and that your sons and successors in the said office and charge may likewise entitle and call themselves Don, and Admiral and Viceroy and Governor thereof; and that you may have power to use and exercise the said office of Admiral, together with the said office of Viceroy and Governor of the said islands and mainland . . . and to hear and determine all the suits and causes civil and criminal appertaining to the said office of Admiralty, Viceroy, and Governor according as you shall find by law, . . . and may have power to punish and chastise delinquents, and exercise the said offices . . . in all that concerns and appertains to the said offices . . . and that you shall have and levy the fees and salaries annexed, belonging and appertaining to the said offices and to each of them, according as our High Admiral in the Admiralty of our kingdoms levies and is accustomed to levy them.

Appendix C

Ships' Crew as Recorded on the First Voyage of Christopher Columbus[235]

Christopher Columbus, captain-general.

Juan de La Cosa, of Santona, master, and owner of the vessel, *Santa Maria.*

Sancho Ruiz, pilot.

Maestre Alonso, of Moguer, physician.

Maestre Diego, boatswain (contramaestre).

Rodrigo Sanchez, of Segovia, inspector (veedor).

Terreros, steward (maestresala).

Rodrigo de Jerez, of Ayamonte.

Ruiz Garcia, of Santona.

Rodrigo de Escobar.

Francisco de Huelva, of Huelva.

Rui Fernandez, of Huelva.

Pedro de Bilbao, of Larrabezua.

Pedro de Villa, of Santona.

Diego de Salcedo, servant of Columbus.

Pedro de Acevedo, cabin boy.

Luis de Torres, converted Jew, interpreter.

Martin Alonso Pinzon, of Palos, captain of the *Pinta.*

Francisco Martin Pinzon, of Palos, master.

Cristobal Garcia Xalmiento, pilot.

Juan de Jerez, of Palos, mariner.

Bartolome Garcia, of Palos, boatswain.

Juan Perez Vizcaino, of Palos, caulker.

Rodrigo de Triana, of Lepe.

Juan Rodriguez Bermejo, of Molinos.

Juan de Sevilla.

Garcia Hernandez, of Palos, steward (despensero).

Garcia Alonso, of Palos.

Gomez Rascon, of Palos,

Cristobal Quintero, of Palos,

Juan Quintero, of Palos. } owners of the vessel.

Diego Bermudez, of Palos.

Juan Bermudez, of Palos.

Francisco Garcia Gallego, of Moguer.

Francisco Garcia Vallejo, of Moguer.

Pedro de Arcos, of Palos.

Vicente Yanez Pinzon, of Palos, captain of the *Niña*.

Juan Nino, of Moguer, master.

Pero Alonso Nino, of Moguer, pilot.

Bartolome Roldan, of Palos, pilot.

Francisco Nino, of Moguer.

Gutierre Perez, of Palos.

Juan Ortiz, of Palos.

Alonzo Gutierrez Querido, of Palos.

Those Who Were Left In Hispaniola, And Perished, Most Of Them Murdered By The Natives: -

Pedro Gutierrez, keeper of the king's drawing room.

Rodrigo de Escobedo, of Segovia, notary.

Diego de Arana, of Cordova, high constable (alguazil mayor).

Alonso Velez de Mendoza, of Seville.

Alvar Perez Osorio, of Castrojeriz.

Antonio de Jaen, of Jaen.

The bachelor Bernardino de Tapia, of Ledesma.

Cristobal del Alamo, of Niebla.

Castillo, silversmith and assayer, of Seville.

Diego Garcia, of Jerez.

Diego de Tordoya, of Cabeza de Buey, in Estremadura.

Diego de Capilla, of Almaden.

Diego de Torpa.

Diego de Mables, of Mables.

Diego de Mendoza, of Guadalajara.

Diego de Montalban, of Jaen.

Domingo de Bermeo.

Francisco Fernandez.

Francisco de Godoy, of Seville.

Francisco de Aranda, of Aranda.

Francisco de Henao, of Avila.

Francisco Ximenez, of Seville.

Gabriel Baraona, of Belmonte.

Gonzalo Fernandez de Segovia, of Leon.

Gonzalo Fernandez de Segovia, of Segovia.

Guillermo Ires, [qy. William Irish, or William Harris?], of Galney [i.e. Galway], Ireland.

Fernando de Porcuna.

Jorge Gonzalez, of Trigueros.

Maestre Juan, surgeon.

Juan de Urniga.

Juan Morcillo, of Villanueva de la Serena.

Juan de Cueva, of Castuera.

Juan Patino, of La Serena.

Juan del Barco, of Barco de Avila.

Juan de Villar, of Villar.

Juan de Mendoza.

Martin de Logrosa, of Logrosa.

Pedro Corbacho, of Caceres.

Pedro de Talavera.

Pedro de Foronda.

Sebastian de Mayorga, of Majorca.

Tristan de San Jorge.

Tallarte de Lages [qy. Arthur Laws, or Larkins?], of England.

Appendix D

The Admiral Christopher Columbus' Letter to King Ferdinand of Spain

Following the Return from his First Voyage

Sir, As I know that you will be pleased at the great victory with which Our Lord has crowned my voyage, I write this to you, from which you will learn how in thirty-three days, I passed from the Canary Islands to the Indies with the fleet which the most illustrious king and queen, our sovereigns, gave to me. And there I found very many islands filled with people innumerable, and of them all I have taken possession for their highnesses, by proclamation made and with the royal standard unfurled, and no opposition was offered to me. To the first island which I found, I gave the name *San Salvador,* in remembrance of the Divine Majesty, Who has marvelously bestowed all this; the Indians call it "Guanahani." To the second, I gave the name *Isla de Santa Maria de Conception;* to the third, *Fernandina;* to the fourth, *Isabella;* to the fifth, *Isla Juana,* and so to each one I gave a new name.

When I reached Juana, I followed its coast to the westward, and I found it to be so extensive that I thought that it must be the mainland, the province of Catayo. And since there were neither towns nor villages on the seashore, but only small hamlets, with the people which I could not have speech, because they all fled immediately, I went forward on the same course, thinking that I should not fail to find great cities and towns. And, at the end of many leagues, seeing that there was no change and that the coast was bearing me northwards, which I wished to avoid, since winter was already beginning and I proposed to make from it to the south, and as moreover the wind was carrying me forward, I determined not to wait for a change in the weather and retraced my path as far as a certain harbour known to me. And from that point, I sent two men inland to learn if there were a king or great cities. They traveled three days' journey and found an infinity of small hamlets and people without number, but nothing of importance. For this reason, they returned.

I understood sufficiently from other Indians, whom I had already taken, that this land was nothing but an island. And therefore I followed its coast eastwards for one hundred and seven leagues to the point where it ended. And from that cape, I saw another island, distant eighteen leagues from the former, to the east, to which I at once gave the name "Espanola." And I went there and followed its northern coast, as I had in the case of Juana, to the eastward for one hundred and eighty-eight great leagues in a straight line. This island and all the others are very fertile to a limitless degree, and this island is extremely so. In it there are many harbors on the coast of the sea, beyond comparison with others which I know in Christendom, and many rivers, good and large, which is marvelous. Its lands are high, and there are in it very many sierras and very lofty mountains, beyond comparison with the island of Teneriffe. All are most beautiful, of a thousand shapes, and all are accessible and filled with trees of a thousand kinds and tall, and they seem to touch the sky. And I am told that they never lose their foliage, as I can understand, for I saw them as green and as lovely as they are in Spain in May, and some of them were flowering, some bearing fruit, and some in another stage, according to their nature. And the nightingale was singing and other birds of a thousand kinds in the month of November there where I went. There are six or eight kinds of palm, which are a wonder to behold on account of their beautiful variety, but so are the other trees and fruits and plants. In it are marvelous pine groves, and there are very large tracts of cultivatable lands, and there is honey, and there are birds of many kinds and fruits in great diversity. In the interior are mines of metals, and the population is without number. Espanola is a marvel.

The sierras and mountains, the plains and arable lands and pastures, are so lovely and rich for planting and sowing, for breeding cattle of every kind, for building towns and villages. The harbors of the sea here are such as cannot be believed to exist unless they have been seen, and so with the rivers, many and great, and good waters, the majority of which contain gold. In the trees and fruits and plants, there is a great difference from those of Juana. In this island, there are many spices and great mines of gold and of other metals.

The people of this island, and of all the other islands which I have found and of which I have information, all go naked, men and women, as their mothers bore them, although some women cover a single place with the leaf of a plant or with a net of cotton which they make for the purpose. They have no iron or steel or weapons, nor are they fitted to use them, not because they are not well built men and of handsome stature, but because they are very marvelously timorous. They have no other arms than weapons made of canes, cut in seeding time, to the ends of which they fix a small sharpened stick. And they do not dare to make use of these, for many times it has happened that I have sent ashore two or three men to some town to have speech, and countless people have come out to them, and as soon as they have seen my men approaching they have fled, even a father not waiting for his son. And this, not because ill has been done to anyone; on the contrary, at every point where I have been and have been able to have speech, I have given to them of all that I had, such as cloth and many other things, without receiving anything for it; but so they are, incurably timid. It is true that, after they have been reassured and have lost their fear, they are so guileless and so generous with all they possess, that no one would believe it who has not seen it. They never refuse anything which they possess, if it be asked of them; on the contrary, they invite anyone to share it, and display as much love as if they would give their hearts, and whether the thing be of value or whether it be of small price, at once with whatever trifle of whatever kind it may be that is given to them, with that they are content. I forbade that they should be given things so worthless as fragments of broken crockery and scraps of broken glass, and ends of straps, although when they were able to get them, they fancied that they possessed the best jewel in the world. So it was found that a sailor for a strap received gold to the weight of two and a half *castellanos,* and others much more for other things which were worth much less. As for new *blancas,* for them they would give everything which they had, although it might be two or three *castellanos'* weight of gold or an *arroba* or two of spun cotton. . . . They took even the pieces of the broken hoops of the wine barrels and, like savages, gave what they had, so that it seemed to me to be wrong and I forbade it. And I gave a thousand handsome good things, which I had brought, in order that they might conceive affection, and more than that, might become Christians and be inclined to the love and service of their highnesses and of the whole Castilian nation, and strive to aid us and to give us of the things which they have in abundance and which are necessary to us. And they do not know any creed and are not idolaters; only they all believe that power and good are in the heavens, and :hey are very firmly convinced that I, with these ships and men, came from the heavens, and in this belief they everywhere received me, after they had overcome their fear. And this does not come because they are ignorant; on the contrary, they are of a very acute intelligence and are men who navigate all those seas, so that it is amazing how good an account they give of everything, but it is because they have never seen people clothed or ships of such a kind.

And as soon as I arrived in the Indies, in the first island which I found, I took by force some of them, in order that they might learn and give me information of that which there is in those parts, and so it was that they soon understood us, and we them, either by speech or signs, and they have been very serviceable. I still take them with me, and they are always assured that I come from Heaven, for all the intercourse which they have had with me; and they were the first to announce this wherever I went, and the others went running from house to house and to the neighboring towns, with loud cries of, "Come! Come to see the people from Heaven!" So all, men and women alike, when their minds were set at rest concerning us, came, so that not one, great or small, remained behind, and all brought something to eat and drink, which they gave with extraordinary affection. In all the island, they have very many canoes, like rowing *fustas,* some larger, some smaller, and some are larger than a *fusta* of eighteen benches. They are not so broad, because they are made of a single log of wood, but a *fusta* would not keep up with them in rowing, since their speed is a thing incredible. And in these they navigate among all those islands, which are innumerable, and carry their goods. One of these canoes I have seen with seventy and eighty men in her, and each one with his oar.

In all these islands, I saw no great diversity in the appearance of the people or in their manners and language. On the contrary, they all understand one another, which is a very curious thing, on account of which I hope that their highnesses will determine upon their conversion to our holy faith, towards which they are very inclined.

I have already said how I have gone one hundred and seven leagues in a straight line from west to east along the seashore of the island Juana, and as a result of that voyage, I can say that this island is larger than England and Scotland together, for, beyond these one hundred and seven leagues, there remain to the westward two provinces to which I have not gone. One of these provinces they call "Avan," and there the people are born with tails; and these provinces cannot have a length of less than fifty or sixty leagues, as I could understand from those Indians whom I have and who know all the islands.

The other, Espanola, has a circumference greater than all Spain, from Colibre, by the sea-coast, to Fuenterabia in Vizcaya, since I voyaged along one side one hundred and eighty-eight great leagues in a straight line from west to east. It is a land to be desired and, seen, it is never to be left. And in it, although of all I have taken possession for their highnesses and all are more richly endowed than I know how, or am able, to say, and I hold them all for their highnesses, so that they may dispose of them as, and as absolutely as, of the kingdoms of Castile, in this Espanola, in the situation most convenient and in the best position for the mines of gold and for all intercourse as well with the mainland here as with that there, belonging to the Grand Khan, where will be great trade and gain, I have taken possession of a large town, to which I gave the name *Villa de Navidad*, and in it I have made fortifications and a fort, which now will by this time be entirely finished, and I have left in it sufficient men for such a purpose with arms and artillery and provisions for more than a year, and a *fusta,* and one, a master of all sea craft, to build others, and great friendship with the king of that land, so much so, that he was proud to call me, and to treat me as, a brother. And even if he were to change his attitude to one of hostility towards these men, he and his do not know what arms are and they go naked, as I have already said, and are the most timorous people that there are in the world, so that the men whom I have left there alone would suffice to destroy all that land, and the island is without danger for their persons, if they know how to govern themselves.

In all these islands, it seems to me that all men are content with one woman, and to their chief or king they give as many as twenty. It appears to me that the women work more than the men. And I have not been able to learn if they hold private property; what seemed to me to appear was that, in that which one had, all took a share, especially of eatable things.

In these islands I have so far found no human monstrosities, as many expected, but on the contrary the whole population is very well-formed, nor are they negros as in Guinea, but their hair is flowing, and they are not born where there is intense force in the rays of the sun; it is true that the sun has there great power, although it is distant from the equinoctial line twenty-six degrees. In these islands, where there are high mountains, the cold was severe this winter, but they endure it, being used to it and with the help of meats which they eat with many and extremely hot spices. As I have found no monsters, so I have had no report of any, except in an island "Quaris," the second at the coming into the Indies, which is inhabited by a people who are regarded in all the islands as very fierce and who eat human flesh. They have many canoes with which they range through all the islands of India and pillage and take as many as they can. They are no more malformed than the others, except that they have the custom of wearing their hair long like women, and they use bows and arrows of the same cane stems, with a small piece of wood at the end, owing to lack of iron which they do not possess. They are ferocious among these other people who are cowardly to an excessive degree, but I make no more account of them than of the rest. These are those who have intercourse with the women of "Matinino," which is the first island met on the way from Spain to the Indies, in which there is not a man. These women engage in no feminine occupation, but use bows and arrows of cane, like those already mentioned, and they arm and protect themselves with plates of copper, of which they have much.

In another island, which they assure me is larger than Espanola, the people have no hair. In it, there is gold incalculable, and from it and from the other islands, I bring with me Indians as evidence.

In conclusion, to speak only of that which has been accomplished on this voyage, which was so hasty, their highnesses can see that I will give them as much gold as they may need, if their highnesses will render me very slight assistance; moreover, spice and cotton, as much as their highnesses shall command; and mastic, as much as they shall order to be shipped and which, up to now, has been found only in Greece, in the island of Chios, and the Seignory sells it for what it pleases; and aloe wood, as much as they shall order to be shipped, and slaves, as many as they shall order to be shipped and who will be from the idolaters. And I believe that I have found rhubarb and cinnamon, and I shall find a thousand other things of value, which the people whom I have left there will have discovered, for I have not delayed at any point, so far as the wind allowed me to sail, except in the town of Navidad, in order to leave it secured and well established, and in truth, I should have done much more, if the ships had served me, as reason demanded.

This is enough . . . and the eternal God, our Lord, Who gives to all those who walk in His way triumph over things which appear to be impossible, and this was notably one; for, although men have talked or have written of these lands, all was conjectural, without suggestion of ocular evidence, but amounted only to this, that those who heard for the most part listened and judged it to be rather a fable than as having any vestige of truth. So that, since Our Redeemer has given this victory to our most illustrious king and queen, and to their renowned kingdoms, in so great a matter, for this all Christendom ought to feel delight and make great feasts and give solemn thanks to the Holy Trinity with many solemn prayers for the great exaltation which they shall have, in the turning of so many peoples to our holy faith, and afterwards for temporal benefits, for not only Spain but all Christians will have hence refreshment and gain.

This, in accordance with that which has been accomplished, thus briefly.

Done in the caravel, off the Canary Islands, on the fifteenth of February, in the year one thousand four hundred and ninety-three.

At your orders. El Almirante.

Appendix E

Letter addressed to the noble Lord Raphael Sanchez,
Treasurer to their most invincible Majesties, Ferdinand
and Isabella, King and Queen of Spain, by Christopher
Columbus, to whom our age is greatly indebted, treating of
the islands of India secently discovered beyond the Ganges,
to explore which he had been sent eight months before under
the auspices and at the expense of their said Majesties.

Knowing that it will afford you pleasure to learn that I have brought my undertaking to a successful termination, I have decided upon writing you this letter to acquaint you with all the events which have occurred in my voyage, and the discoveries which have resulted from it.

Thirty-three days after my departure from Cadiz I reached the Indian sea, where I discovered many islands, thickly peopled, of which I took possession without resistance in the name of our most illustrious Monarch, by public proclamation and with unfurled banners. To the first of these islands, which is called by the Indians Guanahani, I gave the name of the blessed Saviour (San Salvador), relying upon whose protection I had reached this as well as the other islands; to each of these I also gave a name, ordering that one should be called Santa Maria de la Concepcion, another Fernandina, the third Isabella, the fourth Juana, and so with all the rest respectively.

As soon as we arrived at that, which as I have said was named Juana, I proceeded along its coast a short distance westward, and found it to be so large and apparently without termination, that I could not suppose it to be an island, but the continental province of Cathay. Seeing, however, no towns or populous places on the sea coast, but only a few detached houses and cottages, with whose inhabitants I was unable to communicate, because they fled as soon as they saw us, I went further on, thinking that in my progress I should certainly find some city or village. At length, after proceeding a great way and finding that nothing new presented itself, and that the line of coast was leading us northwards (which I wished to avoid, because it was winter, and it was my intention to move southwards; and because moreover the winds were contrary), I resolved not to attempt any further progress, but rather to turn back and retrace my course to a certain bay that I had observed, and from which I afterwards dispatched two of our men to ascertain whether there were a king or any cities in that province. These men reconnoitered the country for three days, and found a most numerous population, and great numbers of houses, though small, and built without any regard to order: with which information they returned to us.

In the mean time I had learned from some Indians whom I had seized, that that country was certainly an island: and therefore I sailed towards the east, coasting to the distance of three hundred and twenty- two miles, which brought us to the extremity of it; from this point I saw lying eastwards another island, fifty-four miles distant from Juana, to which I gave the name of Espanola: I went thither, and steered my course eastward as I had done at Juana, even to the distance of five hundred and sixty-four miles along the north coast.

This said island of Juana is exceedingly fertile, as indeed are all the others; it is surrounded with many bays, spacious, very secure, and surpassing any that I have ever seen; numerous large and healthful rivers intersect it, and it also contains many very lofty mountains. All these islands are very beautiful, and distinguished by a diversity of scenery; they are filled with a great variety of trees of immense height, and which I believe to retain their foliage in all seasons; for when I saw them they were as verdant and luxuriant as they usually are in Spain in the month of May,—some of them were blossoming, some bearing fruit, and all flourishing in the greatest perfection, according to their respective stages of growth, and the nature and quality of each: yet the islands are not so thickly wooded as to be impassable. The nightingale and various birds were singing in countless numbers, and that in November, the month in which I arrived there. There are besides in the same island of Juana seven or eight kinds of palm trees, which, like all the other trees, herbs, and fruits, considerably surpass ours in height and beauty. The pines also are very handsome, and there are very extensive fields and meadows, a variety of birds, different kinds of honey, and many sorts of metals, but no iron.

In that island also which I have before said we named Espanola, there are mountains of very great size and beauty, vast plains, groves, and very fruitful fields, admirably adapted for tillage, pasture, and habitation. The convenience and excellence of the harbours in this island, and the abundance of the rivers, so indispensable to the health of man, surpass anything that would be believed by one who had not seen it. The trees, herbage, and fruits of Espanola are very different from those of Juana, and moreover it abounds in various kinds of spices, gold, and other metals.

The inhabitants of both sexes in this island, and in all the others which I have seen, or of which I have received information, go always naked as they were born, with the exception of some of the women, who use the covering of a leaf, or small bough, or an apron of cotton which they prepare for that purpose. None of them, as I have already said, are possessed of any iron, neither have they weapons, being unacquainted with, and indeed incompetent to use them, not from any deformity of body (for they are well-formed), but because they are timid and full of fear. They carry however in lieu of arms, canes dried in the sun, on the ends of which they fix heads of dried wood sharpened to a point, and even these they dare not use habitually; for it has often occurred when I have sent two or three of my men to any of the villages to speak with the natives, that they have come out in a disorderly troop, and have fled in such haste at the approach of our men, that the fathers forsook their children and the children their fathers. This timidity did not arise from any loss or injury that they had received from us; for, on the contrary, I gave to all I approached whatever articles I had about me, such as cloth and many other things, taking nothing of theirs in return: but they are naturally timid and fearful. As soon however as they see that they are safe, and have laid aside all fear, they are very simple and honest, and exceedingly liberal with all they have; none of them refusing any thing he may possess when he is asked for it, but on the contrary inviting us to ask them. They exhibit great love towards all others in preference to themselves: they also give objects of great value for trifles, and content themselves with very little or nothing in return. I however forbad that these trifles and articles of no value (such as pieces of dishes, plates, and glass, keys, and leather straps) should be given to them, although if they could obtain them, they imagined themselves to be possessed of the most beautiful trinkets in the world.

It even happened that a sailor received for a leather strap as much gold as was worth three golden nobles, and for things of more trifling value offered by our men, especially newly coined blancas, or any gold coins, the Indians would give whatever the seller required; as, for instance, an ounce and a half or two ounces of gold, or thirty or forty pounds of cotton, with which commodity they were already acquainted. Thus they bartered, like idiots,cotton and gold for fragments of bows, glasses, bottles, and jars; which I forbad as being unjust, and myself gave them many beautiful and acceptable articles which I had brought with me, taking nothing from them in return; I did this in order that I might the more easily conciliate them, that they might be led to become Christians, and be inclined to entertain a regard for the King and Queen, our Princes and all Spaniards, and that I might induce them to take an interest in seeking out, and collecting, and delivering to us such things as they possessed in abundance, but which we greatly needed.

They practice no kind of idolatry, but have a firm belief that all strength and power, and indeed all good things, are in heaven, and that I had descended from thence with these ships and sailors, and under this impression was I received after they had thrown aside their fears. Nor are they slow or stupid, but of very clear understanding; and those men who have crossed to the neighbouring islands give an admirable description of everything they observed; but they never saw any people clothed, nor any ships like ours.

On my arrival at that sea, I had taken some Indians by force from the first island that I came to, in order that they might learn our language, and communicate to us what they knew respecting the country; which plan succeeded excellently, and was a great advantage to us, for in a short time, either by gestures and signs, or by words, we were enabled to understand each other. These men are still travelling with me, and although they have been with us now a long time, they continue to entertain the idea that I have descended from heaven; and on our arrival at any new place they published this, crying out immediately with a loud voice to the other Indians, "Come, come and look upon beings of a celestial race": upon which both women and men, children and adults, young men and old, when they got rid of the fear they at first entertained, would come out in throngs, crowding the roads to see us, some bringing food, others drink, with astonishing affection and kindness.

Each of these islands has a great number of canoes, built of solid wood, narrow and not unlike our double- banked boats in length and shape, but swifter in their motion: they steer them only by the oar. These canoes are of various sizes, but the greater number are constructed with eighteen banks of oars, and with these they cross to the other islands, which are of countless number, to carry on traffic with the people. I saw some of these canoes that held as many as seventy-eight rowers.

In all these islands there is no difference of physiognomy, of manners, or of language, but they all clearly understand each other, a circumstance very propitious for the realization of what I conceive to be the principal wish of our most serene King, namely, the conversion of these people to the holy faith of Christ, to which indeed, as far as I can judge, they are very favourable and well-disposed.

I said before, that I went three hundred and twenty-two miles in a direct line from west to east, along the coast of the island of Juana; Judging by which voyage, and the length of the passage, I can assert that it is larger than England and Scotland united; for independent of the said three hundred and twenty-two miles, there are in the western part of the island two provinces which I did not visit; one of these is called by the Indiane Anam, and its inhabitants are born with tails.

These provinces extend to a hundred and fifty-three miles in length, as I have learnt from the Indians whom I have brought with me, and who are well acquainted with the country. But the extent of Espanola is greater than all Spain from Catalonia to Fontarabia, which is easily proved, because one of its four sides which I myself coasted in a direct line, from west to east, measures five hundred and forty miles. This island is to be regarded with especial interest, and not to be slighted; for although as I have said I took possession of all these islands in the name of our invincible King, and the government of them is unreservedly committed to his said Majesty, yet there was one large town in Espanola of which especially I took possession, situated in a remarkably favourable spot, and in every way convenient for the purposes of gain and commerce.

To this town I gave the name of Navidad del Senor, and ordered a fortress to be built there, which must by this time be completed, in which I left as many men as I thought necessary, with all sorts of arms, and enough provisions for more than a year. I also left them one caravel, and skilful workmen both in ship-building and other arts, and engaged the favor and friendship of the King of the island in their behalf, to a degree that would not be believed, for these people are so amiable and friendly that even the King took a pride in calling me his brother. But supposing their feelings should become changed, and they should wish to injure those who have remained in the fortress, they could not do so, for they have no arms, they go naked, and are moreover too cowardly; ao that those who hold the said fortress, can easily keep the whole island in check, without any pressing danger to themaelves, provided they do not transgress the directions and regulations which I have given them.

As far as I have learned, every man throughout these islands is united to but one wife, with the exception of the kings and princes, who are allowed to have twenty: the women seem to work more than the men. I could not clearly understand whether the people possess any private property, for I observed that one man had the charge of distributing various things to the rest, but especially meat and provisions and the like. I did not find, as some of us had expected, any cannibals amongst them, but on the contrary men of great deference and kindness. Neither are they black, like the Ethiopians: their hair is smooth and straight: for they do not dwell where the rays of the sun strike most vividly,—and the sun has intense power there, the distance from the equinoctial line being, it appears, but six-and-twenty degrees. On the tops of the mountains the cold is very great, but the effect of this upon the Indians is lessened by their being accustomed to the climate, and by their frequently indulging in the use of very hot meats and drinks. Thus, as I have already said, I saw no cannibals, nor did I hear of any, except in a certain island called Charis, which is the second from Espanola on the side towards India, where dwell a people who are considered by the neighbouring islanders as most ferocious: and these feed upon human flesh. The same people have many kinds of canoes, in which they cross to all the surrounding islands and rob and plunder wherever they can; they are not different from the other islanders, except that they wear their hair long, like women, and make use of the bows and javelins of cane, with sharpened spear-points fixed on the thickest end, which I have before described, and therefore they are looked upon as ferocious, and regarded by the other Indians with unbounded fear; but I think no more of them than of the rest. These are the men who form unions with certain women, who dwell alone in the island Matenin, which lies next to Espanola on the side towards India; these latter employ themselves in no labour suitable to their own sex, for they use bows and javelins as I have already described their paramours as doing, and for defensive armour have plates of brass, of which metal they possess great abundance. They assure me that there is another island larger than Espanola, whose inhabitants have no hair, and which abounds in gold more than any of the rest. I bring with me individuals of this island and of the others that I have seen, who are proofs of the facts which I state.

Finally, to compress into few words the entire summary of my voyage and speedy return, and of the advantages derivable therefrom, I promise, that with a little assistance afforded me by our most invincible sovereigns, I will procure them as much gold as they need, as great a quantity of spices, of cotton, and of mastic (which is only found in Chios), and as many men for the service of the navy as their Majesties may require. I promise also rhubarb and other sorts of drugs, which I am persuaded the men whom I have left in the aforesaid fortress have found already and will continue to find; for I myself have tarried no where longer than I was compelled to do by the winds, except in the city of Navidad, while I provided for the building of the fortress, and took the necessary precautions for the perfect security of the men I left there. Although all I have related may appear to be wonderful and unheard of, yet the results of my voyage would have been more astonishing if I had had at my disposal such ships as I required. But these great and marvellous results are not to be attributed to any merit of mine, but to the holy Christian faith, and to the piety and religion of our Sovereigns; for that which the unaided intellect of man could not compass, the spirit of God has granted to human exertions, for God is wont to hear the prayers of his servants who love his precepts even to the performance of apparent impossibilities. Thus it has happened to me in the present instance, who have accomplished a task to which the powers of mortal men had never hitherto attained; for if there have been those who have anywhere written or spoken of these islands, they have done so with doubts and conjectures, and no one has ever asserted that he has seen them, on which account their writings have been looked upon as little else than fables. Therefore let the king and queen, our princes and their most happy kingdoms, and all the other provinces of Christendom, render thanks to our Lord and Saviour Jesus Christ, who has granted us so great a victory and such prosperity. Let processions be made, and sacred feasts be held, and the temples be adorned with festive boughs. Let Christ rejoice on earth, as he rejoices in heaven in the prospect of the salvation of the souls of so many nations hitherto lost. Let us also rejoice, as well on account of the exaltation of our faith, as on account of the increase of our temporal prosperity, of which not only Spain, but all Christendom will be partakers.

Such are the events which I have briefly described.

Farewell.

Lisbon, the 14th of March.

CHRISTOPHER COLUMBUS,
Admiral of the Fleet of the Ocean.

Pope Alexander VI: The Division of the World (1493)[236]

Alexander, bishop, servant of the servants of God, to the illustrious sovereigns, our very dear son in Christ, Ferdinand, king, and our very dear daughter in Christ, Isabella, queen of Castile. . . .

We have indeed learned that you, who for a long time had intended to seek out and discover certain islands and mainlands remote and unknown and not hitherto discovered by others, to the end that you might bring to the worship of our Redeemer and the profession of the Catholic faith their residents and inhabitants, having been up to the present time greatly engaged in the siege and recovery of the kingdom itself of Granada were unable to accomplish this holy and praiseworthy purpose; but the said kingdom having at length been regained, as was pleasing to the Lord, with a wish to fulfill your desire, chose our beloved son, Christopher Columbus . . . whom you furnished with ships and men equipped for like designs, not without the greatest hardships, dangers, and expenses, to make diligent quest for these remote and unknown mainlands and islands through the sea, where hitherto no one had sailed; and they at length with divine aid and with the utmost diligence sailing in the ocean sea, discovered certain very remote islands and even mainlands that hitherto had not been discovered by others; wherein dwell very many peoples living in peace, and, as reported, going unclothed, and not eating flesh. . . .

Wherefore, as becomes Catholic kings and princes . . . you have purposed . . . to bring under your sway the said mainlands and islands . . . . And in order that you may enter upon so great an undertaking with greater readiness and heartiness endowed with the benefit of our apostolic favor, we, of our own accord, not at your instance nor the request of anyone else in your regard, but out of our own sole largess and certain knowledge and out of the fullness of our apostolic power, by the authority of Almighty God conferred upon us in blessed Peter and of the vicarship of Jesus Christ, which we hold on earth, do by tenor of these presents, should any of said islands have been found by your envoys and captains, give, grant, and assign to you and your heirs and successors, kings of Castile and Leon, forever, together with all their dominions, cities, camps, places, and villages, and all rights, jurisdictions, and appurtenances, all islands and mainlands found and to be found, discovered and to be discovered towards the west and the south, by drawing and establishing a line from the Arctic pole, namely the north, to the Antarctic pole, namely the south, no matter whether the said mainlands and islands are found and to be found in the direction of India or towards any other quarter, the said line to be distant one hundred leagues towards the west and south from any of the islands commonly known as the Azores and Cape Verde. With this proviso, however, that none of the islands and mainlands, found and to be found, discovered and to be discovered, beyond that said line towards the west and south, be in the actual possession of any Christian king or prince up to the birthday of our Lord Jesus Christ just past from which the present year 1493 begins. . . .

Furthermore, under penalty of excommunication *late sententie* to be incurred *ipso facto*, should anyone thus contravene, we strictly forbid all persons of whatsoever rank, even imperial and royal, or of whatsoever estate, degree, order, or condition, to dare without your special permit or that of your aforesaid heirs and successors, to go for the purpose of trade or any other reason to the islands or mainlands . . . apostolic constitutions and ordinances and other decrees whatsoever to the contrary notwithstanding. . . .

Let no one therefore, infringe, or with rash boldness contravene, this our recommendation, exhortation, requisition, gift, grant, assignment, constitution, deputation, decree, mandate, prohibition, and will. Should anyone presume to attempt this, be it known to him that he will incur the wrath of Almighty God and of the blessed apostles Peter and Paul.

Given at Rome, at St. Peter's,
in the year of the incarnation of our Lord 1493,
the fourth of May,
and the first year of our pontificate.

Appendix G

LAST WILL AND TESTAMENT OF THE ADMIRAL— CHRISTOPHER COLUMBUS[237]

The Will of Christopher Columbus Certified Copy in the Collection of the Duke of Veragua, Madrid

In the name of the Most Holy trinity, who inspired me with the idea and afterward made it perfectly clear to me, that I could navigate and go to the Indies from Spain, by traversing the ocean westwardly; which I communicated to the King, Don Ferdinand, and to the Queen, Dona Isabella, our Sovereigns; and they were pleased to furnish me the necessary equipment of men and ships, and to make me their Admiral over the said ocean, in all parts lying to the west of an imaginary line drawn from pole to pole, a hundred leagues west of the Cape de Verde and Azore Islands, also appointing me their Viceroy and Governor over all the continents and islands that I might discover beyond the said line westwardly; with the right of being succeeded in the said offices by my eldest son and his heirs forever, and a grant of the tenth part of all things found in the said jurisdiction; and of all rents and revenues arising from it; and the eights of all the lands and everything else, together with the salary corresponding to my rank of Admiral, Viceroy and Governor, and all other emoluments accruing thereto, as is more fully expressed in the title and agreement sanctioned by their Highnesses.

And I pleased the Lord Almighty that in the year one thousand four hundred and ninety-two, I should discover the continent of the Indies and many islands, among them Espanola, which the Indians call Ayte and the Menicongos, Cipango. I then returned to Castile to their highnesses, who approved of my undertaking a second enterprise for further discoveries and settlements, and the Lord gave me victory over the Island of Espanola, which extends six hundred leagues, and I conquered it and made it tributary; and I discovered many islands inhabited by cannibals, and seven hundred to the west of Espanola, among which is Jamaica, which we call Santiago; and three hundred and thirty-three leagues of continent from south to west, besides a hundred and seven to the north, which I discovered on my first voyage; together with many islands, as may more clearly, be seen by my letters, memorials and maritime charts. And as we hope in God that before long a good and great revenue will be derived from the above islands and continent, of which, for the reason aforesaid, belong to me the tenth and the eighth, with the salaries and emoluments specified above; and considering that we are mortal, and that it is proper for everyone to settle his affairs, and to leave declared to his heirs and successors the property he possesses or may have a right to: Wherefore, I have concluded to create an entailed estate (mayorazgo) out of the said eighth of the lands, places and revenues, in the manner which I now proceed to state:

In the first place I am to be succeeded by Don Diego, my son, who, in case of death without children, is to be succeeded by my other son, Ferdinand; and should God dispose of him also without leaving children and without my having any other son, then my brother, Don Bartholomew, is to succeed; and after him his eldest son; and if God should dispose of him without heirs, he shall be succeeded by his sons from one to another forever; or in the failure of a son, to be succeeded by Don Ferdinand, after the same manner, from son to son, successively; or in their place by my brothers, Bartholomew and Diego. And should it please the Lord that the estate, after having continued sometime in the line of any of the above successors, should stand in need of an immediate and lawful male heir, the succession shall then devolve to the nearest relative being a man of legitimate birth and bearing the name of Columbus derived from his father and his ancestors. This entailed estate shall in nowise be inherited by a woman, except in the case that no male is to be found, either in this or any other quarter of the world, of my real lineage, whose name as well as that of his ancestors, shall have always been Columbus. In such an event (which may God forefend) than the female of legitimate birth most nearly related to the preceding possessor of the estate shall succeed to it; and this is to be under the conditions herein stipulated at foot, which must be understood to extend as well to Don Diego, my son, as to the aforesaid and their heirs, every one of them, to be fulfilled by them; and failing to do so they are to be deprived of the succession for not having complied with what shall herein be expressed; and the estate to pass to the person most nearly related to the one who held the right; and the person thus succeeding shall in like manner forfeit the estate, should he also fail to comply with said conditions; and another person, the nearest of my lineage shall succeed, provided he abide by them, so that they may be observed in the form prescribed. This forfeiture is not to be incurred for trifling matters, originating in lawsuits, but in important cases, when the glory of God, or my own, or that of my family may be concerned which supposes a perfect fulfillment of all the things hereby ordained; all which I recommend to the Courts of Justice. And I supplicate His Holiness, who now is, and those who may succeed to the holy church, that if it should happen that this, my will and testament, has need of his holy order and command for its fulfillment, that such order be issued by virtue of obedience and under penalty of excommunication, and that it shall not be in any wise disfigured. And I also pray the King and Queen, our Sovereigns, and their eldest born, Prince Don Juan, our Lord and their successors, for the sake of the services I have done them, and because it is just, and that it may please them not to permit this, my will and constitution of my entailed estate to be any way altered, but to leave it in the form and manner which I have ordained forever, for the greater glory of the Almighty, and that it may be the root and basis of my lineage, and a memento of the services I have rendered their Highnesses; that, being born in Genoa, I came over to serve them in Castile and discovered to the west of terra firma the Indies and islands before mentioned. I accordingly pray their Highnesses to order that this, my privilege and testament, be held valid and be executed summarily, and without any opposition of demur, according to this letter. I also pray the grandees of the realm and the lords of the council, and all others having administration of justice to be pleased not to suffer this, my will and testament, to be of no avail, but to cause it to be fulfilled as by me ordained; it being just that a noble, who has served the King and Queen and the kingdom, should be respected in the disposition of his estate by will, testament, institution of entail or inheritance, and that the same be not infringed either in whole or in part.

In the first place, my son, Don Diego, and all my successors and descendants, as well as my brothers, Bartholomew and Diego, shall bear my arms, such as I shall leave them after my days, without inserting anything else in them; and they shall be their seal to seal with all. Don Diego, my son, or any other who may inherit this estate, on coming in possession of the inheritance, shall sign with the signature which I now make use of, which is an X with an S over it, and an M with a Roman A over it, and over that an S, and then a Greek Y with an S over it, with its lines and points as is my custom, as may be seen by my signatures, of which there are many, and it will be seen by the present one.

He shall write "The Admiral," whatever other titles the Kind may have conferred on him. This is to be understood as respects his signature, but not the enumeration of his titles, which he can make at full length if agreeable, only the signature is to be "The Admiral."

The said Don Diego, or any other inheritor of this estate, shall possess my offices of the Admiral of the Ocean, which is to the west of an imaginary line, which His Highness ordered to be drawn, running from pole to pole, a hundred leagues beyond the Azores, and as many more beyond the Cape de Verde Islands, over all of which I was made by their order, their Admiral of the Sea, with all the pre-eminences held by Don Henrique in the Admiralty of Castile; and they made me their Governor and Viceroy perpetually and forever, over all the islands and mainlands discovered, or to be discovered, for myself and heirs, and is more fully shown by my treaty and privileges as above mentioned.

Item: The said Don Diego, or any other inheritor of this estate, shall distribute the revenue which it may please our Lord to grant him, in the following manner, under the above penalty.

First: Of the whole income of this estate, now and at all times, and of whatever maybe had or collected from it, he shall give the fourth part of it to my brother, Don Bartholomew Columbus, Adelantado of the Indies, and this is to continue until he shall have acquired an income of a million maravedis [approximately thirty-five hundred dollars] for his support, and for the services he has rendered and will continue to render to this entailed estate; which million he is to receive as stated, every year, if the said fourth amount to so much, and the he have nothing else; but if he possesses a part or the whole of that amount in rents, that henceforth, he shall not enjoy the said million, nor any part of it, except that he shall have in the fourth year part unto the said quantity of a million, if it should amount to so much; and as much as he shall have a revenue besides this fourth part, whatever sum of maravedis of known rent from property or offices shall be discontinued; and from said million shall be reserved whatever marriage portion he may receive with any female he may acquire or may have over and above his wife's dowry; and when it shall please God that he or his heirs or descendants shall derive from their property and offices a revenue of a million arising from rents, neither he nor his heirs shall enjoy any longer anything from the said fourth part of the entailed estate which shall remain with Don Diego, or whoever may inherit.

Item: From the revenues of the said estate, or from any fourth part of it (should it amount be adequate to it), shall be paid every year to my son Ferdinand two millions, till such time as his revenue shall amount to tow millions, in the same form, and in manner as in the case of Bartholomew, who, as well as his heirs, are to have the million or the part that may be wanting.\

Item: The said Don Diego or Don Bartholomew shall make out of the said estate, for my brother Diego, such provision as may enable him to live decently, as he is my brother, to whom I assign no particular sum, as he has attached himself to the church, and that will be give him which is right; and this is to be given him in a mass, and before anything shall have been received by Ferdinand, my son, or

Bartholomew, my brother, or their heirs; and also according to the amount of the income of the estate. And in case of discord, the case is to be referred to two of our relations or other men of honor; and should they disagree among themselves, they will choose a third person as arbitrator, being virtuous and not distrusted by either party.

Item: All this revenue which I bequeath to Bartholomew, to Ferdinand, and to Diego, shall be delivered to and received to them as prescribed under the obligation of being faithful and loyal to Diego, my son, or his heirs, they as well as their children; and should it appear that they, or any of them, had proceeded against him in anything touching his honor, or the prosperity of the family or of the estate either in word or deed, whereby might come a scandal and debasement to my family, and a detriment to my estate in that case, nothing further shall be given to them or his from that time forward, inasmuch as they are always faithful to Diego and his successors.

Item: As it was my intention, when I first instituted this entailed estate, to dispose, or that my son Diego should dispose for me, of the tenth part of the income in favor of necessitous persons, as a tithe, and in commemoration of the Almighty, and Eternal God; and persisting still in this opinion, and hoping that his High Majesty will assist me, and those who may inherit it, in this or the New World, I have resolved that the said tithe shall be paid in the manner following:

First. It is to be understood that the fourth part of the revenue of the estate which I have ordained and directed to be given to Don Bartholomew, until he have an income of one million, includes the tenth of the whole revenue of the estate; and that, as in proportion as the income of my brother Don Bartholomew shall increase, as it has to be discounted from the revenue of the fourth part of entailed estate, that the said revenue of the fourth part of entailed estate, that the said revenue has to be calculated, to know how much the tenth part amounts to; and the part which exceeds what is necessary to make up the million for Don Bartholomew shall be received by each of my family as may most stand in need of it, discounting it from the said tenth, if their income do not amount to the fifty thousand maravedis; and should any of these come to have an income to this amount, such a part shall be awarded to them as two persons, chosen for the purpose, may determine along with Don Diego or his heirs. Thus, it is to be understood that the million which I leave to Bartholomew comprehends the tenth of the whole revenue of the estate; which revenue is to be distributed among my nearest and most needy relations in the manner I have directed; and when Don Bartholomew has an income of one million, and that nothing more shall be due to him on account of said fourth part, then Don Diego, my son, or the persons which I shall herein point out, shall inspect the accounts and so direct that the tenth of the revenue shall still continue to be paid to the most necessitous members of my family that may be found in this or any other quarter of the world, who shall diligently be sought out; and they are to be paid out of the fourth part from which Don Bartholomew is to derive his million, which sums are to be taken into account, and deducted from the said tenth, which, should it amount to more, the overplus, as it arises from the fourth part, shall be given to the most necessitous persons as aforementioned; and should it not be sufficient, that Don Bartholomew shall have it until his own state goes on increasing, leaving the said million in part or in whole.

Item: The said Don Diego, my son, or whoever may be the inheritor, shall appoint two persons of conscience and authority, and most nearly related to the family who are to examine the revenue and its amount carefully, and to cause the tenth to be paid out of the fourth from which Don Bartholomew is to receive his million to his most necessitous members of my family who may be found here or elsewhere, whom they shall look for diligently upon their consciences; and as it might happen that said Don Diego or others after him, for reasons which may concern their own welfare, or the credit support of the estate, may be unwilling to make known the full amount of the income, nevertheless I charge him on his conscience to pay the sum aforesaid and charge them on their souls and consciences not to denounce or make it known, except with the consent of Don Diego, or the person that may succeed him, but let the aboe tithe be paid in the manner I have directed.

Item: In order to avoid all disputes in the choice of the two nearest relations who are to act with Don Diego or his heirs, I hereby elect Don Bartholomew, my brother, for one, and Don Fernando, my son, for the other; and when these two shall enter upon the business they shall choose two other persons among the most trusty, and most nearly related, and these again shall elect two others, when it shall be question of commencing the examination; and thus it shall be managed with diligence from one to the other, as well as in this as in the other government, for the service and glory of God, and the benefit of the said entailed estate.

Item: I also enjoin Diego, or any one that may inherit the estate, to have and maintain in the city of Genoa one person of our lineage to reside there with his wife, and appoint him a sufficient revenue to enable him to live decently, as a person closely connected with the family, of which he is to be the root and basis in that city; from which great good may accrue to him inasmuch as I was born there, and came from thence.

Item: The said Don Diego, or whoever shall inherit the estate, must remit in bills, or in any other way, all sums as he may be able to save out of the revenue of the estate, and direct purchases to be made in his name, or that of his heirs, in a fund in the Bank of St. George [the great financial corporation of Genoa], which gives an interest of six percent, and is secure money; and this shall be devoted to the purpose I am about to explain.

Item: As it becomes every man of rank and property to serve God, either personally or by means of his wealth, and as all moneys deposited with St. George are quite safe, and Genoa is a noble city and powerful by the sea, and as at the same time that I undertook to set out upon that discovery of the Indies, it was with the intention of supplicating the King and Queen, our lords, that whatever moneys should be derived from the said Indies, should be invested in the conquest of Jerusalem; and as I did so supplicate them, if they do this, it will be well; if not, at all events the said Diego, or such persons as may succeed him in this trust, to collect together all the money he can, and accompany the King, our lord, should he go to the conquest of Jerusalem, or else go there himself with all the force he can command; and in pursuing this intention, it will please the Lord to assist toward the accomplishment of the plan; and should he not be able to effect the conquest of the whole, no doubt he will achieve in part. Let him therefore collect and make a fund of all his wealth in St. George in Genoa, and let it multiply there until such time as it may appear to him that something of consequence may be effected as respects the project on Jerusalem; for I believe that when their Highnesses see that this is contemplated, they will wish to realize it themselves, or will afford him, as their servant and vassal, the means of doing it for them.

Item: I charge my son Diego and my descendants, especially whoever may inherit this estate, which consists, as aforesaid, of the tenth of whatsoever may be had or found in the Indies, and the eighth part of the lands and rents, all which, together with my rights and emoluments as admiral, viceroy, and governor, amount to more than twenty-five percent, I say, that I require him to employ all this revenue, as well as his person, and all the means in his power, in well and faithfully serving and supporting their Highnesses, or their successors, even to the loss of life and property; since it was their Highnesses, next to God, who first gave the means of getting and achieving this property, although it is true, I came over these realms to invite them to the enterprise, and that a long time elapsed before any provision was made for carrying in into execution; which, however, is not surprising, as this was an undertaking of which all the world was ignorant, and no one had any faith in it; wherefore, I am by so much more indebted to them, as well as because they have since also much favored and promoted me.

Item: I also require of Diego, or whosoever may be in possession of the estate, that in the case of any schism taking place in the church of God, or that any person of whatever class or condition should attempt to despoil it of its property and honors they hasten to offer at the feet of his Holiness, that is, if they are not heretics (which God forbid), their persons, power and wealth, for the purpose of suppressing such schism, and preventing any spoliation of the honor and property of the church.

Item: I command the said Diego, or whoever may possess the said estate, to labor and strive for the honor, welfare, and aggrandizement of the city of Genoa, and to make use of all his power and means in defending and enhancing the good and credit of the republic, in all things not contrary to the service of the church of God, or the high dignity of the King and Queen, our lords and their successors.

Item: The said Diego, or whoever may possess or succeed to the estate, out of the fourth part of the whole revenue, from which, as aforesaid, is to be taken a tenth, when Don Bartholomew or his heirs shall have saved the two millions, or part of them, and when the time shall come for making a distribution among our relations, shall apply and invest the said tenth in providing marriages for such daughters of our lineage as may require it, and in so doing all the good in their power.

Item: When a suitable time shall arrive, he shall order a church to be built in the island of Espanola, and in the most convenient spot, to be called Santa Maria de la Conception; to which is to be annexed an hospital, upon the best possible plan, like those of Italy and Castile, and a chapel is to be erected in which to say mas for the good of my soul, and those of my ancestors and successors with great devotion, since no doubt it will please the Lord to give us a sufficient revenue for this and the aforementioned purposes.

Item: I also order Diego, my son, or whosoever may inherit after him, to spare no pains in having and maintaining in the island of Espanola, four good professors in theology, to the end and aim of their studying and laboring to convert to our holy faith the inhabitants of the Indies; and in proportion as by God's will the revenue of the estate shall increase in the same degree shall the number of teachers and devout persons increase, who are to strive to make Christians of the natives; in attaining which no expense should be thought too great. And in commemoration of all that I hereby ordain, and of the foregoing, a monument of marble shall be erected in the said church of La Conception, in the most conspicuous place, to serve as a record of what I here enjoin on the said Diego, as well as to other persons who may look upon it; which marble shall contain an inscription to the same effect.

Item: I also require of Diego, my son, and whosoever may succeed him in the estate, that every time, and as often as he confesses, he first show his obligation, or a copy of it, to the confessor, praying him to read it through, that he may be enabled to inquire respecting its fulfillment; from which will redound great good and happiness to his soul.[238]

Appendix C

THE LETTER OF COLUMBUS TO LUIS DE SANT ANGEL ANNOUNCING HIS DISCOVERY

(1493)

As I know you will be rejoiced at the glorious success that our Lord has given me in my voyage, I write this to tell you how in thirty-three days I sailed to the Indies with the fleet that the illustrious King and Queen, our Sovereigns, gave me, where I discovered a great many islands, inhabited by numberless people; and of all I have taken possession for their Highnesses by proclamation and display of the Royal Standard without opposition. To the first island I discovered I gave the name of San Salvador, in commemoration of His Divine Majesty, who has wonderfully granted all this. The Indians call it Guanaham. The second I named the Island of Santa Maria de Concepcion; the third, Fernandina; the fourth, Isabella; the fifth, Juana; and thus to each one I gave a new name. When I came to Juana, I followed the coast of that isle toward the west, and found it so extensive that I thought it might be the mainland, the province of Cathay; and as I found no towns nor villages on the sea-coast, except a few small settlements, where it was impossible to speak to the people, because they fled at once, I continued the said route, thinking I could not fail to see some great cities or towns; and finding at the end of many leagues that nothing new appeared, and that the coast led northward, contrary to my wish, because the winter had already set in, I decided to make for the south, and as the wind also was against my proceeding, I determined not to wait there longer, and turned back to a certain harbor whence I sent two men to find out whether there was any king or large city. They explored for three days, and found countless small communities and people, without number, but with no kind of government, so they returned.

I heard from other Indians I had already taken that this land was an island, and thus followed the eastern coast for one hundred and seven leagues, until I came to the end of it. From that point I saw another isle to the eastward, at eighteen leagues' distance, to which I gave the name of Hispaniola. I went thither and followed its northern coast to the east, as I had done in Juana, one hundred and seventy-eight leagues eastward, as in Juana. This island, like all the others, is most extensive. It has many ports along the sea-coast excelling any in Christendom—and many fine, large, flowing rivers. The land there is elevated, with many mountains and peaks incomparably higher than in the centre isle. They are most beautiful, of a thousand varied forms, accessible, and full of trees of endless varieties, so high that they seem to touch the sky, and I have been told that they never lose their foliage. I saw them as green and lovely as trees are in Spain in the month of May. Some of them were covered with blossoms, some with fruit, and some in other conditions, according to their kind. The nightingale and other small birds of a thousand kinds were singing in the month of November when I was there. There were palm trees of six or eight varieties, the graceful peculiarities of each one of them being worthy of admiration as are the other trees, fruits and grasses. There are wonderful pine woods, and very extensive ranges of meadow land. There is honey, and there are many kinds of birds, and a great variety of fruits. Inland there are numerous mines of metals and innumerable people. Hispaniola is a marvel. Its hills and mountains, fine plains and open country, are rich and fertile for planting and for pasturage, and for building towns and villages. The seaports there are incredibly fine, as also the magnificent rivers, most of which bear gold. The trees, fruits and grasses differ widely from those in Juana. There are many spices and vast mines of gold and other metals in this island. They have no iron, nor steel, nor weapons, nor are they fit for them, because although they are well-made men of commanding stature, they appear extraordinarily timid. The only arms they have are sticks of cane, cut when in seed, with a sharpened stick at the end, and they are afraid to use these. Often I have sent two or three men ashore to some town to converse with them, and the natives came out in great numbers, and as soon as they saw our men arrive, fled without a moment's delay although I protected them from all injury.

At every point where I landed, and succeeded in talking to them, I gave them some of everything I had—cloth and many other things— without receiving anything in return, but they are a hopelessly timid people. It is true that since they have gained more confidence and are losing this fear, they are so unsuspicious and so generous with what they possess, that no one who had not seen it would believe it. They never refuse anything that is asked for. They even offer it themselves, and show so much love that they would give their very hearts. Whether it be anything of great or small value, with any trifle of whatever kind, they are satisfied. I forbade worthless things being given to them, such as bits of broken bowls, pieces of glass, and old straps, although they were as much pleased to get them as if they were the finest jewels in the world. One sailor was found to have got for a leathern strap, gold of the weight of two and a half castellanos, and others for even more worthless things much more; while for a new blancas they would give all they had, were it two or three castellanos of pure gold or an arroba or two of spun cotton. Even bits of the broken hoops of wine casks they accepted, and gave in return what they had, like fools, and it seemed wrong to me. I forbade it, and gave a thousand good and pretty things that I had to win their love, and to induce them to become Christians, and to love and serve their Highnesses and the whole Castilian nation, and help to get for us things they have in abundance, which are necessary to us. They have no religion, nor idolatry, except that they all believe power and goodness to be in heaven. They firmly believed that I, with my ships and men, came from heaven, and with this idea I have been received everywhere, since they lost fear of me. They are, however, far from being ignorant. They are most ingenious men, and navigate these seas in a wonderful way, and describe everything well, but they never before saw people wearing clothes, nor vessels like ours. Directly I reached the Indies in the first isle I discovered, I took by force some of the natives, that from them we might gain some information of what there was in these parts; and so it was that we immediately understood each other, either by words or signs. They are still with me and still believe that I come from heaven. They were the first to declare this wherever I went, and the others ran from house to house, and to the towns around, crying out, "Come ! come! and see the man from heaven!" Then all, both men and women, as soon as they were reassured about us, came, both small and great, all bringing something to eat and to drink, which they presented with marvellous kindness. In these isles there are a great many canoes, something like rowing boats, of all sizes, and most of them are larger than an eighteen-oared galley. They are not so broad, as they are made of a single plank, but a galley could not keep up with them in rowing, because they go with incredible speed, and with these they row about among all these islands, which are innumerable, and carry on their commerce. I have seen some of these canoes with seventy and eighty men in them, and each had an oar. In all the islands I observed little difference in the appearance of the people, or in their habits and language, except that they understand each other, which is remarkable. Therefore I hope that their Highnesses will decide upon the conversion of these people to our holy faith, to which they seem much inclined. I have already stated how I sailed one hundred and seven leagues along the sea-coast of Juana, in a straight line from west to east. I can therefore assert that this island is larger than England and Scotland together, since beyond these one hundred and seven leagues there remained at the west point two provinces where I did not go, one of which they call Avan, the home of men with tails. These provinces are computed to be fifty or sixty leagues in length, as far as can be gathered from the Indians with me, who are acquainted with all these islands. This other, Hispaniola, is larger in circumference than all Spain from Catalonia to Fuentarabia in Biscay, since upon one of its four sides I sailed one hundred and eighty-eight leagues from west to east. This is worth having, and must on no account be given up. I have taken possession of all these islands, for their Highnesses, and all may be more extensive than I know, or can say, and I hold them for their Highnesses, who can command them as absolutely as the kingdoms of Castile. In Hispaniola, in the most convenient place, most accessible for the gold mines and all commerce with the mainland on this side or with that of the great Khan, on the other, with which there would be great trade and profit, I have taken possession of a large town, which I have named the City of Navidad. I began fortifications there which should be completed by this time, and I have left in it men enough to hold it, with arms, artillery, and provisions for more than a year; and a boat with a master seaman skilled in the arts necessary to make others; I am so friendly with the king of that country that he was proud to call me his brother and hold me as such. Even should he change his mind and wish to quarrel with my men, neither he nor his subjects know what arms are, nor wear clothes, as I have said. They are the most timid people in the world, so that only the men remaining there could destroy the whole region, and run no risk if they know how to behave themselves properly. In all these islands the men seem to be satisfied with one wife except they allow as many as twenty to their chief or men. The women appear to me to work harder than the men, and so far as I can hear they have nothing of their own, for I think I perceived that what one had others shared, especially food. In the islands so far, I have found no monsters, as some expected, but, on the contrary, they are people of very handsome appearance. They are not black as in Guinea, though their hair is straight and coarse, as it does not grow where the sun's rays are too ardent. And in truth the sun has extreme power here, since it is within twenty-six degrees of the equinoctial line. In these islands there are mountains where the cold this winter was very severe, but the people endure it from habit, and with the aid of the meat they eat with very hot spices.

As for monsters, I have found not trace of them except at the point in the second isle as one enters the Indies, which is inhabited by a people considered in all the isles as most ferocious, who eat human flesh. They possess many canoes, with which they overrun all the isles of India, stealing and seizing all they can. They are not worse looking than the others, except that they wear their hair long like women, and use bows and arrows of the same cane, with a sharp stick at the end for want of iron, of which they have none. They are ferocious compared to these other races, who are extremely cowardly; but I only hear this from the others. They are said to make treaties of marriage with the women in the first isle to be met with coming from Spain to the Indies, where there are no men. These women have no feminine occupation, but use bows and arrows of cane like those before mentioned, and cover and arm themselves with plates of copper, of which they have a great quantity. Another island, I am told, is larger than Hispaniola, where the natives have no hair, and where there is countless gold; and from them all I bring Indians to testify to this. To speak, in conclusion, only of what has been done during this hurried voyage, their Highnesses will see that I can give them as much gold as they desire, if they will give me a little assistance, spices, cotton, as much as their Highnesses may command to be shipped, and mastic as much as their Highnesses choose to send for, which until now has only been found in Greece, in the isle of Chios, and the Signoria can get its own price for it; as much lign-aloe as they command to be shipped, and as many slaves as they choose to send for, all heathens. I think I have found rhubarb and cinnamon. Many other things of value will be discovered by the men I left behind me, as I stayed nowhere when the wind allowed me to pursue my voyage, except in the City of Navidad, which I left fortified and safe. Indeed, I might have accomplished much more, had the crews served me as they ought to have done. The eternal and almighty God, our Lord, it is Who gives to all who walk in His way, victory over things apparently impossible, and in this case signally so, because although these lands had been imagined and talked of before they were seen, most men listened incredulously to what was thought to be but an idle tale. But our Redeemer has given victory to our most illustrious King and Queen, and to their kingdoms rendered famous by this glorious event, at which all Christendom should rejoice, celebrating it with great festivities and solemn Thanksgivings to the Holy Trinity, with fervent prayers for the high distinction that will accrue to them from turning so many peoples to our holy faith; and also from the temporal benefits that not only Spain but all Christian nations will obtain. Thus I record what has happened in a brief note written on board the *Caravel*, off the Canary Isles, on the 15th of February, 1493. Yours to command,

THE ADMIRAL

Postscript within the letter
Since writing the above, being in the Sea of Castile, so much wind arose south southeast, that I was forced to lighten the vessels, to run into this port of Lisbon to-day which was the most extraordinary thing in the world, from whence I resolved to write to their Highnesses. In all the Indies I always found the temperature like that of May. Where I went in thirty-three days I returned in twenty-eight, except that these gales have detained me fourteen days, knocking about in this sea, Here all seamen say that there has never been so rough a winter, nor so many vessels lost. Done the 14th day of March.[239]

Appendix I

THE TREATMENT OF HERETICS, 1229–1235

Thomas Aquinas

A. REGULATIONS OF THE SYNOD OF TOULOUSE CONCERNING THE INQUISITION, 1229

1. BISHOPS must bind under oath when necessary in each parish, within and outside a city, a priest and two or more lay people of good reputation to diligently, faithfully, and often search out heretics in their parishes, individual suspicious houses, subterranean rooms and additions to houses, and other hiding places. If they discover a heretic, follower, patron, or protector of heretics, they must, taking precaution that they do not escape, quickly notify the bishop and mayor of the place or his bailiff so they will be duly punished (command of the episcopal inquisition according to the practice of the synods of Verona, Bourges, Narbonne, and the twelfth general synod).

2. Exempt abbots, who are not subject to episcopal jurisdiction, must act in the same way as the bishops.

3. The governors of the respective districts should order diligent search of country residences, houses, and forests for heretics and destroy their hiding places.

4. Whoever, allowing a heretic to stay on his property either for money or any other cause, if he confesses or is convicted, loses his property forever and his body is handed over to the civil authority for punishment.

5. He also is subject to legal punishment whose property, although without his knowledge but by negligence, has become an abode of heretics.

✦ ✦ ✦

1. The house where a heretic is found must be torn down and the property must be confiscated.

2. The bailiff who lives in a suspicious place and is not diligent in searching for heretics loses his office and is not permitted to be employed either there or in any other place.

3. In order to prevent an innocent person from being punished or slanderously accused of heresy we command that no one shall be punished as a heretic or follower of heresy before he is so declared by a bishop or other clerical persons.

4. All are permitted to search for heretics in others' territories, and the bailiffs must help them. The king can, accordingly, search for heretics in the territory of the count of Toulouse, and the count of Toulouse in the king's land.

5. If one who is tainted with heresy voluntarily gives up the heresy he is not allowed to remain in the house where he formerly lived in case the house was under suspicion of heresy. He must be moved into a Catholic house which is free from suspicion. Besides, he must wear two crosses on his coat; the one on the right and the other on the left, and of a different color from his coat. Such persons cannot hold public office or be admitted to legal actions unless they are fully re-instated after due penance by the pope or his legate.

✦ ✦ ✦

11. Whoever has involuntarily returned to the Church, through fear of death or for any other reason, must be imprisoned by the bishop so he can perform his penance or not be able to seduce others. Whoever retains his property must, by order of the prelate, provide for his own necessities. If he possesses nothing, then the prelate must provide for him.

12. All members of a parish shall vow to the bishop under oath that they will preserve the Catholic faith and will persecute heretics according to their power. This oath must be renewed every two years.

13. Males and females who have attained the use of reason must confess their sins to a priest three times a year, or with their priest's permission to another priest. They must perform the imposed penances humbly and according to their strength and receive the holy sacrament of the Eucharist three times a year. Whoever does not do this is under suspicion of being a heretic.

14. Lay people are not permitted to possess the books of the Old and New Testament, only the Psalter, Breviary, or the Little Office of the Blessed Virgin, and these books not in the vernacular language.

15. Whoever is accused of heresy or is only suspected of heresy is not permitted to practice his profession as a doctor. When a sick person has received Holy Communion from his priest he must be careful that no heretic or one suspected of heresy visit him, for terrible things have already happened through such visits....

✦ ✦ ✦

17. No prelate, baron or other superiors shall entrust the office of bailiff or steward to any heretic or follower of heresy, nor keep in his service one who has been condemned or suspected of heresy.

18. He is accused of heresy or is suspected of heresy who has been legally proved by good and honorable people before a bishop of having a bad reputation. ... .

✦ ✦ ✦

42. Women who own castles or fortresses are not permitted to marry enemies of the faith and the peace . . . .

✦ ✦ ✦

44. Whoever is too poor to employ a lawyer has to be provided with one if necessary by the curia.

45. Pastors must explain these regulations to their parishioners four times a year.

Endnotes

1. Benzion Netanyahu, *The Marranos of Spain: From the Late 14th to the Early 16th Century* (Teaneck, NJ: American Academy for Jewish Research, 1966), p. 3.

2. Ibid., pp. 3–4.

3. *The Log of Christopher Columbus' First Voyage to America in the Year 1492*, as copied out in brief by Bartolomé de Las Casas, one of his companions, with illustrations by J. O'H. Cosgrave II (New York: William R. Scott, 1938), Introduction.

4. Mosco Galimir, *Cristobal Colón: The Discoverer of America* (New York: Galimir, 1950), pp. 29–30.

5. Ferdinand Columbus, *The Life of the Admiral Christopher Columbus by His Son Ferdinand*, Translated by Benjamin Keen (New Brunswick, NJ: Rutgers University Press, 1959), pp. 4–5.

6. Samuel Eliot Morison, *Admiral of the Ocean Sea: A Life of Christopher Columbus* (New York: Little Brown and Company, 1942, renewed 1970), p. 12

7. Silvio A. Bedini, Editor Emeritus, The Smithsonian Institution (New York: Simon and Schuster, 1992), pp. 164–165.

8. "Christopher Columbus was a Catalan, and possibly Jewish, scholar says," http://medievalnews. blogspot.com/2009/10/christopher-columbus-was-catalan-and.html; accessed July 2014.

9. Originally published in *Visual Anthropology*, Vol. 5, pp. 211–227 C1993 Harwood Academic Publishers GmbH.

10. John Boyd Thacher, *Christopher Columbus, His Life, His Work, His Remains*, Volume III. (New York: Putnam's Sons, 1904), p. 3.

11. Morison, pp. 44–45.

12. Ferdinand Columbus, p. 9.

13. Morison, p. 45.

14. Christopher Columbus, http://restore-christian-america.org/founders.html; accessed April 2014.

15. Thacher, pp. 192–193.

16. Ferdinand Columbus, p. 10.

17. Oliver Dunn and James Kelley, Jr., *The Diario of Christopher Columbus's First Voyage to America, 1492–1493* (Norman, OK: University of Oklahoma Press; Reprint edition, 1991), p. 253.

18. Morison, p. 24.

19. http://en.wikipedia.org/wiki/Portuguese_navigators; accessed April 2014.

20. Christopher Columbus, from his *Libro de las profecias (Book of Prophecies)*, http://restore-christian-america.org/founders.html; accessed April 2014.

21. Simon Wiesenthal, *Sails of Hope* (New York: McMillan Publishing Co, Inc., 1973), pp. 146–147.

22. Simcha Jacobovici, "Fernando Torres, Jews and Christopher Columbus, October 14, 2013, http://blogs.timesofisrael.com/fernando-torres-jews-and-christopher-columbus/; accessed May 2014.

23. Bedini, p. 178.

24. Morison, p. 42.

25. Morison, p. 60.

26. Bedini, p. 396.

27. Wiesenthal, p. 151.

28. Salvador de Madariaga, *Christopher Columbus: Being the Life of the Very Magnificent Lord Don Christobal Colon* (New York: McMillan, 1940), p. 144.

29. Delno C. West and August Kling, *The Libro de las profecias of Christopher Columbus: An en face edition* (Gainesville, FL: University Press of Florida, 1991), p. 105.

30. http://www.brainyquote.com/quotes/authors/c/christopher_columbus. html#mQeujhH20HEHhH8D.99

31. Americus Vespucius, http://www.godtheoriginalintent.com/web%20pages/Quotes.html; accessed July 2014.

32. Dan Carlinsky, "Christopher Confusion," Modern Maturity (Feb–Mar 1992) Volume 35, pp. 50–55.

33. Bethar, http://www.jewishencyclopedia.com/articles/3222-bethar; accessed April 2014.

34. Pedro de la Caballeria, http://en.wikipedia.org/wiki/De_la_Caballeria; accessed April 2014.

35. Henry Kamen, *Empire: How Spain Became a World Power, 1492–1763*, NewYork: Harper Perennial, 2002), p. 7.

36. Jewish Badge, Jewish Virtual Library, http://www.jewishvirtuallibrary.org/jsource/judaica/ ejud_0002_0003_0_01851.html; accessed April 2014.

37. Jennifer Garza, "Ballot Over San Francisco Measure to Ban Circumcision," *The Sacramento Bee*, July I, 2014, http://www.sanfranciscosentinel.com/?p=134594; accessed July 2014.

38. Abravanel's *Commentary on the First Prophets* (*Pirush Al Nevi'im Rishonim*), end of II Kings, pp. 680–681, Jerusalem 1955 (Hebrew).

39. Professor H. Graetz, *History of the Jews*, Vol. III Philadelphia: The Jewish Publication Society of America, 1894.

40. Ibid, p. 45

41. Solomon Katz, *Monographs of the Mediaeval Academy of America No. 12: The Jews in the Visigothic and Frankish Kingdoms of Spain and Gaul* (Cambridge, Massachusetts: The Mediaeval Society of America, 1937), p. 10.

42. Yom Tov Assis, *The Jews of Spain: From Settlement to Expulsion* (Jerusalem: The Hebrew University of Jerusalem, 1988), p. 10.

43. Katz, p. 13

44. Ibid., p. 16

45. Ibid., p. 21

46. Seventeenth Council of Toledo, http://en.wikipedia.org/wiki/Seventeenth_Council_of_Toledo; accessed April 2014.

47. Norman Roth (1994), *Jews, Visigoths and Muslims in Medieval Spain: Cooperation and Conflict* (Leiden: Brill, 1994), pp. 79–90.

48. Norman Stillman, "Aspects of Jewish Life in Islamic Spain" in *Aspects of Jewish Culture in the Middle Ages*, ed. Paul E. Szarmach (Albany: State University of New York Press, 1979), p. 53.

49. Benzion Netanyahu, *The Origins of the Inquisition in Fifteenth Century Spain* (New York: Random House, 1995), p. 54.

50. Jane Frances Amler, *Christopher Columbus's Jewish Roots* (Northvale, NJ: Jason Aronson, Inc., 1993), p. 64.

51. Madariaga, p. 119.

52. http://skepticism.org/timeline/april-history/4848-pope-innocent-iv-denies-jews-in-cordova-permission-to-build-a-synagogue.html

53. Netanyahu, *The Origins of the Inquisition in Fifteenth Century Spain,* pp. 768–769.

54. Jewish Encyclopedia, http://www.jewishencyclopedia.com/articles/13940-spain; accessed April 2014.

55. Americo Castro, *Structure of Spanish History* (Oxford, England: Oxford University Press, 1954), p. 502.

56. Netanyahu, *The Origins of the Inquisition in Fifteenth Century Spain,* pp. 64–65.

57. Wilhelm Marr, a German agitator and publicist, popularized the term "anti-Semitism" in 1881.

58. *Cortes de Leon y de Castilla,* 1371, section 2 (CLC, II, P. 203).

59. Solomon Alami, *Iggeret Musar,* Ed. Adolf Jellinek (Jerusalem: Ulan Press, 2012), p. 10b. (Passage translated from the Hebrew by Benzion Netanyahu.)

60. Yitzhak Baer, *A History of the Jews in Christian Spain* (Philadelphia: The Jewish Publication Society, 1993), Volume II, p. 193.

61. J. Amador de los Rios, *Historia Social, Politica y Religiosa de los Judios de Espania y Portugal, 1875–1876,* p. 581—as quoted in: Netanyahu, *The Origins of the Inquisition in Fifteenth Century Spain,* p. 131.

62. Ibid., p. 585

63. A religious or moral act that causes others to reverence God; *esp* : religious martyrdom in times of persecution, http://www.merriam-webster.com/dictionary/kiddush%20hashem; accessed April 2014.

64. Nissan Mindel, "The Massacre of 5151," http://www.chabad.org/library/article_cdo/aid/112389/jewish/The-Massacres-of-5151.htm; accessed April 2014.

65. Netanyahu, *The Origins of the Inquisition in Fifteenth Century Spain,* pp. 135–136.

66. A historically controversial area of Western Europe lying in western Germany along both banks of the middle Rhine River.

67. The Jews were often accused of causing the Plague to destroy Christians[f], even though Jews and Muslims were as likely to be infected as Christians. After being tortured, some Jews confessed that they were poisoning wells and other water sources, creating the Plague. As a result, Jews were expelled or killed by the thousands. As a result of forced confessions, the entire Jewish population of Strassburg, Germany, was given the choice to convert to Christianity or be burned on rows of stakes on a platform in the city's burial ground. About 2,000 were killed. Http://facts.randomhistory.com/2009/06/09_black-death.html; accessed May 2014.

68. Helen Rawlings, *The Spanish Inquisition* (Hoboken, NJ: Wiley-Blackwell, 2005), p. 53.

69. At their annual party rally, the Nazis announce new laws that revoke Reich citizenship for Jews and prohibit Jews from marrying or having sexual relations with persons of "German or related blood." "Racial infamy," as this becomes known, is made a criminal offense. The Nuremberg Laws define a "Jew" as someone with three or four Jewish grandparents. Consequently, the Nazis classify as Jews thousands of people who had converted from Judaism to another religion, among them even Roman Catholic priests and nuns and Protestant ministers whose grandparents were Jewish; http://www.ushmm.org/outreach/en/article.php?ModuleId=10007695; accessed May 2014.

70. Netanyahu, *The Origins of the Inquisition in Fifteenth Century Spain*, p. 351.

71. Antonio Martin Gamero, *Historía de la ciudad de Toledo* (University of Michigan, 2007), p. 1038. http://books.google.com/books/about/Historía_de_la_ciudad_de_Toledo.html?id=0JpNAAAAMAAJ; accessed May 2014.

72. Benzion Netanyahu, *Don Isaac Abravanel Statesman & Philosopher* (Ithaca, NY: Cornell University Press: 1953), pp. 42–43.

73. Ibid., p. 43.

74. Anti-Semitism, http://southerninstitute.info/holocaust_education/ds1.html; accessed May 2014.

75. Andres Bernaldez, *Memorias del reinadode los Reyes Catolicos*, ed. Manuel Gomez-Moreno y Juan de M. Carriazo, 1962; p. 920. Translated by Benzion Netanyahu in *The Origins of the Inquisition in Fifteenth Century Spain*, p. 1053.

76. "Deathly Silence," http://southerninstitute.info/holocaust_education/ds1.html; accessed May 2014.

77. *The Free Dictionary*, http://www.thefreedictionary.com/Burghers; accessed April 2014.

78. Netanyahu, *Don Isaac Abravanel Statesman & Philosopher*, p. 45.

79. http://thinkexist.com/quotes/henry_charles_lea/; accessed July 2014.

80. Netanyahu, *The Origins of the Inquisition in Fifteenth Century Spain*, p. xiv.

81. "Thomás de Torquemada and the Spanish Inquisition," http://www.crimelibrary.com/notorious_murders/mass/torquemada/6.html; accessed May 2014.

82. G. CH. Lee, *The History of the Inquisition in the Middle Ages*, "Brokgauz-Efron," Saint Petersburg, 1914 (*in Russian*) as stated on http://godspeakstoday.info/sh_biblio.html#r56; accessed April 2014.

83. Augustine, *Expositions on the Book of Psalms*, IV, Library of Fathers, Vol. 32, Veritatis Splendor Publications 2012, Amazon Digital Services, p. 79.2.

84. "Thomas Aquinas: Treatment of Heretics," Selection A from Conciliengeschichte, trans. by Brother Conrad Zimmermann, O.S.B. (Freiburg im Breisgau: B. Herder, 1886), V, 980–986; selection B from Original Sources of European History, edited by Edward P. Cheyney (Philadelphia: The University of Pennsylvania Press, 1902), III, 14–15; 17–18; selection C from Summa Theologica, trans. by Fathers of English Dominican Province (New York: Benziger Brothers, Inc., 1947), II, 1226–1227, http://www.scrollpublishing.com/store/Aquinas-Heretics. html; accessed July 2014.

85. Dagobert D. Runes, The War Against the Jews (New York, NY: Philosophical Library, Inc., 2008), p. 18.

86. Inquisition, Jewish Encyclopedia, http://jewishencyclopedia.com/articles/8122-inquisition; accessed April 2014.

87. Jane S. Gerber, The Jews of Spain (New York: The Free Press, 1994), p. 127 (See A. Sicroff, Les Controverses des statuts de puerte de sang en Espagna du XVe au Xviie siècle (Paris, 1960).

88. Tomás de Torquemada, http://jewishwebsight.com/bin/articles.cgi?Area=jw&ID=JW1303); accessed April 2014.

89. Luna was constable of Castile, ruler of Castile during much of the reign of the weak John II. He was the illegitimate son of a noble of Aragonese descent and only distinguished statesman during a dismal period in Castilian history. For many years his main efforts were concerned with saving the crown from armed factions of dissident magnates who sought to control it. http://www.britannica.com/EBchecked/topic/351334/Alvaro-de-Luna; accessed May 2014.

90. Netanyahu, The Origins of the Inquisition in Fifteenth Century Spain, p. 500.

91. Nicholas of Lyra, Postillae perpetuae in universam S. Scripturam (Commentary Notes to the Universal Holy Scripture). From 1319 he headed the Franciscans in France and in 1325 founded the College of Burgundy from where he wrote a 50-volume exegesis on the Scriptures; Volume on Deuteronomy, p. 335.

92. Arthur Koestler, The Ghost in the Machine, http://www.goodreads.com/work/quotes/31021-the-ghost-in-the-machine; accessed April 2014.

93. The Phoenician wife of Ahab who according to the account in I and II Kings pressed the cult of Baal on the Israelite kingdom but was finally killed in accordance with Elijah's prophecy, http://www.merriam-webster.com/dictionary/jezebel; accessed April 2014.

94. Cecil Roth, The Spanish Inquisition (New York: W.W. Norton & Co, 1964), p. 267.

95. William Jones, The History of the Christian Church (Great Britain: Ages Software, 1997), p. 88.

96. Tomás de Torquemada, http://deni-edwards.hubpages.com/hub/Torquemadas-Spanish-Inquisition-From-Suspicion-to-Death; accessed May 2014.

97. Miroslav Hroch & Anna Skybova, Ecclesia Militans: The Inquisition (New York: Dorset Press, 1988), p. 145.

98. http://www.catholicpeacefellowship.org/nextpage.asp?m=2272; accessed April 2014.

99. Hroch & Skybova, p. 146.

100. Torture Techniques of the Spanish Inquisition, http://jamesray.hubpages.com/hub/Killing-in-the-Name-of-God; accessed April 2014.

101. Thomas Cahill, Heretics and Heroes: How Renaissance Artists and Reformation Priests Created our World (New York: Doubleday, a division of Randon House, 2013), pp. 49–50.

102. Netanyahu, *The Origins of the Inquisition in Fifteenth Century Spain,* p. 132.

103. One of the most famous victims of the Inquisition was Joan of Arc of France who, following the Battle of Orleans, was tried by the French for sorcery and heresy and was burned at the stake in 1431 at the age of 19.

104. Simon Wiesenthal, *Sails of Hope: The Secret Mission of Christopher Columbus* (translated from German by Richard and Clara Winston); (New York: Macmillan Publishing Co., Inc., 1973), P. 52.

105. "Ships and Sailing," http://www.jewishvirtuallibrary.org/jsource/judaica/ejud_0002_0018_0_18358.html; accessed May 2014.

106. Willie Martin, "Columbus and His Jewish Ancestors," http://www.operationmorningstar.org/columbus_and_his_jewish_ancestor.htm; accessed May 2014.

107. Edward E. Hale, *The Life of Christopher Columbus,* available at http://www.classicreader.com/book/1293/; accessed May 2014.

108. Madariaga, p. 168.

109. Elijah Capsali, *Seder Eliyahu Zuta* ed. A. Shmuelevitz (Tel Aviv University: Jerusalem, 1975), chapter 69.

110. Morison, p. 105.

111. Baer, *A History of the Jews in Christian Spain* (Philadelphia: The Jewish Publication Society, 1993), p. 421.

112. Capsali, chapter 67 as quoted in *The Jews of Spain: A History of the Sephardic Experience* (Jane S. Gerber: New York: The Free Press, 1992), p. 136.

113. Leo W. Schwarz, ed., *Memoirs of My People* (New York: Jewish Publication Society of America, 1945), pp. 46–47.

114. Wiesenthal, p. 54.

115. "The Diary of Luis De Torres," *Los Angeles Jewish Times,* December 24, 1999.

116. Samuel Usque, *Consolation for the Tribulations of Israel,* edited and translated by Martin A. Cohen (Philadelphia: Jewish Publication Society, 1965), pp. 201–202.

117. Netanyahu, *Don Isaac Abravanel Statesman & Philosopher,* pp. 57–58.

118. Steven Weitzman, *Solomon: The Lure of Wisdom* (Ann Arbor, MI: Sheridan Books, 2011).

119. Laura Ackerman Smoller, *History, Prophecy and the Stars* (Princeton University Press, 1994), as quoted on http://thezodiac.com/weird/columbus.htm; accessed May 2014.

120. Young, *Christopher Columbus,* Chapter II.

121. West and Kling, p. 229.

122. 122   Ferdinand Columbus, p. 21.

123. 123   Ibid., p. 22

124. Dr. Gerhard Falk, "Columbus & the Jews," http://jbuff.com/c100903.htm; accessed May 2014.

125. Wiesenthal, p. 107.

126. *The Book of the Prophecies Edited by Christopher Columbus*, Volume III; Roberto Rusconi, Historicaland Textual Editor, Blair Sullivan, Translator (Eugene, OR: Wipf and Stock Publishers, 1997), p. 71.

127. Bedini, p. 749.

128. Leroy Edwin Froom, *The Prophetic Faith of Our Fathers*, Vol. I. (Washington, D.C.: Review and Herald, 1948), pp. 167–171, 173.

129. *The Log of Christopher Columbus' First Voyage to America in the Year 1492*, as copied out in brief by Bartolomé de Las Casas, one of his companions, with illustrations by J. O'H. Cosgrave II (New York: William R. Scott, 1938), September 22 and 23, 1492.

130. Newton Frohlich, "Was the Discoverer of America Jewish?" *Moment*, Dec. 1991, p. 43.

131. Dr. Meir Kayserling, *Christopher Columbus and the Participation of the Jews in the Spanish and Portugese Discoveries* (New York: Hermon Press, 1968), p. 122.

132. Walter F. McEntire, *Was Christopher Columbus a Jew?* (Boston: The Stratford Company, 1925), p. 77.

133. Maurice David, *Who Was Columbus? His Real Name and Fatherland* (New York: The Research Publishing Co., 1933), p. 103.

134. Bedini, p. 629.

135. David, p. 99.

136. *The Log of Christopher Columbus' First Voyage to America in the year 1492*, August 3, 1492.

137. Gerber, p. 133.

138. http://www.gutenberg.org/files/33095/33095-h/33095-h.htm, page 34; accessed July 2014.

139. Wiesenthal, p. 170.

140. Young, *Christopher Columbus.*

141. Jerry Woodfill, "Ships of Exploration: *Santa Maria* and spaceship America," http://er.jsc.nasa.gov/seh/ships.htm; accessed May 2014.

142. "Christopher Columbus' Ships: Vessels that Discovered America," *Marine Insight*, http://www.marineinsight.com/marine/life-at-sea/maritime-history/christopher-columbus-ships-vessels-that-discovered-america/; accessed May 2013.

143. History World International, http://history-world.org/Columbus%2C%20List%20of%20Sailors.htm; accessed May 2014.

144. Shavla Weil, "Hebrew in Chennamangalam," February 16, 2006, http://www.haaretz.com/print-edition/features/hebrew-in-chennamangalam-1.180357; accessed July 2014.

145. Maurice H. Harris, *From the Moslem Conquest of Spain to the Discovery of America* (New York: Block Publishing Co., 1921), pp. 351–352, Internet Archive, http://www.archive.org/stream/historyofmediaev00harr/historyofmediaev00harr_djvu.txt; accessed May 2014. (Translated from the German of Ludwig August Frankl bv Minnie D. Louis.)

146. Netanyahu, *Don Isaac Abravanel Statesman & Philosopher*, p. 63.

147. Ibid., p. 64.

148. Morison, p. 149.

149. The identification of Leviathan is disputed, ranging from an earthly creature to a mythical sea monster in ancient literature.

150. President Ronald Reagan's Speech, Challenger Crew Memorial Service, Johnson Space Center, January 31, 1986, http://astronautmemorial.net/challengermemorial.htm; accessed May 2014.

151. Young, *Christopher Columbus,* Chapter 13.

152. Robert H. Fuson, *The Log of Christopher Columbus* (Camden, ME: International Marine Publishing Co., 1987), p. 71.

153. *The Log of Christopher Columbus' First Voyage to America in the Year 1492,* as copied out in brief by Bartolomé de Las Casas, p. 35.

154. Ferdinand Columbus, p. 58.

155. *The Log of Christopher Columbus' First Voyage to America in the Year 1492,* October 11–12, 1492.

156. Ibid.

157. "Was Christopher Columbus a Messianic Jew?", http://www.ramsheadpress.com/messiah/ch16.html; accessed May 2014.

158. Dunn and Kelly, pp. 65–66.

159. Ibid, p. 65

160. Ibid., p. 69

161. Morison, p. 261

162. Ibid., p. 137

163. "The Indians who greeted Columbus were long believed to have died out. But a journalist's search for their descendants turned up surprising results," Robert M. Poole, *Smithsonian Magazine,* October 2011, http://www.smithsonianmag.com/people-places/what-became-of-the-taino-73824867/?no-ist; accessed June 2014.

164. Paolo Emilio Taviani, *Columbus: The Great Adventure, His Life, His Times, and His Voyages* (New York: Crown Publishing, a subsidiary of Random House, 1991), pp. 130–131.

165. Ernle Bradford, *Christopher Columbus* (New York: Viking, 1971), pp. 127–128.

166. "Shipwreck off Haiti Could be Columbus' Santa Maria, Explorers Say," http://www.marineinsight.com/shipping-news/shipwreck-haiti-columbuss-santa-maria-explorers-say/; accessed May 2014.

167. Fuson, p. 174.

168. Dunn and Kelly, pp. 363–365.

169. Morison, p. 342.

170. Madariaga, p. 243.

171. Ferdinand Columbus, p. 101.

172. Taviani, p. 183.

173. Jane Frances Amler, p. 174.

174. From the works of Girolamo Benzoni (1565), *Historia del Mondo Nuovo*; Venice. English translation *History of the New World by Girolamo Benzoni* (Hakluyt Society, London, 1857).

175. "Native Americans, Treatment of," http://www.encyclopedia.com/doc/1G2-3406400630.html; accessed June 2014.

176. "Christopher Columbus," http://www.ibiblio.org/expo/1492.exhibit/c-Columbus/columbus.html; accessed June 2014.

177. "Walking," Henry David Thoreau, http://www.thoreau-online.org/walking-page7.html; accessed June 2014.

178. Thacher, pp. 101, 105, 108.

179. "Letter of Dr. Chanca on the Second Voyage of Columbus," http://www.americanjourneys.org/aj-065/summary/index.asp; accessed June 2014.

180. Young, Chapter Six.

181. Ferdinand Columbus, pp. 110–111.

182. http://seestjohn.com/st_john_life/virgin-islands/st-john-usvi-history-cannibalism-in-the-caribbean/#sthash.rBnl10hE.dpuf

183. Morison, p. 427.

184. Kathleen Deagan and Jose Maria Cruxent, *Columbus's Outposts Among the Tainos: Spain and America at La Isabela, 1493–1498* (New Haven, CT: Yale University Press, 2002), p. 2.

185. Taviani, p. 160.

186. Samuel M. Wilson, *Hispaniola: Caribbean Chiefdoms in the Age of Columbus* (Tuscaloosa: The University of Alabama Press, 1990), pp. 93–95.

187. Taviani, pp. 169–170.

188. Madariaga, p. 329.

189. *Indian Freedom: The Cause of Bartolomé de Las Casas* ed. Francis Patrick Sullivan (Franklin, WI: Sheed and Ward, 1995), p. 354.

190. Madariaga, p. 290.

191. Christopher Columbus, William Eleroy Curtis, José Ignacio Rodrigues, *The Authentic Letters of Columbus* (Chicago, IL: Stanford University Library, 1894), p. 113, Digitized by Google, http://books.google.com/books?id=TKgKAAAAIAAJ&pg=PA118&source=gbs_toc_r&cad=3#v=onepage&q=Vespucci&f=false; accessed June 2014.

192. Morison, pp. 523–524.

193. Morison, p. 529.

194. "Columbus lands in South America," http://www.history.com/this-day-in-history/columbus-lands-in-south-america, accessed June 2014.

195. Taviani, pp. 196–197.

196. Morison, p. 536.

197. Christopher Columbus, William Eleroy Curtis, José Ignacio Rodrigues, *The Authentic Letters of Columbus* (Chicago, IL: Stanford University Library, 1894), p. 113, Digitized by Google, http://books.google.com/books?id=TKgKAAAAIAAJ&pg=PA118&source=gbs_toc_r&cad=3#v=onepage&q=Vespucci&f=false; accessed June 2014, p. 123.

198. Taviani, p. 208.

199. "Writings of Columbus," Ed. Arthur Stedman, https://ia700407.us.archive.org/1/items/writingsofchrist00coluuoft/writingsofchrist00coluuoft_bw.pdf; accessed June 2014.

200. Martin Dugard, *The Last Voyage of Columbus: Being the Epic Tale of the Great Captain's Fourth Expedition, Including Accounts of Mutiny, Shipwreck, and Discovery Paperback* (New York, NY: Little, Brown and Company, Time Warner Group, 2005), p. 106.

201. Taviani, p. 213.

202. Taviani, p. 257.

203. Christopher Columbus, http://www.nndb.com/people/033/000045895/; accessed June 2014.

204. Filson Young, *Christopher Columbus*, Chapter III, "The Last Voyage," eBook by Project Gutenburg, http://www.gutenberg.org/files/4116/4116-h/4116-h.htm#ch6; accessed May 2014. Chapter III, "The Last Voyage," http://www.gutenberg.org/files/4116/4116-h/4116-h.htm; accessed June 2014.

205. Ibid.

206. Taviani, p. 224.

207. Washington Irving, *The Life and Voyages of Christopher Columbus, Vol. II*, pp. 217–218, http://www.fulltextarchive.com/pdfs/The-Life-and-Voyages-of-Christopher-Columbus.pdf; accessed June 2014.

208. Ibid.

209. "Christopher Columbus Letter from the Fourth Voyage," http://earlyamericas.wordpress.com/anthology/columbus-letter-from-the-fourth-voyage/; accessed June 2014.

210. Morison, pp. 633–634.

211. Keen, pp. 264–265.

212. Morison, pp. 650–651.

213. Irving, p. 239.

214. Filson Young, Chapter III, "The Last Voyage," http://www.gutenberg.org/files/4116/4116-h/4116-h.htm; accessed June 2014.

215. Irving, pp. 145–146.

216. Keen, p. 272.

217. Personal Interview by Mike Evans with Mordechai Gur, 1995.

218. Personal interview by Mike Evans with Chief Rabbi Shlomo Goren, 1995.

219. Anthony Beevor, *The Battle for Spain: The Spanish Civil War, 1936–1939* (London: Penguin Books. 2006), p. 405.

220. Ibid., p. 342.

221. Michael Richards, *A Time of Silence: Civil War and the Culture of Repression in Franco's Spain, 1936–1945* (Cambridge, GB: Cambridge University Press, 1998), p. 11.

222. http://www.ramsheadpress.com/messiah/PDF/CHAPTER16.pdf; accessed June 2014.

223. Galimir, p. 53.

224. Kayserling, p. 122.

225. Madariaga, p. 375.

226. Dugard, p. 253.

227. Keen, p. 282.

228. Keen, p. 284.

229. Ibid.

230. Bedini, p. 752.

231. Bedini, p. 24.

232. "Christopher Columbus, MOT," May 30, 2012, http://www.abqjew.net/2012/05/christopher-columbus-mot.html; accessed July 2014.

233. Edict of Expulsion, http://www.sephardicstudies.org/decree.html; accessed May 2014.

234. http://college.cengage.com/history/primary_sources/world/agree_columbus.htm; accessed May 2014.

235. See Endnote 132 above.

236. http://www.thelatinlibrary.com/imperialism/readings/alexander.html

237. Christopher Columbus, William Eleroy Curtis, José Ignacio Rodrigues, *The Authentic Letters of Columbus* (Chicago, IL: Stanford University Library, 1894), p. 113, Digitized by Google, http://books.google.com/books?id=TKgKAAAAIAAJ&pg=PA118&source=gbs_toc_r&cad=3#v=onepage&q=Vespucci&f=false; accessed June 2014.

238. William Eleroy Curtis, Honorary Curator, Department of Columbus Memorial, *The Authentic Letters of Columbus*, May 1895, Chicago, IL, http://www.archive.org/stream/authenticletters00colu/authenticletters00colu_djvu.txt; accessed July 2014.

239. http://www.ushistory.org/documents/columbus.htm; accessed July 2014.

Bibliography

A

Abravanel's Commentary on the First Prophets (Pirush Al Nevi'im Rishonim), End of II Kings, Jerusalem 1955 (Hebrew).

Alami, Solomon, Iggeret Musar (Ed. Adolf Jellenik) (Jerusalem: Ulan Press, 2012).

Amler, Jane Frances Christopher Columbus's Jewish Roots (Northvale, NJ: Jason Aronson, Inc., 1993).

Assis, Yom Tov The Jews of Spain: From Settlement to Expulsion, (Jerusalem: The Hebrew University of Jerusalem, 1988).

B

Baer, Yitzhak A History of the Jews in Christian Spain, Volume II (Philadelphia: The Jewish Publication Society, 1993).

Benzoni, Girolamo, From the works of (1565), Historia del Mondo Nuovo; Venice. English translation History of the New World by Girolamo Benzoni, (Hakluyt Society, London, 1857.)

Bradford, Ernle Christopher Columbus (New York: Viking, 1971).

Brinkbäumer, Klaus The voyage of the Vizcaína: the mystery of Christopher Columbus's last ship (Chicago: Houghton Mifflin Harcourt, 2006).

C

Cahill, Thomas Heretics and Heroes: How Renaissance Artists and Reformation Priests Created our World (New York: Doubleday, a division of Random House, 2013).

Capsali, Elijah Seder Eliyahu Zuta (ed. A. Shmuelevitz) (Tel Aviv University: Jerusalem, 1975).

Carlinsky, Dan "Christopher Confusion," Volume 35
Modern Maturity (Feb-Mar 1992).

Castro, Americo Structure of Spanish History
(Oxford, England: Oxford University Press, 1954).

Columbus, Christopher; Curtis, William; Eleroy, Rodrigues;
José Ignacio The Authentic Letters of Columbus
(Chicago, IL: Stanford University Library, 1894).

Columbus, Christopher The Book of the Prophecies Edited by Christopher Columbus,
Volume III; Roberto Rusconi, Historical and Textual Editor, Blair Sullivan,
Translator
(Eugene, OR: Wipf and Stock Publishers, 1997).

D

David, Maurice Who Was Columbus? His Real Name and Fatherland
(New York: The Research Publishing Co., 1933).

De Madariaga, Salvador Christopher Columbus: Being the Life of the Very
Magnificent Lord Don Christobal Colon
(New York: McMillan, 1940).

Deagan, Kathleen and Cruzent, Jose Maria Columbus's Outposts Among the Tainos:
Spain and America at La Isabela, 1493-1498
(New Haven, CT: Yale University Press, 2002).

Dugard, Martin The Last Voyage of Columbus: Being the Epic Tale of the Great
Captain's Fourth Expedition, Including Accounts of Mutiny, Shipwreck,
and Discovery Paperback
(New York, NY: Little, Brown and Company, Time Warner Group, 2005).

Dunn, Oliver and Kelley, Jr. James, The Diario of Christopher Columbus's
First Voyage to America, 1492–1493
(Norman, OK: University of Oklahoma Press; Reprint edition, 1991.

E

Elijah Capsali, Seder Eliyahu Zuta ed. A. Shmuelevitz
(Tel Aviv University: Jerusalem, 1975).

F

Froom, Leroy Edwin The Prophetic Faith of our Fathers, Vol. I.
(Washington, D.C.: Review and Herald, 1948).

Fuson, Robert H. The Log of Christopher Columbus
(Camden, ME: International Marine Publishing Co., 1987).

G

Gaetz, Professor H. History of the Jews, Vol. III
(Philadelphia: The Jewish Publication Society of America, 1894).

Galimir, Mosco Cristobal Colón, The Discoverer of America
(New York: Galimir, 1950).

Gamero, Antonio Martin Historía de la ciudad de Toledo
(University of Michigan, 2007).

Gerber, Jane S. The Jews of Spain, a History of the Sephardic Experience
(Jane S. Gerber: New York: The Free Press, 1992.)

H

Helen Rawlings The Spanish Inquisition
(Hoboken, NJ: Wiley-Blackwell, 2005).

Hroch, Miroslav & Skybova, Anna Ecclesia Militans: The Inquisition
(New York: Dorset Press, 1988).

J

Jones, William The History of the Christian Church
(Great Britain: Ages Software, 1997).

K

Kamen, Henry Empire: how Spain became a World Power, 1492-1763
(New York: Harper Perennial, 2002).

Katz, Solomon Monographs of the Mediaeval Academy of America No. 12:
The Jews in the Visigothic and Frankish Kingdoms of Spain and Gaul
(Cambridge, Massachusetts: The Mediaeval Society of America, 1937).

Kayserling, Dr. Meir Christopher Columbus and The Participation of the Jews in the
      Spanish and Portugese Discoveries
      (New York: Hermon Press, 1968).

Keen, Benjamin Ferdinand Columbus The Life of the Admiral Christopher Columbus
      by His Son Ferdinand, Translated by
      (New Brunswick, NJ: Rutgers University Press, 1959).

L

Las Casas, The Log of Christopher Columbus' First Voyage to America in the year
      1492, as copied out in brief by Bartholomew Las Casas, one of his companions,
      with illustrations by J. O'H. Cosgrave II
      (New York: William R. Scott, 1938).

Lester, C. Edwards The Life and Voyages of Americus Vespucius
      (Ann Arbor, MI: Scholarly Publishing Office,
      University of Michigan Press, 2005)

Lyra, Nicholas of Postillae perpetuae in universam S. Scripturam,
      (Commentary)

M

McEntire, Walter F. Was Christopher Columbus a Jew
      (Boston: The Stratford Company, 1925).

Morison, Samuel Eliot Admiral of the Ocean Sea: A life of Christopher Columbus
      (New York: Little Brown and Company, 1942, Silvio A. Bedini, Editor Emeritus,
      The Smithsonian Institution (New York: Simon and Schuster, 1992).

N

Netanyahu, Benzion Don Isaac Abravanel Statesman & Philosopher
      (Ithaca, NY: Cornell University Press: 1953).

Netanyahu, Benzion The Marranos of Spain:
      From the Late 14th to the Early 16th Century
      (Teaneck, NJ: American Academy for Jewish Research, 1966).

Netanyahu, Benzion The Origins of the Inquisition in Fifteenth Century Spain
      (New York: Random House, 1995).

R

Rawlings, Helen The Spanish Inquisition
(Hoboken, NJ: Wiley-Blackwell, 2005).

Richards, Michael A Time of Silence; Civil War and the Culture of Repression
in Franco's Spain, 1936-1945
(Cambridge, GB: Cambridge University Press, 1998).

Rios, J. Amador de los Historia Social, Politica y Religiosa de los Judios
de Espania y Portugal, 1875-1876—as quoted in: Netanyahu,
The Origins of the Inquisition in Fifteenth Century Spain.

Roth, Cecil The Spanish Inquisition
(New York: W.W. Norton & Co, 1964).

Roth, Norman (1994), Jews, Visigoths and Muslims
in Medieval Spain: Cooperation and Conflict
(Leiden: Brill, 1994).

Runes, Dagobert D. The War Agai+nst +the Jews
(New York: Philosophical Library, Inc., 2008).

S

Schwarz, Leo W. Memoirs of My People
(New York: Jewish Publication Society of America, 1945).

Smoller, Laura Ackerman History, Prophecy and the Stars
(Princeton University Press, 1994).

Stillman, Norman "Aspects of Jewish Life in Islamic Spain" in Aspects
of Jewish Culture in the Middle Ages, ed. Paul E. Szarmach
(Albany: State University of New York Press, 1979).

Sullivan, Francis Patrick Indian Freedom: The Cause of Bartolomé de Las Casas
(Franklin, WI: Sheed and Ward, 1995).

T

Taviani, Paolo Emilio Columbus: The Great Adventure,
His Life, His Times, and His Voyages
(New York: Crown Publishing a subsidiary of Random House.)

Thacher, John Boyd Christopher Columbus,
    His Life, His Work, His Remains, Volume III.
    (New York: Putnam's Sons, 1904.)

U

Usque, Samuel Consolation for the Tribulations of Israel
    edited and translated by Martin A. Cohen
    (Philadelphia: Jewish Publication Society, 1965).

W

Weitzman, Steven Solomon: The Lure of Wisdom
    (New Haven and London: Yale University Press, 2011)

West, Delno C. and Kling, August The Libro de las profecias
    of Christopher Columbus: An en face edition
    (Gainesville, FL: University Press of Florida, 1991).

Wiesenthal, Simon Sails of Hope: The Secret Mission of Christopher Columbus
    (translated from German by Richard and Clara Winston).
    (New York: Macmillan Publishing Co., Inc., 1973).

Wilford, John Noble The Mysterious History of Columbus.
    An Exploration of the man, the Myth, the legacy
    (New York: Alfred A. Knopf 1991).

Wilson, Samuel M. Hispaniola: Caribbean Chiefdoms in the Age of Columbus
    (Tuscaloosa: The University of Alabama Press, 1990).

Y

Young, Filson Christopher Columbus and the New World of His
    Discovery, (Philadelphia: J.B. Lippincott, 1906).

Index

T

MICHAEL DAVID EVANS, the #1 *New York Times* bestselling author, is an award-winning journalist/Middle East analyst. Dr. Evans has appeared on hundreds of network television and radio shows including *Good Morning America, Crossfire* and *Nightline*, and *The Rush Limbaugh Show*, and on Fox Network, *CNN World News*, NBC, ABC, and CBS. His articles have been published in the *Wall Street Journal, USA Today, Washington Times, Jerusalem Post* and newspapers worldwide. More than twenty-five million copies of his books are in print, and he is the award-winning producer of nine documentaries based on his books.

Dr. Evans is considered one of the world's leading experts on Israel and the Middle East, and is one of the most sought-after speakers on that subject. He is the chairman of the board of the Ten Boom Holocaust Museum in Haarlem, Holland, and is the founder of Israel's first Christian museum—Friends of Zion: Heroes and History—in Jerusalem.

Dr. Evans has authored a number of books including: *History of Christian Zionism, Showdown with Nuclear Iran, Atomic Iran, The Next Move Beyond Iraq, The Final Move Beyond Iraq*, and *Countdown*. His body of work also includes he novels *Seven Days, GameChanger, The Samson Option, The Four Horsemen, The Locket, Born Again: 1967, and his most recent, The Columbus Code*.

✦ ✦ ✦

Michael David Evans is available to speak or for interviews.
Contact: EVENTS@drmichaeldevans.com.

BOOKS BY: MIKE EVANS

Israel: America's Key to Survival

Save Jerusalem

The Return

Jerusalem D.C.

Purity and Peace of Mind

Who Cries for the Hurting?

Living Fear Free

I Shall Not Want

Let My People Go

Jerusalem Betrayed

Seven Years of Shaking: A Vision

The Nuclear Bomb of Islam

Jerusalem Prophecies

Pray For Peace of Jerusalem

America's War: The Beginning of the End

The Jerusalem Scroll

The Prayer of David

The Unanswered Prayers of Jesus

God Wrestling

The American Prophecies

Beyond Iraq: The Next Move

The Final Move beyond Iraq

Showdown with Nuclear Iran

Jimmy Carter: The Liberal Left and World Chaos

Atomic Iran

Cursed

Betrayed

The Light

Corrie's Reflections & Meditations

GAMECHANGER SERIES:
   GameChanger
   Samson Option
   The Four Horsemen

THE PROTOCOLS SERIES:
   The Protocols
   The Candidate

The Revolution

The Final Generation

Seven Days

The Locket

Living in the F.O.G.

Persia: The Final Jihad

Jerusalem

The History of Christian Zionism

Countdown

Ten Boom: Betsie, Promise of God

Commanded Blessing

Born Again: 1948

Born Again: 1967

Presidents in Prophecy

Stand with Israel

Prayer, Power and Purpose

Turning Your Pain Into Gain

The Columbus Code

Christopher Columbus, Secret Jew

TO PURCHASE, CONTACT: orders@timeworthybooks.com

P. O. BOX 30000, PHOENIX, AZ 85046